T0291928

OPTIMUM-PATH FOREST

OPTIMUM-PATH FOREST

FOREST

Theory, Algorithms, and Applications

Edited by

ALEXANDRE XAVIER FALCÃO

JOÃO PAULO PAPA

ACADEMIC PRESS
An imprint of Elsevier

Academic Press is an imprint of Elsevier
125 London Wall, London EC2Y 5AS, United Kingdom
525 B Street, Suite 1650, San Diego, CA 92101, United States
50 Hampshire Street, 5th Floor, Cambridge, MA 02139, United States
The Boulevard, Langford Lane, Kidlington, Oxford OX5 1GB, United Kingdom

Notices

Knowledge and best practice in this field are constantly changing. As new research and experience
broaden our understanding, changes in research methods, professional practices, or medical
treatment may become necessary.

Practitioners and researchers must always rely on their own experience and knowledge in
evaluating and using any information, methods, compounds, or experiments described herein. In
using such information or methods they should be mindful of their own safety and the safety of
others, including parties for whom they have a professional responsibility.

To the fullest extent of the law, neither the Publisher nor the authors, contributors, or editors,
assume any liability for any injury and/or damage to persons or property as a matter of products
liability, negligence or otherwise, or from any use or operation of any methods, products,
instructions, or ideas contained in the material herein.

Library of Congress Cataloging-in-Publication Data
A catalog record for this book is available from the Library of Congress

British Library Cataloguing-in-Publication Data
A catalogue record for this book is available from the British Library

ISBN: 978-0-12-822688-9

For information on all Academic Press publications
visit our website at https://www.elsevier.com/books-and-journals

Publisher: Mara Conner
Acquisitions Editor: Tim Pitts
Editorial Project Manager: Fernanda A. Oliveira
Production Project Manager: Kamesh Ramajogi
Designer: Vicky Pearson Esser

Typeset by VTeX

Working together
to grow libraries in
developing countries

www.elsevier.com • www.bookaid.org

Dedication

To God, my wife, Daiane, and my sons, Bento and Mateo (coming soon). Last but not least, to my father, Mauro (In memoriam), to my mother, Maria, to my sisters, and the whole family.

João Paulo Papa

I would like to dedicate this work to my mother, Darcy, wife Paula, daughter, Clara, and son, Pedro.

Alexandre Xavier Falcão

Contents

List of contributors   *xi*
Biography of the editors   *xiii*
Preface   *xv*

1. **Introduction**   **1**
   Alexandre Xavier Falcão and João Paulo Papa

   References   4

2. **Theoretical background and related works**   **5**
   Luis C.S. Afonso, Alexandre Xavier Falcão, and João Paulo Papa

   2.1. Introduction   5
   2.2. The optimum-path forest framework   7
   2.3. Applications   22
   2.4. Conclusions and future trends   36
   Acknowledgments   37
   References   37

3. **Real-time application of OPF-based classifier in Snort IDS**   **55**
   Luan Utimura, Kelton Costa, and Rafał Scherer

   3.1. Introduction   55
   3.2. Intrusion detection systems   58
   3.3. Machine learning   62
   3.4. Methodology   66
   3.5. Experiments and results   73
   3.6. Final considerations   89
   Acknowledgments   90
   References   90

4. **Optimum-path forest and active learning approaches for
   content-based medical image retrieval**   **95**
   Rafael S. Bressan, Pedro H. Bugatti, and Priscila T.M. Saito

   4.1. Introduction   95
   4.2. Methodology   96
   4.3. Experiments   99
   4.4. Conclusion   104
   4.5. Funding and acknowledgments   105
   References   105

5. **Hybrid and modified OPFs for intrusion detection systems and
    large-scale problems**   **109**
    Mansour Sheikhan and Hamid Bostani

    5.1. Introduction   109
    5.2. Modified OPF-based IDS using unsupervised learning and social network
          concept   111
    5.3. Hybrid IDS using unsupervised OPF based on MapReduce approach   114
    5.4. Hybrid IDS using modified OPF and selected features   117
    5.5. Modified OPF using Markov cluster process algorithm   119
    5.6. Modified OPF based on coreset concept   123
    5.7. Enhancement of MOPF using k-medoids algorithm   132
    References   133

6. **Detecting atherosclerotic plaque calcifications of the carotid
    artery through optimum-path forest**   **137**
    Danilo Samuel Jodas, Mateus Roder, Rafael Pires,
    Marcos Cleison Silva Santana, Luis A. de Souza Jr., and
    Leandro Aparecido Passos

    6.1. Introduction   137
    6.2. Theoretical background   140
    6.3. Methodology   144
    6.4. Experimental results   148
    6.5. Conclusions and future works   150
    References   151

7. **Learning to weight similarity measures with Siamese networks:
    a case study on optimum-path forest**   **155**
    Gustavo H. de Rosa and João Paulo Papa

    7.1. Introduction   155
    7.2. Theoretical background   157
    7.3. Methodology   160
    7.4. Experimental results   163
    7.5. Conclusion   170
    References   172

8. **An iterative optimum-path forest framework for clustering**   **175**
    David Aparco-Cardenas, Pedro Jussieu de Rezende, and
    Alexandre Xavier Falcão

    8.1. Introduction   175
    8.2. Related work   179
    8.3. The iterative optimum-path forest framework   182
    8.4. Experimental results   191

8.5. Conclusions and future work 213
Acknowledgments 214
References 214

9. Future trends in optimum-path forest classification **217**
João Paulo Papa and Alexandre Xavier Falcão

References 219

Index *221*

List of contributors

Luis C.S. Afonso
UNESP – São Paulo State University, School of Sciences, Bauru, Brazil

David Aparco-Cardenas
Institute of Computing, University of Campinas (UNICAMP), Campinas, São Paulo, Brazil

Hamid Bostani
Young Researchers and Elite Club, South Tehran Branch, Islamic Azad University, Tehran, Iran
Digital Security Group, Radboud University, Nijmegen, The Netherlands

Rafael S. Bressan
Department of Computing, Federal University of Technology – Parana, Cornelio Procopio, Brazil

Pedro H. Bugatti
Department of Computing, Federal University of Technology – Parana, Cornelio Procopio, Brazil

Kelton Costa
São Paulo State University, Department of Computing, Bauru, Brazil

Pedro Jussieu de Rezende
Institute of Computing, University of Campinas (UNICAMP), Campinas, São Paulo, Brazil

Gustavo H. de Rosa
Department of Computing, São Paulo State University, Bauru, Brazil

Luis A. de Souza Jr.
Department of Computing, São Carlos Federal University, São Carlos, Brazil

Alexandre Xavier Falcão
Institute of Computing, University of Campinas (UNICAMP), Campinas, São Paulo, Brazil

Danilo Samuel Jodas
Department of Computing, São Paulo State University, Bauru, Brazil

João Paulo Papa
UNESP – São Paulo State University, School of Sciences, Bauru, Brazil
Department of Computing, São Paulo State University, Bauru, Brazil

Leandro Aparecido Passos
Department of Computing, São Paulo State University, Bauru, Brazil

Rafael Pires
Department of Computing, São Paulo State University, Bauru, Brazil

Mateus Roder
Department of Computing, São Paulo State University, Bauru, Brazil

Priscila T.M. Saito
Department of Computing, Federal University of Technology – Parana, Cornelio Procopio, Brazil

Rafał Scherer
Czestochowa University of Technology, Department of Computing, Częstochowa, Poland

Mansour Sheikhan
Department of Electrical Engineering, South Tehran Branch, Islamic Azad University, Tehran, Iran

Marcos Cleison Silva Santana
Department of Computing, São Paulo State University, Bauru, Brazil

Luan Utimura
São Paulo State University, Department of Computing, Bauru, Brazil

Biography of the editors

Alexandre Xavier Falcão

Alexandre Xavier Falcão (lids.ic.unicamp.br) is a full professor at the Institute of Computing (IC), University of Campinas (Unicamp), where he has worked since 1998.

He attended the Federal University of Pernambuco from 1984–1988, where he received a B.Sc. in Electrical Engineering. He then attended Unicamp, where he got an M.Sc. (1993), and a Ph.D. (1996), in Electrical Engineering, by working on volumetric data visualization and medical image segmentation. During his Ph.D., he worked with the Medical Image Processing Group at the University of Pennsylvania from 1994–1996. In 1997, he developed video quality assessment methods for Globo TV. In 2011–2012, he spent a one-year sabbatical at the Robert W. Holley Center for Agriculture and Health (USDA, Cornell University), working on image analysis applied to plant biology.

He served as Associate Director of IC-Unicamp (2006–2007), Coordinator of its Post-Graduation Program (2009–2011), and Senior Area Editor of IEEE Signal Processing Letters (2016–2020). He is currently a research fellow at the top level for the Brazilian National Council for Scientific and Technological Development (CNPq), President of the Special Commission of Computer Graphics and Image Processing (CEGRAPI) for the Brazilian Computer Society (SBC), and Area Coordinator of Computer Science for the Sao Paulo Research Foundation (FAPESP).

Among several awards, it is worth mentioning three Unicamp inventor awards at the category "License Technology" (2011, 2012, and 2020), three awards of academic excellence (2006, 2011, 2016) from IC-Unicamp, one award of academic recognition "Zeferino Vaz" from Unicamp (2014), and the best paper award in the year of 2012 from the journal "Pattern Recognition" (received at Stockholm, Sweden, during the conference ICPR 2014).

His research work aims at computational models to learn and interpret the semantic content of images in the domain of several applications. The areas of interest include image and video processing, data visualization, medical image analysis, remote sensing, graph algorithms, image annotation, organization, and retrieval, and (interactive) machine learning and pattern recognition (https://scholar.google.com/citations?user=HTFEUaUAAAAJ&hl=en).

João Paulo Papa

João Paulo Papa received his B.Sc. in Information Systems from the São Paulo State University, SP, Brazil. In 2005, he received his M.Sc. in Computer Science from the Federal University of São Carlos, SP, Brazil. In 2008, he received his Ph.D. in Computer Science from the University of Campinas, SP, Brazil. During 2008–2009, he had worked as a post-doctorate researcher at the same institute, and during 2014–2015 he worked as a visiting scholar at Harvard University. He has been an Associate Professor at the Computer Science Department, São Paulo, State University, since 2016, and his research interests include machine learning, pattern recognition, and image processing. He is also the recipient of the Alexander von Humboldt fellowship and an IEEE Senior Member.

Among several awards, it is worth mentioning the best paper award in the year of 2012 from the journal "Pattern Recognition" (received at Stockholm, Sweden, during the conference ICPR 2014, and the Unicamp inventor award at the category "License Technology" in 2019.

He is currently a research fellow for the Brazilian National Council for Scientific and Technological Development (CNPq), Senior Area Editor of IEEE Signal Processing Letters, Brazilian representative at the International Association for Pattern Recognition, and Associate Editor for the following journals: Computers in Biology and Medicine, SN Computer Science. He is also member of the advisory board of the Integrated Computer-Aided Engineering.

Preface

The Optimum-Path Forest (OPF) story dates back to 2004 with a paper called "The image foresting transform: Theory, algorithms, and applications" published on the well-known IEEE Transactions on Pattern Analysis and Machine Intelligence, IEEE PAMI for short. The Image Foresting Transform (IFT) came up to deal with image analysis based on the comprehensive framework provided by Graph Theory. By modeling pixels as graph nodes and establishing a proper adjacency relation, IFT became a powerful tool for multiscale skeletonization, distance transforms, morphological reconstructions, and image segmentation.

A mindful reader may be aware that a fine line separates image segmentation from image classification. Pixels become feature vectors and segmenting an object turns out to be classifying (labeling) its pixels accordingly. Half a decade later, in 2009, one of the most prominent papers concerning the OPF was published. What followed then was many papers that either tried to apply OPF on a different application or to improve its learning procedure. Remote sensing, medicine, speech recognition, and engineering are just a few applications that benefited from the OPF framework.

Now the family has grown. The reader can find supervised, semi-supervised, and unsupervised variants of the OPF classifier. For sure, deep learning has not been forgotten. Papers have shown how to replace softmax layers with an OPF classifier with considerably higher accuracies. We tried, in this book, to provide a complete workflow of OPF history, i.e., we refreshed our minds with an exciting survey of works and a brief theoretical background to open the reader's mind to the OPF world. We hope this book will serve as introductory and advanced material so that newcomers and experienced researchers can take advantage of the OPF capabilities.

As we usually say, OPF is not a classifier but a framework for designing classifiers based on optimum-path forest. By just changing some pieces, you can design your own OPF classifier and enjoy it! Which one are you going to pick?

The authors

CHAPTER 1

Introduction

Alexandre Xavier Falcão[a] and João Paulo Papa[b]

[a]Institute of Computing, University of Campinas (UNICAMP), Campinas, São Paulo, Brazil
[b]UNESP – São Paulo State University, School of Sciences, Bauru, Brazil

Pattern recognition techniques have been consistently applied in a broad range of domains, varying from remote sensing and medicine to engineering, among others. The literature is vast and dominated mainly by Neural Networks [1] in the past, followed by Support Vector Machines [2], and recently by the so-called "Deep Learning" approaches [3]. These latter techniques shifted the way we think about problem engineering. Instead of handcrafting features, we can use raw data to feed models that learn the best information that the data describes. On the other hand, we need considerably large data sets to train the models, which are not always available.

According to the well-known "No Free Lunch Paradigm," there is no single technique that shall fit better in all situations and data sets. Motivated by such assumption, Papa et al. [4] presented the first version of the supervised Optimum-Path Forest (OPF) classifier, which models data classification as a graph partition problem. The nodes denote samples (i.e., feature vectors) while edges encode the strength of connectivity among them. The idea is to partition the graph into optimum-path trees (OPTs) such that examples from the same class belong to the same tree. Representative samples called "prototypes" are the roots of such OPTs, and they rule the competition process that ends up partitioning the data set. The approach proposed in 2017 showed to be robust and fast for training, besides being parameterless.[1]

We prefer to understand OPF as a framework for designing classifiers based on optimum-path forests rather than a sole classifier. The rationale behind that concerns the fact that OPF is customizable and, therefore, different versions are obtained by choosing a few hyperparameters. The first one is related to the adjacency relation, which is usually set to a complete graph or a k-nn model. Usually, the latter approach provides an intrinsic

---

[1] The authors are grateful to Celso Tetsuo Nagase Suzuki for his former implementation of the OPF classifier.

Optimum-Path Forest
https://doi.org/10.1016/B978-0-12-822688-9.00009-8
1

representation of the data set as a whole, but it comes with the price of computing the k-nearest neighbors for each example. In 2008, Papa and Falcão [5] proposed the first supervised OPF based on such neighborhood formulation, with results that outperformed standard OPF in some situations. The second hyperparameter stands for the methodology to estimate prototypes. A simple and not effective approach is to pick some at random, but initial experiments have shown us that it may lead to poor generalization over unseen examples. Throughout the book, the reader can observe that different approaches can be used to find prototypes, each depending on the preliminary information we have from the data set. Last but not least, the competition process is, essentially, an optimization problem. Therefore, a path–cost function must be adopted to guide the OPF training algorithm into finding a suitable partition of the feature space.

New problems require adaptations. In 2009, Rocha et al. [6] proposed the unsupervised OPF. In the absence of labels, the approach proposed by Papa et al. [7] in the very same year is no longer possible since it requires information form labels beforehand. On the contrary, unsupervised OPF aims at finding regions with the highest density such that prototypes are then picked from these places. In this version, both nodes and arcs are weighted, and a k-neighborhood relation is used to compute a probability density function over each training sample. Semisupervised learning has also been addressed in work by Amorim et al. [8], in which unlabeled training samples are employed to improve classification.

After a considerable number of publications since its first publication, we observed that supervised OPF with a complete graph could improve during training. In 2012, Papa et al. [9] published such an improvement that sorts training samples according to their costs, i.e., examples with the lowest costs are placed on the first positions of the list. When a test sample appears to be classified, we start evaluating the training samples placed in the first positions first.[2] From beyond this point, we could observe OPF has gained popularity around the globe.

The k-neighborhood adjacency relation was further explored by Papa et al. [10]. Inspired by the unsupervised OPF [6], this version also weights nodes and arcs, and prototypes placed at the top of regions with maximum density begin the competition process. This approach's restriction is to estimate the value of k, which is usually accomplished over a validating set [11].

---

[2] The authors are grateful to Thiago Spina for his ideas and insightful comments on this work.

Besides, we observed that ensembles of OPF classifiers composed of versions with different modelings for the adjacency relation could improve effectiveness [12].

Speaking about ensembles, we can refer to some interesting works. Ponti and Papa [13] showed that both OPF training time and accuracy could be enhanced when trained over disjoint training sets. Later on, Ponti and Rossi [14] demonstrated that one could reduce training sets using ensembles of OPF-based classifiers. The subject of reducing training sets has been of considerable importance. In 2010, Papa et al. [15] proposed an approach aiming to obtain reduced but relevant training sets. The idea is to use a validation set to mark training samples that did not participate in any classification process. These samples are thought to be irrelevant, and thus they can be discarded from the learning step. Years later, Fernandes and Papa [16] proposed a similar approach, but to deal with tie zones, i.e., regions in the feature space that contain test samples that have been offered equal costs from training samples during the competition process. Let $C_x(A)$ and $C_x(B)$ be the cost that training samples A and B offered to a given test sample x, respectively, such that $C_x(A) < C_x(B)$. We addressed the following question in this work: if $|C_x(A) - C_x(B)| \le \epsilon$, is there any way to measure both samples' confidence A and B such that B is preferable to A when conquering x? In other words, we aim to learn a confidence measure for each training sample such that the most reliable samples are prone to conquer others, not only the ones that offer the best (i.e., minimum) cost.

There are many other interesting works related to OPF-based classifiers we can refer to. Obviously, there are quite a few shortcomings that are not yet addressed, such as dealing with sparse and high-dimensional feature spaces, among others. On the other hand, OPF has shown to guide Convolutional Neural Networks into better results using semisupervised learning in work by Amorim et al. [17], which aimed at coping with the problem of soybean leaf and herbivorous pest identification.

The main idea of this book is to shed light on recent advances in the context of optimum-path forest-based classification and to provide a concise review of the literature from the past years. We hope this book can also serve as a document to undergraduate and graduate levels, as well as senior researchers. The book comprises applications on several domains, such as intrusion detection in computer networks, active and metric learning, and medicine-driven problems.

References

[1] S. Haykin, Neural Networks: A Comprehensive Foundation, 3rd edition, Prentice-Hall, Inc., Upper Saddle River, NJ, USA, 2007.

[2] C. Cortes, V. Vapnik, Support vector networks, Machine Learning 20 (1995) 273–297.

[3] Y. LeCun, Y. Bengio, G.E. Hinton, Deep learning, Nature 521 (7553) (2015) 436–444.

[4] J. Papa, A. Falcão, P. Miranda, C. Suzuki, N. Mascarenhas, Design of robust pattern classifiers based on optimum-path forests, in: Mathematical Morphology and Its Applications to Signal and Image Processing (ISMM), MCT/INPE, 2007, pp. 337–348.

[5] J.P. Papa, A.X. Falcão, A new variant of the optimum-path forest classifier, in: G. Bebis, R. Boyle, B. Parvin, D. Koracin, P. Remagnino, F. Porikli, J. Peters, J. Klosowski, L. Arns, Y. Chun, T.-M. Rhyne, L. Monroe (Eds.), Advances in Visual Computing, in: Lecture Notes in Computer Science, vol. 5358, Springer Berlin Heidelberg, 2008, pp. 935–944.

[6] L.M. Rocha, F.A.M. Cappabianco, A.X. Falcão, Data clustering as an optimum-path forest problem with applications in image analysis, International Journal of Imaging Systems and Technology 19 (2) (2009) 50–68.

[7] J.P. Papa, A.X. Falcão, C.T.N. Suzuki, Supervised pattern classification based on optimum-path forest, International Journal of Imaging Systems and Technology 19 (2) (2009) 120–131.

[8] W.P. Amorim, A.X. Falcão, J.P. Papa, M.H. Carvalho, Improving semi-supervised learning through optimum connectivity, Pattern Recognition 60 (2016) 72–85.

[9] J.P. Papa, A.X. Falcão, V.H.C. Albuquerque, J.M.R.S. Tavares, Efficient supervised optimum-path forest classification for large datasets, Pattern Recognition 45 (1) (2012) 512–520.

[10] J.P. Papa, S.E.N. Fernandes, A.X. Falcão, Optimum-path forest based on k-connectivity: theory and applications, Pattern Recognition Letters 87 (2017) 117–126.

[11] J.P. Papa, A.X. Falcão, A learning algorithm for the optimum-path forest classifier, in: A. Torsello, F. Escolano, L. Brun (Eds.), Graph-Based Representations in Pattern Recognition, in: Lecture Notes in Computer Science, vol. 5534, Springer Berlin Heidelberg, 2009, pp. 195–204.

[12] P.B. Ribeiro, J.P. Papa, R.A.F. Romero, An ensemble-based approach for breast mass classification in mammography images, in: SPIE Medical Imaging, 2017, pp. 101342N-1–101342N-8.

[13] M.P. Ponti, J.P. Papa, Improving accuracy and speed of optimum-path forest classifier using combination of disjoint training subsets, in: C. Sansone, J. Kittler, F. Roli (Eds.), Multiple Classifier Systems, Springer Berlin Heidelberg, Berlin, Heidelberg, 2011, pp. 237–248.

[14] M.P. Ponti, I. Rossi, Ensembles of optimum-path forest classifiers using input data manipulation and undersampling, in: Z.-H. Zhou, F. Roli, J. Kittler (Eds.), Multiple Classifier Systems, Springer Berlin Heidelberg, Berlin, Heidelberg, 2013, pp. 236–246.

[15] J. Papa, A. Falcão, G. de Freitas, A. Avila, Robust pruning of training patterns for optimum-path forest classification applied to satellite-based rainfall occurrence estimation, IEEE Geoscience and Remote Sensing Letters 7 (2) (2010) 396–400.

[16] S.E.N. Fernandes, J.P. Papa, Improving optimum-path forest learning using bag-of-classifiers and confidence measures, Pattern Analysis & Applications 22 (2019) 703–716.

[17] W. Amorim, E. Tetila, H. Pistori, J. Papa, Semi-supervised learning with convolutional neural networks for uav images automatic recognition, Computers and Electronics in Agriculture 164 (2019) 104932.

CHAPTER 2

Theoretical background and related works

Luis C.S. Afonso[a], Alexandre Xavier Falcão[b], and João Paulo Papa[a]
[a]UNESP – São Paulo State University, School of Sciences, Bauru, Brazil
[b]Institute of Computing, University of Campinas (UNICAMP), Campinas, São Paulo, Brazil

2.1 Introduction

Pattern recognition (PR) techniques have been widely employed to solve different and complex problems in many research fields. The motivation in the development of such techniques is to perform recognition tasks more accurately, faster, or just to aid in the mechanical and repetitive ones [142]. The basic idea behind PR techniques is to compute a model capable of classifying unknown samples by a learning data distribution over the feature space. The learning process requires a training set that might carry information (i.e., label) that helps to minimize the classification error in the training set. Therefore, the existence or not of such labeled training data creates three fundamental problems in pattern recognition: (i) supervised, (ii) unsupervised, and more recently the (iii) semisupervised learning [102].

Supervised learning-based algorithms take advantage of a fully labeled data set, which enables to build more robust models. Artificial Neural Networks using Multi-Layer Perceptrons (ANN-MLP) [87], Support Vector Machines (SVM) [26], and Bayesian classifier (BC) [96] figure among the most popular ones. Although well-established in the literature, the mentioned classifiers have their drawbacks, such as to find an optimum set of parameters for better accuracy rates, computational cost, and especially the difficult to handle nonseparable classes in the feature space. For instance, ANN-MLP could have its performance improved if more layers are added, but that comes with the increase of computational cost. Nonlinear problems require SVM to map data into higher-dimensional spaces, which also makes the method costly, and BC makes a decision based on the probability density of each class. If such information is not available, one must be estimated, besides assuming independence among features.

In the opposite way, unsupervised problems do not have any labeled information regarding the training samples at their disposal, which makes

Optimum-Path Forest
https://doi.org/10.1016/B978-0-12-822688-9.00010-4
5

the learning task more difficult. Hence, the fundamental problem in unsupervised learning is to identify clusters in an unlabeled data set, such
that samples from the same cluster should share some level of similarity.
Many methods were proposed where the learning problem is addressed
with different perspectives, such as data clustering and density estimation,
just to mention a few [231]. Self-Organizing Maps and k-means figure
among the most common unsupervised algorithms. Self-Organizing Maps
(SOM) [101] is a very popular unsupervised neural-network model for the
analysis of high-dimensional input data. Difficulties in using SOM comprise
to define the map size, which is related to the number of input data, and hierarchical representations are hard to be identified [205]. The k-means [95]
is one of the simplest clustering algorithms that partitions data in an iterative fashion using k-centroids. The parameter k is defined a priori, which is
not a straightforward task. Also, its random initialization has a considerable
impact on the final result, besides assuming the clusters have a spherical
shape.

Semisupervised learning is a more recent problem in pattern recognition [88]. Many of the real-world problems have an incredibly high amount
of data and label it completely is very much costly. Therefore, the training
set is comprised of labeled and unlabeled samples, which requires a three-
step training process: (i) training using the labeled data, (ii) propagating the
labels to the unlabeled training data, and (iii) training using the fully labeled
training set. Generative models are referred to as the oldest semisupervised
learning technique. The technique builds a model based on the input data
distribution and may fail if the model is computed incorrectly or the input data is not correlated with the classification task. Approaches such as
transductive or semisupervised SVMs may fail when the classes are strongly
overlapped since they assume a high density within a class and low density
among classes [189].

Graph-based machine learning techniques have their appeal as well.
Basically, such methods model the machine learning task as a problem for-
mulated in the Graph Theory: the data set samples, which are represented
by their corresponding feature vectors, are encoded by the graph nodes,
that are further connected by an adjacency relation. Without loss of gener-
ality, a graph-based method aims at removing or adding edges using some
heuristic to create connected components, which stand for a group of samples that share similar characteristics [29].

The Optimum-Path Forest (OPF) is a framework for the design of
graph-based classifiers, and comprises three models: (i) supervised [146,

150,153,155], (ii) semisupervised [19,20], and (iii) unsupervised [212]. The traditional OPF algorithm models samples as the nodes of a graph, which are connected to each other based on some predefined adjacency relation. Learning and classification phases are carried out by a competition-based process ruled by a few "key" samples called *prototypes*, which are responsible for conquering the remaining samples by offering them optimum-path costs. The outcome of such a process is a set of optimum-path trees (forest), each rooted at a different prototype. As to be further discussed, the set of prototypes are defined based on the model employed.

Although being a recent approach, OPF has been applied in numerous applications, such as network security, image and video analysis, and disease identification, just to mention a few. Moreover, it has shown competitive accuracy rates, outperforming some well-known and state-of-art classifiers (e.g., SVM, k-NN, and BC). OPF-based classifiers are quite fast in both training and classification process since it does not interpret pattern recognition problems as a separating hyperplanes task [148]. However, to the best of our knowledge, we have not observed any survey concerning OPF-based classifiers up-to-date. Therefore, the main contributions of this paper are two-fold:

• To provide a survey concerning OPF-based classifiers and a wide spectrum of the problems that applied them;
• To shed a light over OPF-based classifiers by compiling the theory behind them.

The paper is organized as follows: Section 2.2 provides details about the general OPF framework and its variations for supervised, semisupervised, and unsupervised learning. Section 2.3 presents the applications of the OPF in pattern recognition and general problems, and Section 2.4 states the final remarks and future research directions.

2.2 The optimum-path forest framework

This section introduces the general idea of the optimum-path forest, which is a framework for the design of simple, fast, and native multiclass graph-based classifiers.

2.2.1 Theoretical background

A weighted graph $\mathcal{G} = (\mathcal{C}, \mathcal{E}, w)$ is formally defined as a triplet, in which $\mathcal{C}$ denotes the set of vertices (nodes) and $\mathcal{E}$ stands for the set of edges or arcs. Besides, $w : \mathcal{C} \times \mathcal{C} \to \Re^+$ stands for a function that weights each arc of the graph. An edge defines a connection between any two adjacent nodes and the connections are established according to an *adjacency relation* $\mathcal{A}$ (i.e., an irreflexive binary relation between nodes). The edges allow to perform the so-called "walks on the graph" and to find paths among nodes. A path π_s is defined as a sequence of adjacent nodes starting from any node and with terminus at node $s \in C$, and it is called trivial when composed of a single node s being represented as $\langle s \rangle$. An optimum-path is the one with a value $f(\pi_s)$ that satisfies $f(\pi_s) \le f(\tau_s)$, being τ_s any other path in the graph with terminus at sample s, and f a real-valued path-cost function. Fig. 2.1 depicts a few possible paths in a graph.[1]

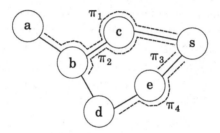

Figure 2.1 The dashed lines represent four possible paths to node s: $\pi_1 = \{a, b, c, s\}$, $\pi_2 = \{b, c, s\}$, $\pi_3 = \{e, s\}$, and $\pi_4 = \{d, e, s\}$.

The main idea behind OPF is to partition a graph into a forest (i.e., set of trees), such that all trees are comprised of optimum paths, and the nodes within a tree share similar properties. In such a way, OPF can be understood as a generalization of Dijkstra's algorithm that works with any smooth path-cost function and is capable of finding optimum-paths from multiple sources [70]. *Why does the OPF working mechanism is restricted to smooth path-cost functions?* The answer comes from the work by Falcão et al. [70] that describes the generalization of Dijkstra's algorithm works essentially with monotonic-incremental cost functions (i.e., a function whose values always increase within a certain interval). However, a few nonmonotonic-incremental functions are also eligible as a path-cost function (e.g., the 4-connected adjacency and $f_{euc}(\pi)$, which defines the Euclidean distance between the endpoints of π). Hence, the authors defined more general conditions to cover such cases, which where further revisited by Ciesielski et al. [37].

---

[1] In the pattern recognition context, the nodes encode the feature vectors.

The conditions capture the essential features of such functions and the ones that satisfy them are called *smooth*. Moreover, the path-cost functions are comprised of two terms: (i) the initialization term $f(\langle s \rangle)$ that assigns an initial value to the trivial paths, usually according to the type of node (i.e., prototype or nonprototype); and (ii) the propagation term $f(\pi_s \cdot \langle s, t \rangle)$, which defines the path cost to be offered to a node during the bidding process.

Let $\mathcal{Z} = \{z_1, z_2, \ldots, z_m\}$ be a data set of samples such that $z_i \in \mathcal{R}^n$. The optimum-path forest encodes each sample as a node in the graph $\mathcal{G} = (\mathcal{Z}, \mathcal{A})$, and the graph-partitioning task is performed in a bidding-like process where the bid is the cost defined by a smooth-path cost function. As aforementioned, the OPF is capable of computing optimum-path trees from multiple sources, called *prototypes*, which are a subset of samples $\mathcal{P} \in \mathcal{Z}$. The heuristic implemented to select the set of prototypes varies according to the application. For instance, they can be selected at random, by computing minimum spanning trees, or by some probability density function. For the sake of explanation, let us consider the set $\mathcal{P}$ is already defined. After defining the path-cost function and the set of prototypes, the next step concerns computing the optimum-path trees (OPTs).

The optimum-path trees are computed in a bidding-like process where the prototypes play as bidders and the remaining samples (i.e., the non-prototype samples) are the prize. In the first step, all paths are trivial and initialized with a cost according to the type of node they are associated (i.e., prototype or nonprototype).

In the OPF context, the bidding order is defined by a priority queue whose ordering is defined by the trivial-path cost. The targets (i.e., prize-nodes) of each node are its adjacent ones and the value to be offered is a path cost. The winner is the one that offers the optimum-path cost and the prize-node is added to its "collection" (i.e., optimum-path tree). *What if multiple prototypes offer the same optimum-path cost?* In this case, OPF applies the first-takes-the-prize policy (i.e., first-in-first-out – FIFO), but any policy can be implemented as well. Fig. 2.2 provides an overview of the process for a given adjacency relation $\mathcal{A}$.

Following, we present a toy example that computes optimum-paths from multiple sources considering the f_{sum} path-cost function:

$$f_{sum}(\langle s \rangle) = \begin{cases} 0 & \text{if } s \in \mathcal{P} \\ +\infty & \text{otherwise,} \end{cases}$$

$$f_{sum}(\pi_s \cdot \langle s, t \rangle) = f_{sum}(\pi_s) + d(s, t). \tag{2.1}$$

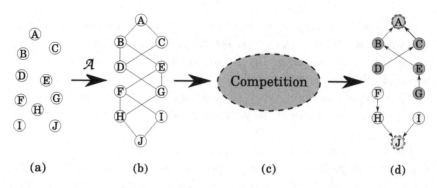

(a)   **(b)**   **(c)**   **(d)**

Figure 2.2 Overview of the OPF working mechanism: (a) initial data set, (b) derived graph $\mathcal{G}$ according to $\mathcal{A}$, (c) computing the optimum-path trees, and (d) the resulting optimum-path forest with the prototypes highlighted (dashed circles).

Fig. 2.3 illustrates the entire process from the (a) initialization of the graph to (l) its optimum-path forest. The values in red (dark gray in print version) stand for the trivial-path cost of the nodes, in which each node $s \in \mathcal{Z}$ is initialized with a value according to its type and stored in a priority queue $\mathcal{Q}$.

The values in green (gray in print version) stand for the weight of the edges defined by $d(s, t)$, which can be any distance or similarity metric computed over the arc $(s, t) \in \mathcal{A}$. The prototypes are represented as dashed-circled nodes (i.e., nodes a and j), and on the right side of each graph is shown the current priority queue $\mathcal{Q}$. The node in yellow (light gray in print version) is the one that has been removed from $\mathcal{Q}$, and the pink (mid gray in print version) ones are its adjacent that are still in $\mathcal{Q}$. The priority queue stores the nodes in increasing order of costs and the ones with minimum values are the first to be popped out. Notice that $\mathcal{Q}$ is implemented using a binary heap. For the sake of explanation, we have a min-heap since we are trying to minimize the cost of each sample.

In the toy example, node a is the first to be removed and tries to conquer its adjacent node b (Fig. 2.3b) by offering a cost $C_a(b) = 0.0 + 0.8$. Since $C_a(b) < C(b)$, where $C(b)$ stands for the current cost of node b, node b is conquered by node a. Now, $\mathcal{O}(b) = \{a\}$ and b points to a where $\mathcal{O}$ is the predecessor map. The process is repeated for the next adjacent node of a (i.e., node c). Similar to node b, the node c is also conquered by a with a cost of 0.7. Notice the priority queue is updated every time a node is conquered.

The next node in the queue is j, and its adjacency is analyzed in the same way as it was done for a. The bidding is performed until $\mathcal{Q}$ is empty.

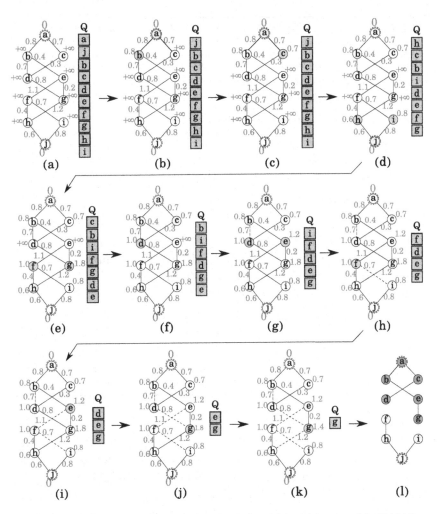

Figure 2.3 General working mechanism of OPF from: (a) initialization, (b)–(k) bidding process to (l) optimum-path forest.

Notice the case of a tie in (j) where *d* tries to conquer *g* but it does not due to the FIFO policy. Also, notice in (k) where the conqueror of *g* changes to *e*. The entire process is implemented in Algorithm 2.1, in which *f* sums up all arc-weights along a path.

One of the main applications of the optimum-path forest concerns general pattern recognition problems, but it is not restricted to them. By performing a few modifications in its general formulation, OPF becomes a powerful classification algorithm capable of learning under dif-

---

Algorithm 2.1: Optimum-Path Forest Algorithm for Shortest-Path Computation

---

Input: A set of samples $\mathcal{Z}$, set of prototypes $\mathcal{P} \subset \mathcal{Z}$, a path-cost function f, and an adjacency relation $\mathcal{A}$.
Output: Predecessor map $\mathcal{O}$ and path-cost map $\mathcal{C}$.
Auxiliary: Priority queue $\mathcal{Q}$, and variable cst.

---

1    $\mathcal{Q}(s) \leftarrow 0$
2   **for** *all* $s \in \mathcal{Z}$ **do**
3      $\mathcal{O}(s) \leftarrow nil$, $\mathcal{C}(s) \leftarrow +\infty$, $\mathcal{Q} \leftarrow \{s\}$;
4   **if** $s \subset \mathcal{P}$ **then**
5      $\mathcal{C}(s) \leftarrow 0$
6   **while** $\mathcal{Q} \neq \{\}$ **do**
7   Remove from $\mathcal{Q}$ a sample s such that $\mathcal{C}(s)$ is minimum;
8   **for** *each sample* $t \in \mathcal{A}(s)$ *and* $t \in \mathcal{Q}$ **do**
9        $cst = f(\mathcal{O}(s), d(s, t))$;
10   **if** $cst < \mathcal{C}(t)$ **then**
11        $\mathcal{O}(t) \leftarrow s$, $\mathcal{C}(t) \leftarrow cst$;
12   Update $\mathcal{Q}$;
13   **return** $\mathcal{O}, \mathcal{C}$

---

ferent assumptions (i.e., supervised, semi-supervised, and unsupervised). OPF-based classifiers explore the connectivity strength among samples to group the similar ones and their main advantages are two-fold: (i) the native treatment for multiclass problems, and (ii) the fact the attribute space geometry is not considered, which provides better results for data sets comprised of outliers or overlapping classes.

2.2.2 Supervised learning

This section introduces two strategies for supervised learning using OPF. They differ from each other on the adjacency relation, path-cost function, and the heuristic to select the prototypes.

2.2.2.1 OPF using complete graph

The strategy introduced by Papa et al. [146] implements the complete graph as an adjacency relation, i.e., there is an arc connecting any pair of nodes.

Let $\mathcal{Z}$ be a λ-labeled data set, and $\mathcal{Z}_1$, $\mathcal{Z}_2$, and $\mathcal{Z}_3$ stand for the training, validation, and testing sets, respectively, such that $\mathcal{Z} = \mathcal{Z}_1 \cup \mathcal{Z}_2 \cup \mathcal{Z}_3$, and $\mathcal{Z}_1 \cap \mathcal{Z}_3 = \emptyset$. The OPF with complete graph (OPF_{cg}) builds $\mathcal{P} \subseteq \mathcal{Z}_1$ by computing a minimum spanning tree (MST) over the complete graph $\mathcal{G} = (\mathcal{Z}_1, \mathcal{A})$. The outcome is an undirected acyclic graph where the edges are weighted by the distance between the adjacent feature vectors. Such spanning tree is optimum in the sense the sum of the weights of its edges is minimum if compared to any other spanning tree of the complete graph. The MST holds some theoretical properties, and it guarantees no error during training under certain circumstances [14].

Since training aims at minimizing the classification error, the prototypes will be the samples in the resulting MST that are connected and belong to distinct classes, i.e., samples located at the decision boundaries. The option for such samples is based on the fact they are more likely to be misclassified due to the proximity to the influence region of other classes. By disconnecting such samples, we obtain the set of prototypes $\mathcal{P}$ and the bidding is performed through Algorithm 2.2, which uses the f_{max} as path-cost function:

$$f_{max}(\langle s \rangle) = \begin{cases} 0 & \text{if } s \in \mathcal{P} \\ +\infty & \text{otherwise,} \end{cases}$$

$$f_{max}(\pi_s \cdot (s, t)) = \max\{f_{max}(\pi_s), d(s, t)\}. \tag{2.2}$$

Lines 1–4 initialize the cost map by assigning cost 0 to the prototypes and $+\infty$ to the remaining samples. All samples have their predecessors set as *nil*, and the prototypes are inserted into the priority queue $\mathcal{Q}$. The loop at Line 5 iterates over all samples $s \in \mathcal{P}$ first to start the competition process: if the cost offered *cst* is lower than the current cost of the prize-node t, the sample t is labeled with the same label as sample s and added to its tree (Line 12). Notice the classes can be represented by multiple optimum-path trees, and there must be at least one per class.

The classification of a sample $t \in \mathcal{Z}_3$ is performed by connecting it to all samples $s \in \mathcal{Z}_1$ and making t part of the graph. By considering all possible paths between $\mathcal{P}$ and t, we aim at finding the optimum-path to t with the same class of its most strongly connected prototype. Such path can be found by evaluating the optimum-path cost $\mathcal{C}(t)$ as follows:

$$\mathcal{C}(t) = \min\{\max\{\mathcal{C}(s), d(s, t)\}\}, \forall s \in \mathcal{Z}_1. \tag{2.3}$$

Algorithm 2.2: Supervised training using complete graph

Input: A λ-labeled training set $\mathcal{Z}_1$, set of prototypes $\mathcal{P} \subset \mathcal{Z}_1$ and a
function d for distance computation.
Output: Predecessor map $\mathcal{O}$, path-cost map $\mathcal{C}$, and label map $\mathcal{L}$.
Auxiliary: Priority queue $\mathcal{Q}$ and variable cst.

1   **for** *all* $s \in \mathcal{Z}_1$ **do**
2      $\mathcal{O}(s) \leftarrow nil$, $\mathcal{C}(s) \leftarrow +\infty$;
3   **for** *all* $s \in \mathcal{P}$ **do**
4      $\mathcal{C}(s) \leftarrow 0$, $\mathcal{L}(s) = \lambda(s)$, $\mathcal{Q} \leftarrow s$
5   **while** $\mathcal{Q} \neq \{\}$ **do**
6   Remove from $\mathcal{Q}$ a sample s such that $\mathcal{C}(s)$ is minimum;
7   **for** *each sample* $t \in \mathcal{Z}_1$ *such that* $s \neq t$ *and* $\mathcal{C}(t) > \mathcal{C}(s)$ **do**
8        $cst \leftarrow \max\{\mathcal{C}(s), d(s, t)\}$;
9   **if** $cst < \mathcal{C}(t)$ **then**
10   **if** $\mathcal{C}(t) \neq +\infty$ **then**
11   Remove t from $\mathcal{Q}$;
12          $\mathcal{L}(t) \leftarrow \mathcal{L}(s)$, $\mathcal{O}(t) \leftarrow s$, $\mathcal{C}(t) \leftarrow cst$;
13          $\mathcal{Q} \leftarrow t$;

14   **return** $\mathcal{O}, \mathcal{C}, \mathcal{L}$;

Let $s^* \in \mathcal{Z}_1$ be the node that satisfies Eq. (2.3). The classification assigns $\mathcal{L}(s^*)$ as the label of t. A misclassification happens when $\mathcal{L}(s^*) \neq \lambda(t)$. Fig. 2.4 depicts the training (a)–(c) and classification (d)–(f) phases.

The OPF with complete graph works similar to the nearest-neighbor (NN) classifier only when all training samples are prototypes, which is very rare and indicates that the set of attributes may not be the most appropriate to represent the samples. Moreover, OPF-based classifiers differentiate from NN-based ones on how decisions are made. The latter makes local-based decisions whereas the former is capable of global solutions based on the connectivity strength among samples.

2.2.2.2 OPF using k-nn graph

The second approach for supervised classification (OPF_{knn}) was proposed by Papa et al. [147,148,155], whose primary motivation was to explore different path-cost functions, adjacency relations, and heuristics to select

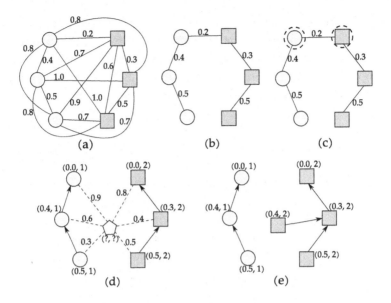

Figure 2.4 OPF$_{cg}$: training and classification phases.

prototypes. Their approach also encodes samples as nodes in a graph, but it employs a k-NN adjacency relation ($\mathcal{A}_k$). Since a k-NN graph does not guarantee a connected graph, computing the prototypes via MST is no longer an option. Hence, OPF$_{knn}$ implements a strategy similar to selecting elements nearby the centroids of clusters [223], where the nodes located in areas of higher concentration of samples are chosen to build $\mathcal{P}$.

The density of each node $s \in \mathcal{Z}_1$ is computed by a probability density function (pdf) as follows:

$$\rho(s) = \frac{1}{\sqrt{2\pi\sigma^2}|\mathcal{A}_k(s)|} \sum_{\forall t \in \mathcal{A}_k(s)} \exp\left(\frac{-d^2(s, t)}{2\sigma^2}\right), \tag{2.4}$$

where $\sigma = d_{max}/3$ and $d_{max} = \max\{d(s, t) \in (\mathcal{Z}_1, \mathcal{A}_k)\}$. A coverage of 99.7% of the nodes within $d(s, t) \in [0, 3\sigma]$ can be guaranteed in the computation of $\rho(s)$ by applying a Gaussian function. Moreover, the pdf is a Parzen-window estimation based on isotropic Gaussian kernel when the arcs are defined by $(s, t) \in \mathcal{A}$ if $d(s, t) \leq d_f$, being d_{max}.

Imagine that the plotting of the density values gives us a surface where the variations of density create valleys and peaks, and the regions with the same values define plateaus. In cases where the plateau is a maximum of the pdf, it is urged to guarantee the connectivity between any pair of nodes at that maximum, so that any node can reach the remaining ones of the plateau and their influence zone via an optimum path. This condition is essential to avoid the segmentation of the plateau in too many OPTs (i.e., too many prototypes), where there should be only a few or even a single one. One can overcome this issue by modifying the adjacency relation $\mathcal{A}_k$ to a symmetric one of type $\mathcal{A}_2$:

$$\text{if } t \in (\mathcal{A}_k(s)), \text{ and } s \notin \mathcal{A}_k(t), \text{ and } \rho(s) = \rho(t), \text{ then } \mathcal{A}_2(t) \leftarrow \mathcal{A}_k(t) \cup \{s\}. \tag{2.5}$$

In a theoretical situation where each maximum is comprised of a single sample, the following path-cost function can be applied:

$$f_1(\langle s \rangle) = \begin{cases} \rho(s) & \text{if } s \in \mathcal{P} \\ -\infty & \text{otherwise,} \end{cases}$$

$$f_1(\pi_s \cdot \langle s, t \rangle) = \min\{f_1(\pi_s), \rho(t)\}. \tag{2.6}$$

Every sample $s \in \mathcal{P}$ defines a trivial path $\langle s \rangle$ since it is not possible to reach s from any other maximum of the pdf without going through nodes of values lower than $\rho(s)$. Hence, any path originated in $\mathcal{P}$ will have a greater value since the remaining trivial paths are initialized with a value $-\infty$. Considering all possible paths from $\mathcal{P}$ to all samples $t \notin \mathcal{P}$, the optimum path $\mathcal{O}^*(t)$ will be the one whose lowest density value is the maximum.

However, in a practical situation, a maximum may be represented by a set of nodes leading us to change the connectivity function in such way that an initial value h defines the relevant pdf maxima (i.e., a single node is selected per maximum). By applying $f_1(\langle s \rangle) = h(s) < \rho(s), \forall s \in \mathcal{Z}_1$, a few pdf maxima are preserved and others are reached by paths from other maxima, whose values are greater than their initial ones. Given that $h(s)$ can be computed as follows:

$$h(t) = \rho(t) - \delta \tag{2.7}$$

$$\delta = \min_{(s,t) \in \mathcal{A} | \rho(t) \neq \rho(s)} |\rho(t) - \rho(s)|,$$

all maxima of ρ are preserved and the regions with a value lower than δ will not define influence zones. According to Rocha et al. [213], the number of maxima can be reduced by:

• increasing the value of δ or by computing an antiextensive morphological operation: the plateaus of height below δ are removed;

- applying connected filters, such as area and volume openings as antiextensive operators: the plateaus of area or volume below δ are removed.

As aforementioned, it is desired to avoid any division of the influence zone of a maximum into multiple influence zones each rooted by one sample from that maximum. In this sense, $\mathcal{P}$ is built by adding to it a single node per maximum, which is the first one detected by OPF_{knn} in each maximum. The nodes in $\mathcal{P}$ will have their cost exchanged from $h(s)$ to $\rho(s)$ and they will be able to conquer the remaining ones in their maximum zone as well. Thus the final connectivity function f_2 is given by

$$f_2(\langle s \rangle) = \begin{cases} \rho(s) & \text{if } s \in \mathcal{P} \\ h(s) & \text{otherwise} \end{cases}$$

$$f_2(\pi_s \cdot \langle s, t \rangle) = \min\{f(\pi_s), \rho(t)\}, \tag{2.8}$$

and training can be performed.

The OPF_{knn} accuracy is influenced by the value k for $\mathcal{A}_k$. Papa et al. [154] proposed an additional step prior the final training that computes the best value $k^* \in [1, k_{max}]$ that maximizes the accuracy Acc over an evaluating set $\mathcal{Z}_2$. The idea is to obtain more relevant samples to the training by swapping samples from $\mathcal{Z}_2$ that were incorrectly classified for any randomly selected samples from $\mathcal{Z}_1$, except the prototypes, and minimize the misclassification rate. The accuracy Acc takes into account unbalanced data sets (i.e., a data set whose classes are comprised of a different amount of samples) and defined as follows:

$$Acc = \frac{2c - \sum_{i=1}^{c} E(i)}{2c} = 1 - \frac{\sum_{i=1}^{c} E(i)}{2c}, \tag{2.9}$$

where i stands for the class, c is the number of classes, and the term $E(i)$ is given by

$$E(i) = \frac{FP(i)}{|\mathcal{Z}_2| - |\mathcal{Z}_2(i)|} + \frac{FN(i)}{|\mathcal{Z}_2(i)|}, \quad i = 1, 2, \ldots, c, \tag{2.10}$$

where $FP(i)$ and $FN(i)$ are the values of false positive and false negative for class i, respectively, and $\mathcal{Z}_2(i)$ stands for the number of samples in class i. In summary, it is computed a classification model for each $k \in [1, k_{max}]$ with accuracy evaluated over $\mathcal{Z}_2$. Then the model that achieves the highest accuracy is used to classify $\mathcal{Z}_3$.

The resulting optimum-path forest from $\mathcal{Z}_1$ must have each class represented by at least one maximum of the pdf. However, such condition may not be satisfied if Eq. (2.8) is applied. To ensure such property, k^* is computed using Eq. (2.8) and then the final training using the best model is performed through the training Algorithm 2.3 applying f_{min}:

$$f_{min}(\langle s \rangle) = \begin{cases} \rho(s) & \text{if } s \in \mathcal{P} \\ h(s) & \text{otherwise,} \end{cases}$$

$$f_{min}(\pi_s \cdot \langle s, t \rangle) = \begin{cases} -\infty & \text{if } \lambda(t) \neq \lambda(s) \\ \min\{f_2(\pi_s), \rho(s)\} & \text{otherwise,} \end{cases} \qquad (2.11)$$

By assigning $-\infty$ to all edges $(s, t) \in \mathcal{A}_k$ where $\lambda(t) \neq \lambda(s)$, we avoid such arcs to be part of an optimum path.

Algorithm 2.3: Supervised training using k-nn graph

Input: A k-nn graph $(\mathcal{Z}_1, \mathcal{A}_k)$, $\lambda(s)$ for all $s \in \mathcal{Z}_1$ and a path-cost function f_1.
Output: Predecessor map $\mathcal{O}$, path cost map $\mathcal{C}$, and label map $\mathcal{L}$.
Auxiliary: Priority queue $\mathcal{Q}$ and variable cst.

1 **for** *all $s \in \mathcal{Z}_1$* **do**
2 | $\mathcal{O}(s) \leftarrow nil$, $\mathcal{C}(s) \leftarrow \rho(s) - \delta$, $\mathcal{L}(s) \leftarrow \lambda(s)$;
3 | Insert s in $\mathcal{Q}$;

4 **while** $\mathcal{Q} \neq \{\}$ **do**
5 | Remove from $\mathcal{Q}$ a sample s such that $\mathcal{C}(s)$ is maximum;
6 | **if** $\mathcal{O}(s) = nil$ **then**
7 | | $\mathcal{C}(s) \leftarrow \rho(s)$;
8 | **for** *each sample $t \in \mathcal{A}_k(s)$ and $\mathcal{C}(t) < \mathcal{C}(s)$* **do**
9 | | $cst \leftarrow \min\{\mathcal{C}(s), \rho(t)\}$;
10 | | **if** $cst > \mathcal{C}(t)$ **then**
11 | | | $\mathcal{L}(t) \leftarrow \mathcal{L}(s)$, $\mathcal{O}(t) \leftarrow s$, $\mathcal{C}(t) \leftarrow cst$;
12 | | | Update the position of t in $\mathcal{Q}$;

13 **return** $\mathcal{O}, \mathcal{C}, \mathcal{L}$;

Concerning the training algorithm, the loop defined in Line 1 initializes the trivial paths and predecessor map, and add all nodes to the priority queue $\mathcal{Q}$. At first, the trivial paths have assigned a cost $f(\langle s \rangle) = \rho(s) - \delta$, and none of them have a predecessor node. Differently from OPF_{cg}, the priority queue in OPF_{knn} is in decreasing order, being the nodes of higher cost the ones with higher priority. The main loop that begins in Line 4 iterates over all nodes that will try to conquer its adjacent ones (i.e., loop in Line 8). If the node t is conquered by a node s, s becomes the predecessor of t, and s assigns its label to node t. The cost and position of node t in Q are also updated. Notice the maxima are defined in Line 6. The outcomes of the algorithm are the optimum–path forest (i.e., predecessor map), path cost map, and label map.

The classification of samples in $\mathcal{Z}_3$ is performed similar to the conquering process (Fig. 2.5). The first step computes the k-nearest neighbors of t and then it is verified which node $s^* \in \mathcal{Z}_1$ satisfies the equation below:

$$C(t) = \arg\max_{s \in \mathcal{Z}_1} \min\{C(s), \rho(t)\}. \tag{2.12}$$

Therefore OPF_{knn} can be understood as a dual version of OPF_{cg} (minimization problem) since it aims at maximizing the cost of each sample, as follows:

$$\max f(\pi_s), \ \forall s \in \mathcal{Z}_1. \tag{2.13}$$

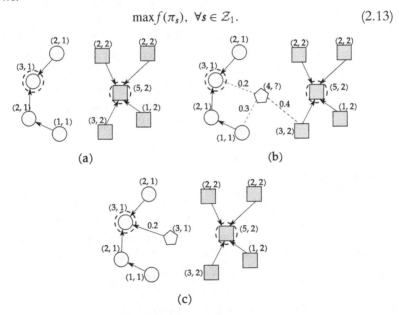

Figure 2.5 OPF k-nn: (a) optimum-path forest after training, (b) sample to be classified, and (c) sample after classification.

2.2.3 Semisupervised learning

The semisupervised learning is characterized by a training set $\mathcal{Z}_1$ comprised of labeled $\mathcal{Z}_1^l$ and unlabeled $\mathcal{Z}_1^u$ sets of samples where $\mathcal{Z}_1 = \mathcal{Z}_1^l \cup \mathcal{Z}_1^u$

and $\mathcal{Z}_1^l \cap \mathcal{Z}_1^u = \emptyset$. The learning process assumes the unlabeled training samples are correctly labeled by the labeled training samples to compute the final model. By taking such assumption, Amorim et al. [18] proposed the semisupervised Optimum-Path Forest classifier (OPF_{ssp}) by assuming that a reasonable amount of unlabeled samples in the training set are correctly labeled by a supervised version of OPF. Therefore the training phase is divided into three steps: (i) computing the set of prototypes from $\mathcal{Z}_1^l$, (ii) labeling the samples in $\mathcal{Z}_1^u$, and (iii) performing the training in $\mathcal{Z}_1$.

The set $\mathcal{P}$ is computed similar to OPF_{cg} by deriving a graph $\mathcal{G} = (\mathcal{Z}_1^l, \mathcal{A})$, being $\mathcal{A}$ a complete graph adjacency relation, and further computing an MST over $\mathcal{G}$. The prototypes will be those samples that are connected to a sample of a different label. Once $\mathcal{P}$ is defined, $\mathcal{Z}_1^u$ is labeled through the bidding-like process described in Algorithm 2.2. The outcome is a set $\mathcal{Z}_1'$ completely labeled. Notice that the labels are propagated only by the prototypes or by samples that already have a label assigned through the propagation term of Eq. (2.11). Furthermore, the winner node assigns its label to the prize-node and becomes the prize-node's predecessor (i.e., Line 12 in Algorithm 2.3). Finally, a complete training over $\mathcal{Z}_1'$ is performed, i.e., computing an MST over $(\mathcal{Z}_1', \mathcal{A})$ to define the new set $\mathcal{P}$ and running Algorithm 2.2. Amorim et al. [18] observed that the training using $\mathcal{Z}_1'$ improves the set of prototypes because relevant samples from $\mathcal{Z}_1^u$ are incorporated. Finally, the classification by OPF_{ssp} is performed in the same way as by OPF_{cg}. The testing sample $t \in \mathcal{Z}_3$ is connected to all samples in $s \in \mathcal{Z}_1'$ and the one that satisfies Eq. (2.3) assigns its label to t.

2.2.4 Unsupervised learning

The unsupervised version of the optimum-path forest classifier was proposed by Rocha et al. [213] based on the well-known mean-shift algorithm that computes clusters as influence zones of the maxima of a probability density function. The unsupervised OPF (OPF_{uns}) also exploits the identification of natural groups in a data set using the pdf of the samples, but with the advantages of being less sensitive to the pdf's gradient estimation and finding clusters more closely to the desired amount.

OPF_{uns} works similar to OPF_{knn} by performing two major steps: (i) defining the set of prototypes $\mathcal{P}$, and (ii) computing the influence zones (i.e., clusters), which are rooted in $\mathcal{P}$. The maxima of a pdf can be implicitly found by computing the density of each node through Eq. (2.4) for a neighborhood defined by a k-NN adjacency relation. As mentioned in Section 2.2.2.2, a maxima of the pdf may be comprised of multiple nodes and many of them are irrelevant for clustering (i.e., overclustering issue rises if all nodes are taken as maxima). Hence, the filter defined in Eq. (2.8) is applied to obtain the relevant maxima that will compose $\mathcal{P}$, and a distinct label is assigned to each maximum.

The next step is to define the influence zones through Algorithm 2.4. The samples are initialized (Line 2) and inserted into the queue $\mathcal{Q}$ (Line 3). The relevant maxima are computed on-the-fly through Lines 6 and 7, where a new label is assigned to the sample s that does not have a predecessor, and its cost changed to $\rho(s)$. By updating the cost, we allow the first sample that leaves the priority queue to propagate its label throughout its influence zone, which includes the nodes in the same maxima area. The label propagation is performed in the loop in Lines 8–12 where a sample s tries to conquer its neighbors. The outputs are an optimum-path cost map $\mathcal{V}$ and a predecessor map $\mathcal{P}$.

Algorithm 2.4: Clustering by OPF

Input: Graph $(\mathcal{Z}, \mathcal{A}_k)$ and functions h and ρ, such that $h(s) < \rho(s)$, $\forall s \in \mathcal{Z}$.

Output: Predecessor map $\mathcal{O}$, path-value map $\mathcal{C}$, and label map $\mathcal{L}$.

Auxiliary: Priority queue $\mathcal{Q}$, variables tmp and $l \leftarrow 1$.

1   **for** *all $s \in \mathcal{Z}$* **do**
2     $\mathcal{O}(s) \leftarrow nil$, $\mathcal{C}(s) \leftarrow \rho(s) - \delta$;
3   Insert s in $\mathcal{Q}$;

4   **while** $\mathcal{Q} \neq \{\}$ **do**
5   Remove from $\mathcal{Q}$ a sample s such that $\mathcal{C}(s)$ is maximum;
6   **if** $\mathcal{O}(s) = nil$ **then**
7       $\mathcal{L}(s) \leftarrow l$, $l \leftarrow l+1$, $\mathcal{C}(s) \leftarrow \rho(s)$;
8   **for** *each sample $t \in \mathcal{A}_k(s)$ and $\mathcal{C}(t) < \mathcal{C}(s)$* **do**
9       $tmp \leftarrow \min\{\mathcal{C}(s), \rho(t)\}$;
10   **if** $tmp > \mathcal{C}(t)$ **then**
11        $\mathcal{L}(t) \leftarrow \mathcal{L}(s)$, $\mathcal{O}(t) \leftarrow s$, $\mathcal{C}(t) \leftarrow tmp$;
12   Update the position of t in $\mathcal{Q}$;

13 **return** $\mathcal{O}, \mathcal{C}, \mathcal{L}$;

Similarly as in OPF$_{knn}$, the value of k also has some influence over the final model in the OPF$_{uns}$ version. Therefore Rocha et al. [213] proposed finding the best value $k^* \in [1, k_{max}]$ by computing the minimum graph cut provided by clustering results for $k \in [1, k_{max}]$ according to a measurement suggested by Shi and Malik based on graph cuts [232].

2.3 Applications

OPF-based classifiers can be applied to any pattern recognition problem being more commonly used for general supervised and unsupervised (clustering) classification. In many of them, OPF has its overall performance compared against well-known classifiers, such as support vector machines, k-nearest neighbors, and Bayesian classifier. The classifier presented competitive results and outperformed the other classifiers in some situations.

In this section, we enumerate the many applications the OPF classifier has already been explored that were published by June 13, 2020. The applications are organized among the three main versions (i.e., supervised, semisupervised, and unsupervised) and subcategorized according to their main application. Figs. 2.6 and 2.7 depict the distribution of published works among learning methods, and by area/learning method, respectively.

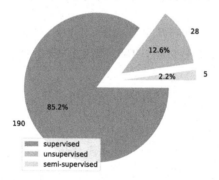

Figure 2.6 Distribution of published works among learning methods.

2.3.1 Supervised

The majority of works were dedicated either to the improvement of the steps of the supervised OPF versions i.e., OPF_{cg} and OPF_{knn}, or to evaluate their performance in distinct contexts. The following sections categorize the works found in the literature based on their main contribution.

2.3.1.1 Improvements in training

Some works were driven to approaches that aim at improving the training set by *pruning* irrelevant samples. The first works in such direction were proposed by Papa and Falcão [149] and Papa et al. [151] that move the

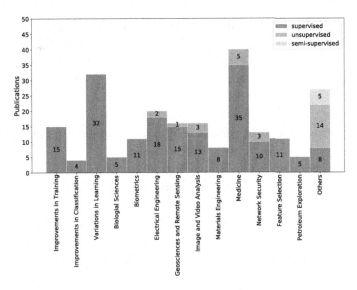

Figure 2.7 Distribution of published works among areas and learning methods.

most relevant samples (misclassified samples) from an evaluation set to the training set and eliminates the irrelevant ones from the training partition. The pruning stopping criterion is an ad hoc measure that computes the deviation between the accuracy over the original evaluating set and the final pruned one. Finding proper values for such a measure, Nakamura et al. [127] explored the Harmony Search algorithm for such purpose. In a later work, Rodrigues et al. [220] extended the problem by applying multi-objective optimization techniques. Barbosa et al. [23] explored genetic algorithms to prune irrelevant training samples and still preserve or even improve accuracy in OPF_{cg} classification. Castelo-Fernández [34] detected and eliminated outliers in the training set based on a penalty computed for each training sample based on the number of false positive and false negative samples. Costa et al. [55] proposed pruning irrelevant training samples based on genetic algorithms, in which reproduction and mutation operators are modified to maintain the number of pruned patterns with a fixed-size.

Iwashita et al. [93] speeded up the path-cost propagation in the training process by exploiting a theoretical relation between a minimum-spanning tree and optimum-path tree when the f_{max} function is applied [14]. Later, Iwashita et al. [92] extended the work by modifying both path- and label-cost propagation to speed-up the training process by computing the MST and the optimum-path forest at the same time.

Afonso et al. [8] applied unsupervised manifold learning to learn better manifolds that capture the contextual information encoded in the feature space. Ponti and Tiva [190] proposed a new training algorithm with incremental capabilities while keeping the properties of the OPF. New instances can be inserted in the model into one of the existing trees, substitute the prototype of a tree, or split a tree. Iwashita et al. [91] introduced the OPF$_{cg}$ classifier in the context of concept drift, using decisions for concept drift handling based on a committee of OPF classifiers.

Some works also considered *parallelizing* the training process. Iwashita et al. [94] implemented the training process for graphic processing units, whereas Culquicondor et al. [43] proposed the parallelization through the OpenMP library. Culquicondor et al. [42] later proposed an efficient parallel implementation for training supervised versions of OPF by replacing the priority queue with an array and a linear search aiming at using a parallel-friendly data structure.

2.3.1.2 Improvements in classification

Concerning the classification task, works were dedicated to improving the OPF$_{cg}$ performance by either speeding it up or making it more robust for huge data sets. Papa et al. [144] employed an ordered set of training nodes sorted by increasing values of costs, which is built during the training phase. Since the node that conquers the testing sample is the one that offers the minimum cost, the probability of one of the first nodes of such set be the conqueror is higher. Later, Papa et al. [150] presented two ideas for speeding up the OPF$_{cg}$ classifier: (i) a new classification algorithm that does not require that all training nodes be visited during the classification, and (ii) a pruning-based approach. Romero et al. [222] implemented the classification process for graphic processing units.

On the other hand, Fernandes et al. [77] aimed at improving the accuracy by considering the optimum-path value from a given sample in the classification process and its confidence value, which is defined by a score index computed through a learning process over a validation set. The idea is to penalize the training samples that are not "strongly" confident.

2.3.1.3 Variations in learning

We can also enumerate the many works that applied distinct learning methods to OPF. The traditional OPF algorithm works naturally with nonlinear situations, but it does not map samples from one space to another as in many kernel-based techniques, such as support vector machines. Hence,

Afonso et al. [10] modified the OPF algorithm to work with distinct *kernel* functions, aiming to improve both training and classification. Fernandes et al. [75] extended OPF_{cg} to a *probabilistic approach* based on the Platt scaling approach.

Contextual-based approaches were also widely explored. Nakamura et al. [125] and Osaku et al. [138] proposed the OPF-MRF (Markov Random Fields), which exploits the contextual information by means of a lattice-based neighborhood model. Later, Osaku et al. [136] proposed using Markovian models along with OPF to address the same context. Osaku et al. [139] proposed a metaheuristic-based optimization framework to find suitable values for the parameter that controls the amount of contextual information used in the classification process. Osaku et al. [140] extended the work in [136] by automatically fine tuning a number of Markovian models for contextual land-use classification in satellite imagery using metaheuristic techniques. Finally, Osaku et al. [137] improved the work proposed in [139] by turning OPF-MRF faster and also more effective by learning the best parameters for the MRF models in different regions of the image.

The work presented by Pereira et al. [175] explored the OPF for *sequential learning* based on four distinct approaches: (i) stacked sequential learning, (ii) sliding window, multiscale sequential learning with (iii) multiresolution, and (iv) pyramid-based decompositions. The approach was evaluated in the context of land-cover classification using both satellite and radar images.

Relevance feedback-based approaches were proposed to overcome the semantic gap by requiring more user interaction than simply the specification of a query image. Silva et al. [49,51] explored such a context by using OPF to decide which database images are relevant or not. Further, Silva et al. [48] proposed improving the retrieval process by incorporating multiple distance spaces that are combined through metaheuristic techniques.

Silva et al. [50] proposed an *active learning* paradigm for contextual-based image retrieval systems based on the optimum-path forest classifier. The work presents a planned method that makes use of samples classified as relevant, but that were close to be classified as irrelevant. Such samples are defined based on their optimum-path cost and showed a gain in effectiveness. Saito et al. [226] proposed an active learning paradigm based on a priori data reduction and organization. Later, Saito et al. [227] proposed a robust active learning for the diagnosis of parasites that performs a data organization by clustering. Then an expert labels the most relevant sample (root) of each cluster and the classifier selects those samples from each cluster whose classification do not match the root's label. Such an approach allows to explore class diversity to select more informative samples for training, and reducing the reprocessing effort.

Pereira et al. [178] introduced a multiple-labeling approach for the optimum-path forest classifier based on the problem transformation method, which was further validated in a multilabeled video classification data set. Amorim et al. [17] modified the OPF_{cg} working mechanism by introducing a local analysis of each class. Such an approach computes k prototypes per class by (i) considering its complete graph, (ii) computing the shortest-path distances among all nodes, (iii) selecting the k shortest-path accumulated distances. The main idea is to select the k most "central" samples of each class as prototypes.

Concerning ensembles, Ponti et al. [97] proposed using a combination of disjoint training subsets and they showed the proposed approach is more effective and faster for training than standard OPF_{cg}. Fernandes et al. [72] proposed pruning ensembles of OPF-based classifiers through metaheuristic algorithms. The work was later extended by Fernandes et al. [74], where it was introduced the concept of quaternions in ensemble pruning strategies. Pereira et al. [176] proposed two ensemble-based approaches to sequential learning, which were validated in the context of land-use classification. Fernandes et al. [73] also presented an ensemble of optimum-path forest classifiers, which consists into combining different instances that compute a score-based confidence level for each training sample to turn the classification process "smarter," i.e., more reliable.

Ponti et al. [193] proposed a framework to combine classifiers using a decision graph under a random field model and a game strategy approach to obtain the final decision. Ponti and Rossi [194] used the optimum-path forest classifier to investigate input data manipulation techniques to use fewer data from the training set without hampering the classification accuracy.

Bostani and Sheikhan [27] proposed applying the Markov cluster algorithm for finding the prototypes. The graph partitioning in the Markov cluster is based on finding key samples named attractors, which attract other related samples so that the obtained attractors can be selected as prototypes for generating optimum-path trees. Diniz et al. [66] proposed a SoC/FPGA (System on a Chip/Field Programmable Gate-Array)-based design and implementation of an architecture for embedded applications, presenting a hardware converted algorithm for an OPF_{cg} classifier. Riva and Ponti [211] investigated the capabilities of an incremental version of the OPF_{cg} classifier in the context of learning new classes and compared its behavior against support vector machines and k-nearest neighbors classifiers. Bostani et al. [28] introduced a novel version of OPF$_{cg}$, which utilizes a coreset approach for reducing the scale of the input data set.

Concerning OPF$_{knn}$, Papa et al. [155] proposed computing the best value k^* as an optimization task using metaheuristic techniques. The basic idea behind metaheuristics is to use a set of agents that walk throughout the search space to find the best solution. Each agent is randomly initialized with a value $k_i \in [1, k_{max}]$ and the solutions are evaluated over the validation set Z_2. Afonso et al. [3] introduced OPF$_{cg}$ and OPF$_{knn}$ in the context of multiple-instance learning where a sample (bag) is classified based on its instances instead of a single one. The supervised versions of OPF were compared to some well-known approaches for multiple-instance learning with competitive results.

2.3.1.4 Biological sciences

The applications in the field of biological sciences comprise the monitoring of species in general. Papa et al. [156] introduced the OPF$_{cg}$ in the context of spermatogenesis monitoring, which is crucial to the species reproduction. Pereira et al. [177] addressed the problem of ecological disorder caused by aquatic weed by proposing the automatic identification of some species using supervised pattern recognition techniques and shape descriptors. Turesson et al. [246] proposed the automatic classification of marmoset vocalizations for the monitoring of captive colonies of highly vocal primates using OPF$_{cg}$. Xu et al. [249] combined a generative adversarial network model with the relevance feedback framework based on the OPF to generate face images. Vieira et al. [248] evaluated the reproductive effects of exposure of adult male rats to gasohol as well as the performance of machine learning algorithms, including OPF$_{cg}$, for pattern recognition and classification of the exposure group.

2.3.1.5 Biometrics

Biometrics has been paramount for the authentication and identification of people and being widely applied for security or people control in many places, such as airports, border control, etc. Some works evaluated their approach through OPF$_{cg}$ for iris characterization [46], large scale iris datasets [4,5], fingerprints [124], and gait recognition [68]. Face recognition was also studied in [36,152], being the later one using infrared images. Amorim et al. [16] addressed the automatic recognition of human faces in images using a composite approach for feature extraction, which was evaluated using Eigenface and Fisher face methods, as well as the optimum-path forest local analysis classifier. Lopes et al. [106] evaluated the OPF_{cg} in the context of tensor-oriented applications, as well as the robustness to space transformations using multilinear principal component analysis in both face and human action recognition tasks considering the image and video data sets. Finizola et al. [80] performed a comparative study between traditional models of machine learning, including OPF_{cg} and deep learning focusing on convolutional neural networks and autoencoders for facial recognition.

Finally, Rodrigues et al. [219] evaluated a binary version of the flower pollination algorithm under different transfer functions to select the best subset of channels that maximizes the accuracy on electroencephalogram-based person identification, which is measured by means of the optimum-path forest classifier.

2.3.1.6 Electrical engineering

The works in electrical engineering aimed at the energy distribution monitoring mainly. The majority of the works cope with the identification of nontechnical losses by applying machine learning-based techniques including OPF_{cg} [195,201–203,244] and its probabilistic version [76]. Also, other works belonging to this category applied metaheuristic algorithms to select the best features along with OPF_{cg} to improve the results [196–199,218], and a hybrid approach using the distribution state estimator and the OPF_{cg} [245].

Other concerns for the energy sector include faults during the distribution and fraud detection. In the former problem, some works studied methods to detect the problem in power transformers [237] and their location in underground systems [61,236]. Detection of frauds and pattern of consumption were also studied in [204] and in [115] that proposed a combination function adapted to the imbalance between classes using F-value as the performance measurement. Filho et al. [206] developed a mobile system to aid the identification and classification of electrical assets using convolutional neural network for feature extraction and evaluated by many classifiers including OPF_{cg}.

2.3.1.7 Geosciences and remote sensing

Remote sensing imagery plays an important role in the study of the surface of the Earth. The images are captured by sensors and usually are comprised of multiple bands. Some works proposed methods to select hyperspectral bands, in which the selection was assessed by classifiers including the OPF_{cg} [126,129]. The images are also important for the study of land cover/usage [184,187,188], landslide recognition [183], classification of river sediment [182], rainfall estimation [59,81,82], to classify desertification areas using hyperspectral images [108], and interactive classification of remote sensing images [69]. There are also works that performed general classification of pixel-based radar images [185], remote sensing images [186], and road recognition [107].

2.3.1.8 Image and video analysis

A considerable number of works were dedicated to image and video applications using OPF for evaluation purposes. The following works were the first ones to introduce the classifier in their context. We can mention the applications of genre-based video classification [117,118], optical character [111] and handwritten digits recognition [105], real-time speed limit sign recognition [83], the evaluation of rotation-invariant and scale-invariant features from texture images [123], evaluation of an approach that identifies blur parameters in images [181], general image categorization [161], evaluation of descriptor combination techniques [109,110]. Lima et al. [60] employed OPF_{cg} with other classifiers to assess features extracted by the combinations of Bag-of-Visual-Words and complex networks. Ponti et al. [191] proposed an algorithm that selects relevant images from a collection based on the aggregation of optimum-path forest-based classifiers. Since small training sets are used, the proposed approach is viable for large data sets. Later, Ponti et al. [192] extended their work in three aspects: (i) analysis of both handcrafted and deep learning features, (ii) using larger image data sets, and (iii) including more methods, such as Support Vector Machines (SVM) ensemble selection, and k-Medoids ensemble selection, compared with OPF-based selection.

2.3.1.9 Materials engineering

The quality of materials is very important for many industrial applications. The evaluation of the material is performed by microstructural characterization, which is a costly task since it is performed manually. Therefore, automated tools are of great importance to aid the task. In this sense, some works applied the OPF for microstructural characterization of different materials [12,57,134,145,158]. The OPF was also applied to automate the segmentation of precipitates [160] and the secondary austenite-phase island [13]. Ivo et al. [90] evaluated OPF_{cg} for the classification of nongrain oriented electrical steel and its electromagnetic efficiency based on the analysis of images obtained by crystalline orientation distribution function.

2.3.1.10 Medicine

A considerable effort has been dedicated to medical applications, in which many works were proposed to aid the identification of diseases. The supervised OPF was employed in a significant amount, such as the identification of oropharyngeal dysphagia [242], Barrett's esophagus [238], and Parkinson's disease [2,9,25,164,170–174,240,241,250]. The supervised OPF was also used for the classification of brain images [30], arrhythmia [47,58], lung diseases [78], aid on the diagnosis of epilepsy [133,179] and ophthalmological diseases [141], detection of Laryngeal pathology [163], human tissue analysis [79], human intestinal parasites from microscopy images [243]. Ribeiro et al. [208] introduced the OPF to the context of breast masses classification. Later, Ribeiro et al. [210] introduced the OPF_{knn} to the context of breast mass identification as well as an ensemble-driven approach. Later, Sasikala et al. [229,230] and Passos et al. [165] also applied OPF_{cg} in the context of breast masses categorization.

Furthermore, OPF_{cg} was evaluated in the contexts of alcoholism detection [56], detection and classification of stroke in skull computed-tomography images [62], diagnosis of skin lesions [135], exudate detection in fundus images [100], heart arrhythmia classification [132], and analysis of brain computed-tomography images [228].

2.3.1.11 Network security

The considerable increase in network traffic generated by many devices as well as concerns on data security motivated many machine learning-based works to aid at traffic monitoring [65], detection of intrusion [99,168,169], and malwares [38,44]. Some others were dedicated to spam filtering [52, 71,234]. Silva et al. [233] introduced the OPF for the task of data mining in Internet-of-Things-oriented applications, such as spam detection in email and web content, as well as intrusion detection in computer networks. The reason for applying OPF concerns its fast learning process, which is paramount for online applications and situations that patterns change or new ones are introduced.

2.3.1.12 Feature selection

Many interesting metaheuristic algorithms have been proposed and applied in a wide variety of optimization problems. Image categorization comprises the steps of extracting features and performing the classification based on them. Numerous features can be considered to create representations, although many may not be relevant for the application. In this sense, metaheuristic techniques have been applied to select the most representative ones, i.e., the ones that maximize the accuracy of a classifier, such as in [130,131,159,162,180,214–217,221,224] that employed the OPF_{cg} to evaluate the set of selected features.

2.3.1.13 Petroleum exploration

Petroleum exploration is comprised of many activities. One of them is the well drilling, which is a very expensive task and subject to a considerable number of events that may cause the loss of the drill, for instance. In this sense, some works were proposed to monitor well drilling operations and to aid the detection of anomalies by using data collected in real-time and machine learning algorithms [84,85,112,113]. Daily drilling reports also figure as an important source of information. Sousa et al. [235] introduced the OPF_{cg} for pattern analysis in drilling reports. The main idea is to perform event classification, i.e., actions taken during drilling, to aid a further activity monitoring.

2.3.1.14 Other applications

Some distinct works also evaluated the supervised versions in different contexts. Marques et al. [114] introduced the OPF_{cg} for musical genre classification aiming a better organization of music data sets for further recommendation. Pedestrian detection requires a good trade-off between processing time and accuracy. Diniz et al. [67] evaluated the OPF_{cg} in such a context, which showed to be a fast and competitive technique against established methods. Amorim et al. [15] introduced OPF_{cg} in for the detection of defects in cowhide.

Souza et al. [239] presented a comparison between the k-nearest neighbors, with an especial focus on the 1-nearest neighbor, and the optimum-path forest supervised classifiers. The study investigates the similarity between k-OPF and kNN classifier. The k-OPF is a variation of OPF_{cg} concerning the classification step, which labels a sample based on the most frequent label present in the root prototypes of the k lower cost paths. The classifiers showed similar accuracies with k-OPF being the fastest. Silva et al. [53] presented a comparison between k-nearest neighbors classifier using Euclidean, city block, cosine and correlation distance metric, self-organizing maps, artificial neural networks and the OPF_{cg}, for the classification of images taken from a low-resolution industrial sensor.

Souza et al. [64] proposed a variation of OPF for fuzzy applications. The proposed approach computes the sample membership through OPF_{uns}

whose values are used for path-cost purposes in OPF_{cg}. Eler et al. [121] developed a visualization tool to support the understanding of OPF training and testing processes. Silva et al. [54] introduced the OPF_{cg} to navigation of unmanned aerial vehicle using deep transfer learning. The approach extracts features using a Convolution Neural Network (CNN), for further feeding machine learning techniques.

2.3.1.15 Voice recognition

Some works were dedicated to automatic speech recognition, which relies on machine learning techniques for automatic processing. However, certain applications require techniques to be efficient and effective at the same time. Due to the features of OPF_{cg}, Papa et al. [157], Iliev et al. [89], and Nakamura et al. [128] opted for applying it for vowel recognition, spoken emotion recognition, and a robot voice interface, respectively. The works employed public data sets with OPF_{cg} performance compared against well-known machine learning techniques, such as the support vector machine, artificial neural networks, Gaussian mixture model, and Bayesian classifier. The OPF_{cg} showed to be the fastest in the applications with comparable or outperforming in accuracy.

2.3.2 Semisupervised

Amorim et al. [19] improved the OPF_{ssp} training phase by reducing the computational complexity from $O(n^2)$ to $O(n \lg n)$, where n is the number of training samples. The adjacency relation of the Improved OPF_{ssp} is defined as the set of arcs resulting from an MST computed over the complete graph of $\mathcal{Z}_1$. Then the set of prototypes $\mathcal{P}$ is comprised of all training samples $\mathcal{Z}_1^l$, and a single training run is performed in time $O(n \lg n)$ where the nodes in $\mathcal{Z}_1^u$ have a label assigned.

Saito et al. [225] introduced an approach that applies active learning to OPF_{ssp}. The idea is to reduce the possibility of selecting an irrelevant sample from a large learning set since a well-chosen size reduction process and an a priori ordering provide essentially good informative samples. Li and Zhu [104] proposed a new self-training method based on the optimum-path forest. The OPF is applied to discover the spatial structure of feature space, and then such information is used to improve the performance of the self-training method.

Amorim et al. [21] explored the optimum connectivity among unlabeled samples through OPF_{ssp} to improve the learning process of CNNs. OPF_{ssp} classifies an unlabeled training set that is used to pretrain a CNN for further fine-tuning using the limited labeled data only. In a latter work, Amorim et al. [22] evaluated their approach for soybean leaf and herbivorous pest identification using images captured by unmanned aerial vehicles.

Last but not least, Benato et al. [24] showed that semisupervised OPF, together with t-SNE [247], obtained better results than other semisupervised approaches. The authors highlighted that such a visualization tool helps toward a better understanding of features extracted by autoencoders in the context of classification tasks.

2.3.3 Unsupervised

In summary, unsupervised learning comprises the task of finding clusters in a given set of samples, such that the samples within the clusters share some level of similarity among them. Some works using OPF_{uns} were dedicated to data clustering. Rocha et al. [212] applied it for image analysis, Afonso et al. [6] learned visual words to compute new representations for images, Martins et al. [116] applied for static video summarization, and Martins et al. [119] proposed a temporal-and spatial-driven video summarization approach based on the OPF.

The unsupervised OPF has the main advantage of computing the clusters on-the-fly, i.e., it does not require the number of clusters prior to computing them, such as in k-means. However, one of its drawbacks is directly related to its strength that is if the user knows the number of clusters and desires to use it. To overcome such an issue, Afonso et al. [11] proposed the Deep-OPF to reach a number of clusters as closest as possible to the one required by that specific application by applying unsupervised learning using different layers. The approach was evaluated on the study of geological formations in seismic images. Later, Afonso et al. [1] proposed hierarchical learning using a variation of the Deep-OPF, which provides a more robust representation that makes use of the content learned by all layers.

The unsupervised optimum-path forest has a single parameter that is used to improve the clustering quality. The traditional approach selects the value through a grid search. Some works were dedicated to the optimization of such a parameter. Costa et al. [45] provided an extensive comparison of evolutionary algorithms for the optimization of OPF_{uns} and validated the approaches in the context of unsupervised network intrusion detection. Later, Costa et al. [39] explored nature-inspired techniques for the optimization of the parameter k_{max}, which was also evaluated in the context of intrusion detection.

Montero et al. [122] proposed a divide-and-conquer approach to OPF_{uns} to overcome the problem of identifying groups naturally related to the semantics of the problem. Chen et al. [35] proposed a new probability density function for OPF_{uns}, which is based on the principle that the cluster centers are based on their densities and the distances between the centers and samples with higher densities.

2.3.3.1 Electrical engineering

Ramos et al. [200] introduced the OPF_{uns} in the context of non-technical losses identification aiding the grouping into subprofiles and minimizing the search for consumers that cause great frauds. Passos et al. [98] proposed an approach for anomaly detection based on the OPF_{uns}, which was evaluated in the same context for situations with little or no information about irregular consumers.

2.3.3.2 Image and video processing

Castelo-Fernández et al. [33] applied the OPF_{uns} for automatic video summarization. According to the authors, the results have shown that the method is both effective and efficient in processing videos containing several thousands of frames, obtaining very meaningful summaries in a quick way. Martins et al. [120] coped with the problem of static video summarization using the unsupervised optimum-path forest to sample the encoded video sequence into frames, and extracting features based on color information or spectral properties.

The task of multiview video summarization aims at efficiently representing the most significant information from a set of videos captured for a certain period of time by multiple cameras. The problem is highly challenging because of the huge size of the data, the presence of many unimportant frames with low activity, interview dependencies, and significant variations in illumination. Kuanar et al. [103] proposed a graph-theoretic solution to the above problems by using semantic features in the form of a visual bag-of-words and visual features like color, texture, and shape to model shot representative frames after temporal segmentation. Gaussian entropy is then applied to filter out frames with low activity. Interview dependencies are captured via bipartite graph matching. Finally, OPF_{uns} is applied for clustering purposes.

2.3.3.3 Medicine

Many medical diagnoses comprise image analysis to identify elements that may indicate abnormalities. Moreover, the images may be 2D or 3D, and their analysis is a costly task. To aid in the identification of unusual elements, some works using OPF_{uns} were dedicated to the segmentation of brain tissue MR-image [31,32], unsupervised breast masses classification [209], and to separate homogeneous regions of magnetic resonance images [143]. Souza et al. [63] introduced the OPF_{uns} classifier to learn visual dictionaries in the context of Barrett's esophagus and automatic adenocarcinoma diagnosis.

2.3.3.4 Network security

Intrusion detection can also be handled as a clustering task. In this sense, Costa et al. [40] introduced the OPF_{uns} in such a context. The work was later extended by Costa et al. [41] that proposed boosting the OPF_{uns} by optimizing its parameters in a discrete lattice using the harmony search algorithm. Recently, Guimarães et al. [86] introduced the anomaly detection-based OPF to detect outliers in wireless sensor networks. The work also proposed fine tuning the OPF_{uns} parameters related to the size of the neighborhood, that is, used to define the clusters and the threshold that defines whether a new sample is an anomaly or not through nature-inspired optimization techniques.

2.3.3.5 Remote sensing images

Pisani et al. [184] proposed to evaluate unsupervised OPF in the context of land use classification. The OPF_{uns} was evaluated in two data sets and had its results compared against the well-known k-means and mean shift algorithms.

2.3.3.6 Other applications

Passos et al. [167] improved the Radial Basis Function Neural Networks (ANN-RBF) by using the optimum-path forest clustering algorithm. The training of an ANN-RBF is comprised of two steps: (i) an unsupervised learning step to finding the parameters of the radial basis functions, and (ii) a supervised learning step that maps the nonlinear input data as a linear combination of the weights. The first step is usually performed by clustering the training data using the well-known k-means. However, applying k-means requires some knowledge of the data to set the parameter k. Therefore, the authors proposed using OPF_{uns} for such a task and achieved suitable results.

Passos et al. [166] proposed to use OPF$_{uns}$ to estimate the parameters of Gaussian distributions aiming to address anomaly detection based on multivariate Gaussian functions. Since this version of OPF$_{uns}$ estimates the prototypes as the highest density regions of the feature space, they are likely to be located in the center of the classes, thus being good candidates to encode the mean values of each Gaussian distribution. Afonso et al. [7] applied the OPF$_{uns}$ for the clustering step of the brain storm optimization algorithm, and Ribeiro and Papa [207] introduced the unsupervised OPF classifier to the Natural Language Processing (NLP) field, more specifically for dialogue act classification task.

2.4 Conclusions and future trends

This paper provided an overview of the fundamentals and algorithms behind the optimum-path forest framework. The survey covers the original algorithms for supervised, semisupervised, and unsupervised learning applications by providing details of their working algorithms. The idea is similar for any of the three learning methods, where samples are encoded as nodes, and the adjacency relation, path–cost function are selected to build the optimum-path forest through a competitive process.

Despite being proposed some years ago, OPF has been applied in many contexts, as well as many other works proposed variations for improvements or applied in new contexts. Its competitive results against well-known classifiers and low training and testing times are very attractive, especially for applications with a considerable amount of data, which justifies the number of works in such a short time (i.e., 190 supervised, 5 semisupervised, and 28 unsupervised, being a total of 223 so far).

The OPF with a complete graph is the most used version with a significant number of works in numerous contexts that include medicine, electrical engineering, and even geosciences. It is also the version that has the highest number of variations associated. However, there is still room for more. The unsupervised OPF also has great potential, especially for not requiring the number of clusters a priori, being mainly employed for learning features. Finally, the semisupervised OPF has been applied to improve learning in different applications.

Regarding future works, there is a clear trend concerning deep learning techniques, which end up generating high-dimensional feature vectors. We have observed some works that employed OPF on top of deep networks and obtained better results than using standard softmax layers. However, these works applied dimensionality reduction techniques before feeding OPF-based classifiers. As the main bottleneck, we shall cite the problem of such techniques in dealing with high-dimensional and sparse feature vectors, which must be addressed in the next works. We also observe a broad horizon for the OPF framework in the context of recommendation systems, information retrieval, and domain adaptation.

Acknowledgments

The authors are grateful to FAPESP grants #2013/07375-0, #2014/12236-1, #2017/25908-6, #2018/21934-5, and #2019/07665-4, CNPq grants #307066/2017-7 and #427968/2018-6. This study was financed in part by the Coordenação de Aperfeiçoamento de Pessoal de Nível Superior - Brasil (CAPES) - Finance Code 001.

References

[1] Luis C.S. Afonso, Clayton R. Pereira, Silke A.T. Weber, Christian Hook, Alexandre X. Falcão, João P. Papa, Hierarchical learning using deep optimum-path forest, Journal of Visual Communication and Image Representation (2020) 102823.

[2] Luis C.S. Afonso, Gustavo H. Rosa, Clayton R. Pereira, Silke A.T. Weber, Christian Hook, Victor Hugo C. Albuquerque, João P. Papa, A recurrence plot-based approach for Parkinson's disease identification, Future Generations Computer Systems 94 (2019) 282–292.

[3] L.C.S. Afonso, D. Colombo, C.R. Pereira, K.A.P. Costa, J.P. Papa, Multiple-instance learning through optimum-path forest, in: 2019 International Joint Conference on Neural Networks (IJCNN), 2019, pp. 1–7.

[4] Luis C.S. Afonso, João P. Papa, Aparecido Nilceu Marana, Ahmad Poursaberi, Svetlana N. Yanushkevich, A fast large scale iris database classification with Optimum-Path Forest technique: a case study, in: The 2012 International Joint Conference on Neural Networks (IJCNN), Brisbane, Australia, June 10–15, 2012, 2012, pp. 1–5.

[5] Luis C.S. Afonso, João P. Papa, Aparecido Nilceu Marana, Ahmad Poursaberi, Svetlana N. Yanushkevich, Marina L. Gavrilova, Optimum-path forest classifier for large scale biometric applications, in: 2012 Third International Conference on Emerging Security Technologies, Lisbon, Portugal, September 5-7, 2012, 2012, pp. 58–61.

[6] Luis C.S. Afonso, João Paulo Papa, Luciene P. Papa, Aparecido Nilceu Marana, Anderson Rocha, Automatic visual dictionary generation through Optimum-Path Forest clustering, in: 19th IEEE International Conference on Image Processing, ICIP 2012, Lake Buena Vista, Orlando, FL, USA, September 30 - October 3, 2012, 2012, pp. 1897–1900.

[7] Luis Claudio Sugi Afonso, Leandro A. Passos, João Paulo Papa, Enhancing brain storm optimization through optimum-path forest, in: 2018 IEEE 12th International Symposium on Applied Computational Intelligence and Informatics (SACI), 2018, pp. 183–188.

[8] Luis Claudio Sugi Afonso, Daniel Carlos Guimarães Pedronette, André N. de Souza, João Paulo Papa, Improving optimum-path forest classification using unsupervised manifold learning, in: 2018 24th International Conference on Pattern Recognition (ICPR), 2018, pp. 560–565.

[9] Luis Claudio Sugi Afonso, Clayton Reginaldo Pereira, Silke Anna Theresa Weber, Christian Hook, João Paulo Papa, Parkinson's disease identification through deep

optimum-path forest clustering, in: 30th SIBGRAPI Conference on Graphics, Patterns and Images, SIBGRAPI 2017, Niterói, Brazil, October 17-20, 2017, 2017, pp. 163–169.

[10] Luis C.S. Afonso, Danillo R. Pereira, João P. Papa, A kernel-based optimum-path forest classifier, in: Marcelo Mendoza, Sergio Velastín (Eds.), Progress in Pattern Recognition, Image Analysis, Computer Vision, and Applications, Springer International Publishing, 2018, pp. 652–660.

[11] Luis C.S. Afonso, Alexandre Campane Vidal, Michelle Kuroda, Alexandre Xavier Falcão, João Paulo Papa, Learning to classify seismic images with deep optimum-path forest, in: 29th SIBGRAPI Conference on Graphics, Patterns and Images, SIBGRAPI 2016, Sao Paulo, Brazil, October 4-7, 2016, 2016, pp. 401–407.

[12] V.H.C. Albuquerque, João Papa, Alexandre Falcão, Pedro Pedrosa Filho, João Tavares, Application of Optimum-Path Forest Classifier for Synthetic Material Porosity Segmentation, 2010, 4 pp.

[13] Victor H.C. Albuquerque, Rodrigo Y.M. Nakamura, Joao P. Papa, Cleiton C. Silva, Joao Manuel R.S. Tavares, Automatic segmentation of the secondary austenite-phase island precipitates in a superduplex stainless steel weld metal, Computational Vision and Medical Image Processing: VipIMAGE 161 (2011).

[14] Cédric Allène, Jean-Yves Audibert, Michel Couprie, Renaud Keriven, Some links between extremum spanning forests, watersheds and min-cuts, Image and Vision Computing 28 (10) (2010) 1460–1471.

[15] W.P. Amorim, F.S.B. Borges, M.C.B. Pache, M.H. Carvalho, H. Pistori, Optimum-Path Forest in the classification of defects in Bovine Leather, in: 2019 XV Workshop de Visão Computacional (WVC), 2019, pp. 49–53.

[16] W.P. Amorim, M.H.D. Cavalho, V.V.V.A. Odakura, Face recognition using optimum-path forest local analysis, in: 2013 Brazilian Conference on Intelligent Systems, 2013, pp. 242–248.

[17] W.P. Amorim, M.H.d. Carvalho, Supervised learning using local analysis in an optimal-path forest, in: 2012 25th SIBGRAPI Conference on Graphics, Patterns and Images, 2012, pp. 330–335.

[18] Willian Paraguassu Amorim, Alexandre Xavier Falcão, Marcelo Henriques de Carvalho, Semi-supervised pattern classification using optimum-path forest, in: 27th SIBGRAPI Conference on Graphics, Patterns and Images, SIBGRAPI 2014, Rio de Janeiro, Brazil, August 27-30, 2014, 2014, pp. 111–118.

[19] Willian Paraguassu Amorim, Alexandre X. Falcão, João P. Papa, Marcelo H. de Carvalho, Improving semi-supervised learning through optimum connectivity, Pattern Recognition 60 (2016) 72–85.

[20] Willian P. Amorim, Alexandre X. Falcão, João P. Papa, Multi-label semi-supervised classification through optimum-path forest, Information Sciences 465 (2018) 86–104.

[21] Willian Paraguassu Amorim, Gustavo Henrique Rosa, Rogério Thomazella, José Eduardo Cogo Castanho, Fábio Romano Lofrano Dotto, Oswaldo Pons Rodrigues Júnior, Aparecido Nilceu Marana, João Paulo Papa, Semi-supervised learning with connectivity-driven convolutional neural networks, Pattern Recognition Letters 128 (2019) 16–22.

[22] Willian Paraguassu Amorim, Everton Castelão Tetila, Hemerson Pistori, João Paulo Papa, Semi-supervised learning with convolutional neural networks for UAV images automatic recognition, Computers and Electronics in Agriculture 164 (2019) 104932.

[23] G. Santos Barbosa, L. da Silva Costa, A. Rêgo da Rocha Neto, A new genetic algorithm-based pruning approach for optimum-path forest, in: 2018 7th Brazilian Conference on Intelligent Systems (BRACIS), 2018, pp. 13–18.

[24] B.C. Benato, A.C. Telea, A.X. Falcão, Semi-supervised learning with interactive label propagation guided by feature space projections, in: 2018 31st SIBGRAPI Conference on Graphics, Patterns and Images (SIBGRAPI), 2018, pp. 392–399.

[25] Lucas S. Bernardo, Angeles Quezada, Roberto Munoz, Fernanda Martins Maia, Clayton R. Pereira, Wanqing Wu, Victor Hugo C. de Albuquerque, Handwritten pattern recognition for early Parkinson's disease diagnosis, Pattern Recognition Letters 125 (2019) 78–84.

[26] Bernhard E. Boser, Isabelle M. Guyon, Vladimir N. Vapnik, A training algorithm for optimal margin classifiers, in: Proceedings of the Fifth Annual Workshop on Computational Learning Theory, ACM, New York, NY, USA, 1992, pp. 144–152.

[27] H. Bostani, M. Sheikhan, Modification of optimum-path forest using Markov cluster process algorithm, in: 2016 2nd International Conference of Signal Processing and Intelligent Systems (ICSPIS), 2016, pp. 1–5.

[28] H. Bostani, M. Sheikhan, B. Mahboobi, Developing a fast supervised optimum-path forest based on coreset, in: 2017 Artificial Intelligence and Signal Processing Conference (AISP), 2017, pp. 172–177.

[29] Horst Bunke, Kaspar Riesen, Recent advances in graph-based pattern recognition with applications in document analysis, Pattern Recognition 44 (5) (2011) 1057–1067.

[30] Fabio A.M. Cappabianco, Alexandre X. Falcão, Leonardo M. Rocha, Clustering by optimum path forest and its application to automatic GM/WM classification in MR-T1 images of the brain, in: Proceedings of the 2008 IEEE International Symposium on Biomedical Imaging: from Nano to Macro, Paris, France, May 14-17, 2008, 2008, pp. 428–431.

[31] Fabio A.M. Cappabianco, Alexandre X. Falcão, Clarissa L. Yasuda, Jayaram K. Udupa, Brain tissue MR-image segmentation via optimum-path forest clustering, Computer Vision and Image Understanding 116 (10) (2012) 1047–1059.

[32] Fabio A.M. Cappabianco, Jaime S. Ide, Alexandre X. Falcão, Chiang-shan Ray Li, Automatic subcortical tissue segmentation of MR images using optimum-path forest clustering, in: 18th IEEE International Conference on Image Processing, ICIP 2011, Brussels, Belgium, September 11-14, 2011, 2011, pp. 2653–2656.

[33] César Castelo-Fernández, Guillermo Calderón-Ruiz, Automatic video summarization using the optimum-path forest unsupervised classifier, in: Alvaro Pardo, Josef Kittler (Eds.), Progress in Pattern Recognition, Image Analysis, Computer Vision, and Applications, Springer International Publishing, 2015, pp. 760–767.

[34] César Castelo-Fernández, Pedro J. De Rezende, Alexandre X. Falcão, João Paulo Papa, Improving the accuracy of the optimum-path forest supervised classifier for large datasets, in: Proceedings of the 15th Iberoamerican Congress Conference on Progress in Pattern Recognition, Image Analysis, Computer Vision, and Applications (CIARP'10), Springer-Verlag, Berlin, Heidelberg, 2010, pp. 467–475.

[35] Siya Chen, Tieli Sun, Fengqin Yang, Hongguang Sun, Yu Guan, An improved optimum-path forest clustering algorithm for remote sensing image segmentation, Computers & Geosciences 112 (2018) 38–46.

[36] G. Chiachia, A.N. Marana, J.P. Papa, A.X. Falcao, Infrared face recognition by optimum-path forest, in: 2009 16th International Conference on Systems, Signals and Image Processing, 2009, pp. 1–4.

[37] Krzysztof Chris Ciesielski, Alexandre Xavier Falcão, Paulo A.V. Miranda, Path-value functions for which Dijkstra's algorithm returns optimal mapping, Journal of Mathematical Imaging and Vision 60 (7) (2018) 1025–1036.

[38] Kelton Costa, Luis Alexandre da Silva, Guilherme Martins, Gustavo de Rosa, Rafael Pires, João Papa, On the evaluation of restricted Boltzmann machines for malware identification, International Journal of Information Security Science 5 (3) (2016) 69–81.

[39] Kelton A.P. Costa, Luis A.M. Pereira, Rodrigo Y.M. Nakamura, Clayton R. Pereira, João P. Papa, Alexandre Xavier Falcão, A nature-inspired approach to speed up

optimum-path forest clustering and its application to intrusion detection in computer networks, Information Sciences 294 (2015) 95–108.

[40] Kelton A.P. Costa, Clayton R. Pereira, Rodrigo Nakamura, João Paulo Papa, Intrusion detection in computer networks using Optimum-Path Forest clustering, in: 37th Annual IEEE Conference on Local Computer Networks, Clearwater Beach, FL, USA, October 22-25, 2012, 2012, pp. 128–131.

[41] Kelton A.P. Costa, Clayton R. Pereira, Rodrigo Nakamura, Luis A.M. Pereira, João Paulo Papa, Boosting Optimum-Path Forest clustering through harmony Search and its applications for intrusion detection in computer networks, in: Fourth International Conference on Computational Aspects of Social Networks, CASoN 2012, Sao Carlos, Brazil, November 21-23, 2012, 2012, pp. 181–185.

[42] Aldo Culquicondor, Alexandro Baldassin, Cesar Castelo-Fernández, João P.L. de Carvalho, João Paulo Papa, An efficient parallel implementation for training supervised optimum-path forest classifiers, Neurocomputing 393 (2020) 259–268.

[43] Aldo Culquicondor, César Castelo-Fernández, João Paulo Papa, A new parallel training algorithm for optimum-path forest-based learning, in: Progress in Pattern Recognition, Image Analysis, Computer Vision, and Applications - 21st Iberoamerican Congress, CIARP 2016, Lima, Peru, November 8-11, 2016, Proceedings, 2016, pp. 192–199.

[44] Kelton A.P. da Costa, Luis A. da Silva, Guilherme B. Martins, Gustavo H. Rosa, Clayton R. Pereira, João Paulo Papa, Malware detection in Android-based mobile environments using optimum-path forest, in: 14th IEEE International Conference on Machine Learning and Applications, ICMLA 2015, Miami, FL, USA, December 9-11, 2015, 2015, pp. 754–759.

[45] Kelton A.P. Da Costa, Clayton R. Pereira, Luis A.M. Pereira, Rodrigo M. Nakamura, João Paulo Papa, A comparison about evolutionary algorithms for optimum-path forest clustering optimization, Journal of Information Assurance and Security 8 (2013) 76–85.

[46] R.M. da Costa, A. Gonzaga, J.P. Papa, A.N. Marana, Human iris characterization through optimum-path forest and dynamic features, in: VII Workshop de Visão Computacional 2011, pp. 1–4.

[47] Eduardo José da S. Luz, Thiago M. Nunes, Victor Hugo C. de Albuquerque, João P. Papa, David Menotti, ECG arrhythmia classification based on optimum-path forest, Expert Systems with Applications 40 (9) (2013) 3561–3573.

[48] André Tavares da Silva, Jefersson Alex dos Santos, Alexandre X. Falcão, Ricardo da Silva Torres, Léo Pini Magalhães, Incorporating multiple distance spaces in optimum-path forest classification to improve feedback-based learning, Computer Vision and Image Understanding 116 (4) (2012) 510–523.

[49] André Tavares da Silva, Alexandre X. Falcão, Léo Pini Magalhães, A new CBIR approach based on relevance feedback and optimum-path forest classification, Journal of WSCG 18 (1–3) (2010) 73–80.

[50] André Tavares da Silva, Alexandre X. Falcão, Léo Pini Magalhães, Active learning paradigms for CBIR systems based on optimum-path forest classification, Pattern Recognition 44 (12) (2011) 2971–2978.

[51] André Tavares da Silva, Léo Pini Magalhães, Alexandre Xavier Falcão, Uma abordagem CBIR baseada em realimentação de relevância e classificação por floresta de caminhos ótimos, in: IV Encontro dos Alunos e Docentes do Departamento de Engenharia de Computação e Automação Industrial-EADCA, 2011, pp. 1–4.

[52] Luis Alexandre da Silva, Kelton Augusto Pontara da Costa, Patricia Bellin Ribeiro, Gustavo Henrique de Rosa, João Paulo Papa, Learning spam features using restricted Boltzmann machines, IADIS-International Journal on Computer Science and Information Systems 11 (1) (2016) 99–114.

[53] R. Dalvit Carvalho da Silva, D.N. Coelho, G.A.P. Thè, M.R. Mendonça, Comparison between k-nearest neighbors, self-organizing maps and optimum-path forest in the recognition of packages using image analysis by Zernike moments, in: 2014 11th IEEE/IAS International Conference on Industry Applications, 2014, pp. 1–6.

[54] S.P.P. da Silva, P. Honório Filho, L.B. Marinho, J.S. Almeida, N.M.M. Nascimento, A.W.d.O. Rodrigues, P.P.R. Filho, A new approach to navigation of unmanned aerial vehicle using deep transfer learning, in: 2019 8th Brazilian Conference on Intelligent Systems (BRACIS), 2019, pp. 222–227.

[55] Leonardo da Silva Costa, Gabriel Santos Barbosa, Ajalmar Rêgo da Rocha Neto, A fixed-size pruning approach for optimum-path forest, in: Ignacio Rojas, Gonzalo Joya, Andreu Catala (Eds.), Advances in Computational Intelligence, Springer International Publishing, Cham, 2019, pp. 723–734.

[56] Jardel das C. Rodrigues, Pedro P. Rebouças Filho, Eugenio Peixoto, Arun Kumar N, Victor Hugo C. de Albuquerque, Classification of EEG signals to detect alcoholism using machine learning techniques, Pattern Recognition Letters 125 (2019) 140–149.

[57] Victor Hugo C. de Albuquerque, Cleisson V. Barbosa, Cleiton C. Silva, Elineudo P. Moura, Pedro Pedrosa Rebouças Filho, João P. Papa, João Manuel R.S. Tavares, Ultrasonic sensor signals and optimum path forest classifier for the microstructural characterization of thermally-aged inconel 625 alloy, Sensors 15 (6) (2015) 12474–12497.

[58] Victor Hugo C. de Albuquerque, Thiago M. Nunes, Danillo R. Pereira, Eduardo José da S. Luz, David Menotti, João P. Papa, João Manuel R.S. Tavares, Robust automated cardiac arrhythmia detection in ECG beat signals, Neural Computing & Applications (2016).

[59] Greice Martins de Freitas, Ana Maria Heuminski de Ávila, João Paulo Papa, Satellite-based rainfall estimation through semi-supervised learning, in: CSIE 2009, 2009 WRI World Congress on Computer Science and Information Engineering, 7 Vols., March 31 - April 2, 2009, Los Angeles, California, USA, 2009, pp. 1–5.

[60] Geovana V.L. de Lima, Priscila T.M. Saito, Fabricio M. Lopes, Pedro H. Bugatti, Classification of texture based on Bag-of-Visual-Words through complex networks, Expert Systems with Applications 133 (2019) 215–224.

[61] André N. de Souza, Pedro da Costa Jr., Paulo S. da Silva, Caio C.O. Ramos, João P. Papa, Efficient fault location in underground distribution systems through optimum-path forest, Applied Artificial Intelligence 26 (5) (2012) 503–515.

[62] João Wellington M. de Souza, Jefferson S. Almeida, Gabriel B. Holanda, Pedro P. Rebouças Filho, New approach to detect and classify stroke in skull CT images via structural co-occurrence matrix and machine learning, in: Rodrigo Costa-Felix, João Carlos Machado, André Victor Alvarenga (Eds.), XXVI Brazilian Congress on Biomedical Engineering, Springer Singapore, Singapore, 2019, pp. 341–348.

[63] Luis A. de Souza, Luis C.S. Afonso, Alanna Ebigbo, Andreas Probst, Helmut Messmann, Robert Mendel, Christian Hook, Christoph Palm, João P. Papa, Learning visual representations with optimum-path forest and its applications to Barrett's esophagus and adenocarcinoma diagnosis, Neural Computing & Applications (2019).

[64] R.W.R. De Souza, J.V.C. De Oliveira, L.A. Passos, W. Ding, J.P. Papa, V. Albuquerque, A novel approach for optimum-path forest classification using fuzzy logic, IEEE Transactions on Fuzzy Systems (2019) 1.

[65] Diego Roberto Colombo Dias, José Remo Ferreira Brega, Luis Carlos Trevelin, Bruno Barberi Gnecco, João Paulo Papa, Marcelo de Paiva Guimarães, 3D network traffic monitoring based on an automatic attack classifier, in: Computational Science and Its Applications - ICCSA 2014 - 14th International Conference, Guimarães, Portugal, June 30 - July 3, 2014, Proceedings, Part II, 2014, pp. 342–351.

[66] Wendell F.S. Diniz, Vincent Fremont, Isabelle Fantoni, Eurípedes G.O. Nóbrega, An FPGA-based architecture for embedded systems performance acceleration ap-

plied to Optimum-Path Forest classifier, Microprocessors and Microsystems 52 (2017) 261–271.

[67] W.F.S. Diniz, V. Fremont, I. Fantoni, E.G.O. Nóbrega, Evaluation of optimum path forest classifier for pedestrian detection, in: 2015 IEEE International Conference on Robotics and Biomimetics (ROBIO), 2015, pp. 899–904.

[68] Claudio Filipi Goncalves dos Santos, Thierry Pinheiro Moreira, Danilo Colombo, João Paulo Papa, Does pooling really matter? An evaluation on gait recognition, in: Ingela Nyström, Yanio Hernández Heredia, Vladimir Milián Núñez (Eds.), Progress in Pattern Recognition, Image Analysis, Computer Vision, and Applications, Springer International Publishing, 2019, pp. 751–760.

[69] Jefersson Alex dos Santos, André Tavares da Silva, Ricardo da Silva Torres, Alexandre Xavier Falcão, Léo P. Magalhães, Rubens A.C. Lamparelli, Interactive classification of remote sensing images by using optimum-path forest and genetic programming, in: Pedro Real, Daniel Diaz-Pernil, Helena Molina-Abril, Ainhoa Berciano, Walter Kropatsch (Eds.), Computer Analysis of Images and Patterns, Springer Berlin Heidelberg, Berlin, Heidelberg, 2011, pp. 300–307.

[70] Alexandre X. Falcão, Jorge Stolfi, Roberto de Alencar Lotufo, The image foresting transform: theory, algorithms, and applications, IEEE Transactions on Pattern Analysis and Machine Intelligence 26 (1) (2004) 19–29.

[71] Dheny Fernandes, Kelton A.P. da Costa, Tiago A. Almeida, João Paulo Papa, SMS spam filtering through optimum-path forest-based classifiers, in: 14th IEEE International Conference on Machine Learning and Applications, ICMLA 2015, Miami, FL, USA, December 9-11, 2015, 2015, pp. 133–137.

[72] Silas Evandro Nachif Fernandes, André Nunes de Souza, Danilo Sinkiti Gastaldello, Danillo Roberto Pereira, João Paulo Papa, Pruning optimum-path forest ensembles using metaheuristic optimization for land-cover classification, International Journal of Remote Sensing 38 (20) (2017) 5736–5762.

[73] Silas Evandro Nachif Fernandes, João Paulo Papa, Improving optimum-path forest learning using bag-of-classifiers and confidence measures, Pattern Analysis & Applications (2017).

[74] Silas Evandro Nachif Fernandes, João Paulo Papa, Pruning optimum-path forest ensembles using quaternion-based optimization, in: 2017 International Joint Conference on Neural Networks, IJCNN 2017, Anchorage, AK, USA, May 14-19, 2017, 2017, pp. 984–991.

[75] Silas Evandro Nachif Fernandes, Danillo Roberto Pereira, Caio C.O. Ramos, André N. de Souza, João Paulo Papa, A probabilistic optimum-path forest classifier for binary classification problems, CoRR, arXiv:1609.00878 [abs], 2016, http://arxiv.org/abs/1609.00878.

[76] S.E.N. Fernandes, D.R. Pereira, C.C.O. Ramos, A.N. Souza, D.S. Gastaldello, J.P. Papa, A probabilistic optimum-path forest classifier for non-technical losses detection, IEEE Transactions on Smart Grid 10 (3) (2019) 3226–3235.

[77] Silas Evandro Nachif Fernandes, Walter J. Scheirer, David D. Cox, João Paulo Papa, Improving optimum-path forest classification using confidence measures, in: Progress in Pattern Recognition, Image Analysis, Computer Vision, and Applications - 20th Iberoamerican Congress, CIARP 2015, Montevideo, Uruguay, November 9-12, 2015, Proceedings, 2015, pp. 619–625.

[78] Pedro P. Rebouças Filho, Antônio C. da Silva Barros, Geraldo L.B. Ramalho, Clayton R. Pereira, João Paulo Papa, Victor Hugo C. de Albuquerque, João Manuel R.S. Tavares, Automated recognition of lung diseases in CT images based on the optimum-path forest classifier, Neural Computing & Applications 31 (2019) 901–914.

[79] Pedro P. Rebouças Filho, Elizângela de S. Rebouças, Leandro B. Marinho, Róger M. Sarmento, João Manuel R.S. Tavares, Victor Hugo C. de Albuquerque, Analysis

of human tissue densities: a new approach to extract features from medical images, Pattern Recognition Letters 94 (2017) 211–218.

[80] J.S. Finizola, J.M. Targino, F.G.S. Teodoro, C.A.M. Lima, Comparative study between deep face, autoencoder and traditional machine learning techniques aiming at biometric facial recognition, in: 2019 International Joint Conference on Neural Networks (IJCNN), 2019, pp. 1–8.

[81] G.M. Freitas, A.M.H. Avila, J.P. Papa, A.X. Falcao, Optimum-path forest-based rainfall estimation, in: 2009 16th International Conference on Systems, Signals and Image Processing, 2009, pp. 1–4.

[82] Greice Martins de Freitas, João Paulo Papa, Ana Maria Heuminski de Avila, Alexandre Xavier Falcão, Hilton Silveira Pinto, Hilton Silveira Pinto, Agricultural areas precipitation occurrence estimation using optimum path forest, Revista Brasileira de Meteorologia 25 (1) (2010) 13–23.

[83] Samuel L. Gomes, Elizângela de S. Rebouças, Edson Cavalcanti Neto, João P. Papa, Victor Hugo C. de Albuquerque, Pedro Pedrosa Rebouças Filho, João Manuel R.S. Tavares, Embedded real-time speed limit sign recognition using image processing and machine learning techniques, Neural Computing & Applications 28 (S-1) (2017) 573–584.

[84] Ivan Rizzo Guilherme, Aparecido Nilceu Marana, João Paulo Papa, Giovani Chiachia, Luis C.S. Afonso, Kazuo Miura, Marcus V.D. Ferreira, Francisco Torres, Petroleum well drilling monitoring through cutting image analysis and artificial intelligence techniques, Engineering Applications of Artificial Intelligence 24 (1) (2011) 201–207.

[85] Ivan Rizzo Guilherme, Aparecido Nilceu Marana, João P. Papa, Giovani Chiachia, Alexandre X. Falcão, Kazuo Miura, Marcus V.D. Ferreira, Francisco Torres, Fast petroleum well drilling monitoring through optimum-path forest, Journal of Next Generation Information Technology 1 (1) (2010) 77–85.

[86] R.R. Guimaraes, L.A. Passos, R.H. Filho, V.H.C.d. Albuquerque, J.J.P.C. Rodrigues, M.M. Komarov, J.P. Papa, Intelligent network security monitoring based on optimum-path forest clustering, IEEE Network 33 (2) (2019) 126–131.

[87] Simon Haykin, Neural Networks: A Comprehensive Foundation, Prentice Hall, 1999.

[88] Te-Ming Huang, Vojislav Kecman, Ivica Kopriva, Kernel Based Algorithms for Mining Huge Data Sets: Supervised, Semi-Supervised, and Unsupervised Learning, Studies in Computational Intelligence, Springer-Verlag, Berlin, Heidelberg, 2006.

[89] Alexander I. Iliev, Michael S. Scordilis, João P. Papa, Alexandre X. Falcão, Spoken emotion recognition through optimum-path forest classification using glottal features, Computer Speech & Language 24 (3) (2010) 445–460.

[90] Roberto Fernandes Ivo, Douglas de Araújo Rodrigues, José Ciro dos Santos, Francisco Nélio Costa Freitas, Luis Fláávio Gaspar Herculano, Hamilton Ferreira Gomes de Abreu, Pedro Pedrosa Rebouças Filho, Study and classification of the Crystallographic Orientation Distribution Function of a non-grain oriented electrical steel using computer vision system, Journal of Materials Research and Technology 8 (1) (2019) 1070–1083.

[91] Adriana Sayuri Iwashita, Victor Hugo C. de Albuquerque, João Paulo Papa, Learning concept drift with ensembles of optimum-path forest-based classifiers, Future Generations Computer Systems 95 (2019) 198–211.

[92] Adriana S. Iwashita, João Paulo Papa, André N. de Souza, Alexandre X. Falcão, Roberto de Alencar Lotufo, V.M. Oliveira, Victor Hugo C. de Albuquerque, João Manuel R.S. Tavares, A path- and label-cost propagation approach to speedup the training of the optimum-path forest classifier, Pattern Recognition Letters 40 (2014) 121–127.

[93]   Adriana S. Iwashita, João P. Papa, Alexandre X. Falcão, Roberto de Alencar Lotufo, Victor M. de Araujo Oliveira, Victor Hugo C. de Albuquerque, João Manuel R.S. Tavares, Speeding up optimum-path forest training by path-cost propagation, in: Proceedings of the 21st International Conference on Pattern Recognition, ICPR 2012, Tsukuba, Japan, November 11-15, 2012, 2012, pp. 1233–1236.

[94]   Adriana S. Iwashita, Marcos V.T. Romero, Alexandro Baldassin, Kelton A.P. Costa, João P. Papa, Training optimum-path forest on graphics processing units, in: VISAPP 2014 - Proceedings of the 9th International Conference on Computer Vision Theory and Applications, Volume 2, Lisbon, Portugal, 5-8 January, 2014, 2014, pp. 581–588.

[95]   Anil K. Jain, Data clustering: 50 years beyond K-means, Pattern Recognition Letters 31 (8) (2010) 651–666.

[96]   A.K. Jain, R.P.W. Duin, J. Mao, Statistical pattern recognition: a review, IEEE Transactions on Pattern Analysis and Machine Intelligence 22 (1) (2000) 4–37.

[97]   Moacir P. Ponti Jr., João P. Papa, Improving accuracy and speed of optimum-path forest classifier using combination of disjoint training subsets, in: Multiple Classifier Systems - 10th International Workshop, MCS 2011, Naples, Italy, June 15-17, 2011, Proceedings, 2011, pp. 237–248.

[98]   Leandro Aparecido Passos Júnior, Caio César Oba Ramos, Douglas Rodrigues, Danillo Roberto Pereira, André Nunes de Souza, Kelton Augusto Pontara da Costa, João Paulo Papa, Unsupervised non-technical losses identification through optimum-path forest, Electric Power Systems Research 140 (Supplement C) (2016) 413–423.

[99]   E. Massato Kakihata, H. Molina Sapia, R. Toshiaki Oiakawa, D. Roberto Pereira, J.P. Papa, V.H. Costa de Albuquerque, F. Assis da Silva, Intrusion detection system based on flows using machine learning algorithms, IEEE Latin America Transactions 15 (10) (2017) 1988–1993.

[100] Parham Khojasteh, Leandro Aparecido Passos Júnior, Tiago Carvalho, Edmar Rezende, Behzad Aliahmad, João Paulo Papa, Dinesh Kant Kumar, Exudate detection in fundus images using deeply-learnable features, Computers in Biology and Medicine 104 (2019) 62–69.

[101] Teuvo Kohonen, The self-organizing map, Proceedings of the IEEE 78 (1990) 1464–1480.

[102] Kidiyo Kpalma, Joseph Ronsin, An overview of advances of pattern recognition systems in computer vision, in: Vision Systems: Segmentation and Pattern Recognition, InTech, 2007.

[103] S.K. Kuanar, K.B. Ranga, A.S. Chowdhury, Multi-view video summarization using bipartite matching constrained optimum-path forest clustering, IEEE Transactions on Multimedia 17 (8) (2015) 1166–1173.

[104] J. Li, Q. Zhu, Semi-supervised self-training method based on an optimum-path forest, IEEE Access 7 (2019) 36388–36399.

[105] G. Siebra Lopes, D. Clifte da Silva, A.W. Oliveira Rodrigues, P.P. Reboucas Filho, Recognition of handwritten digits using the signature features and Optimum-Path Forest Classifier, IEEE Latin America Transactions 14 (5) (2016) 2455–2460.

[106] Ricardo R. Lopes, Kelton A.P. Costa, João P. Papa, On the evaluation of tensor-based representations for optimum-path forest classification, in: Artificial Neural Networks in Pattern Recognition - 7th IAPR TC3 Workshop, ANNPR 2016, Ulm, Germany, September 28-30, 2016, Proceedings, 2016, pp. 117–125.

[107] Marcia Macedo, Maria Maia, Emilia Rabbani, Oswaldo Neto, Remote sensing applied to the extraction of road geometric features based on optimum path forest classifiers, northeastern Brazil, International Journal of Geographical Information Systems 12 (01) (2020) 15–44.

[108] Márcia R.O.B.C. Macedo, Valéria C. Times, George D.C. Cavalcanti, Emilia Rahnemay Kohlman Rabbani, An architecture to classify desertification areas using

hyperspectral images and the optimum path forest algorithm, Electronic Journal Geotechnical Engineering-EJGE 21 (5) (2016) 1881–1895.

[109] Alex Mansano, Jessica Matsuoka, Nikolas Abiuzzi, Luis Afonso, Joao Papa, Fábio Faria, Ricardo Torres, Alexandre Falcao, Swarm-based descriptor combination and its application for image classification, Electronic Letters on Computer Vision and Image Analysis 13 (3) (2014).

[110] Alex F. Mansano, J.A. Matsuoka, Luis C.S. Afonso, João P. Papa, Fábio Augusto Faria, Ricardo da Silva Torres, Improving image classification through descriptor combination, in: 25th SIBGRAPI Conference on Graphics, Patterns and Images, SIBGRAPI 2012, Ouro Preto, Brazil, August 22-25, 2012, 2012, pp. 324–329.

[111] Aparecido Marana, João Papa, Giovani Chiachia, Análise de Desempenho de Classificadores Baseados em Redes Neurais, Máquinas de Vetores de Suporte e Florestas de Caminhos Ótimos para o Reconhecimento de Dígitos Manuscritos, in: Workshop de Visão Computacional 2009, 12 2009.

[112] A.N. Marana, G. Chiachia, I.R. Guilherme, J.P. Papa, An intelligent system for petroleum well drilling cutting analysis, in: 2009 International Conference on Adaptive and Intelligent Systems, 2009, pp. 37–42.

[113] A.N. Marana, J.P. Papa, Marcus V.D. Ferreira, Kazuo Miura, Francisco Assis Cavalcante Torres, An intelligent system to detect drilling problems through drilled-cuttings-return analysis, in: SPE-128916-MS, Society of Petroleum Engineers, 2010.

[114] Caio Miguel Marques, Ivan Rizzo Guilherme, Rodrigo Y.M. Nakamura, João P. Papa, New trends in musical genre classification using optimum-path forest, in: Proceedings of the 12th International Society for Music Information Retrieval Conference, ISMIR 2011, Miami, Florida, USA, October 24-28, 2011, 2011, pp. 699–704.

[115] Matías Di Martino, Federico Decia, Juan Molinelli, Alicia Fernández, Improving electric fraud detection using class imbalance strategies, in: ICPRAM, 2012.

[116] Guilherme B. Martins, Luis C.S. Afonso, Daniel Osaku, Jurandy Almeida, João P. Papa, Static video summarization through optimum-path forest clustering, in: Progress in Pattern Recognition, Image Analysis, Computer Vision, and Applications - 19th Iberoamerican Congress, CIARP 2014, Puerto Vallarta, Mexico, November 2-5, 2014, Proceedings, 2014, pp. 893–900.

[117] Guilherme B. Martins, Jurandy Almeida, João Paulo Papa, Supervised video genre classification using optimum-path forest, in: Progress in Pattern Recognition, Image Analysis, Computer Vision, and Applications - 20th Iberoamerican Congress, CIARP 2015, Montevideo, Uruguay, November 9-12, 2015, Proceedings, 2015, pp. 735–742.

[118] Guilherme B. Martins, Jurandy Almeida, Joao P. Papa, Video Processing and Analysis Through Optimum-Path Forest, 2017.

[119] Guilherme B. Martins, João Paulo Papa, Jurandy Almeida, Temporal-and spatial-driven video summarization using optimum-path forest, in: 29th SIBGRAPI Conference on Graphics, Patterns and Images, SIBGRAPI 2016, Sao Paulo, Brazil, October 4-7, 2016, 2016, pp. 335–339.

[120] Guilherme B. Martins, Danillo R. Pereira, Jurandy G. Almeida, Victor Hugo C. de Albuquerque, João Paulo Papa, OPFSumm: on the video summarization using Optimum-Path Forest, Multimedia Tools and Applications (2018).

[121] D. Medeiros Eler, M. Prachedes Batista, R.E. Garcia, D.R. Pereira, W.E. Marcilio, Visual approach to support analysis of optimum-path forest classifier, in: 2019 8th Brazilian Conference on Intelligent Systems (BRACIS), 2019, pp. 777–782.

[122] Adán Echemendía Montero, Alexandre Xavier Falcao, A divide-and-conquer clustering approach based on optimum-path forest, in: 2018 31st SIBGRAPI Conference on Graphics, Patterns and Images (SIBGRAPI), IEEE, 2018, pp. 416–423.

[123] Javier A. Montoya-Zegarra, João Paulo Papa, Neucimar Jerônimo Leite, Ricardo da Silva Torres, Alexandre X. Falcão, Learning how to extract rotation-invariant and

scale-invariant features from texture images, EURASIP Journal on Advances in Signal Processing 2008 (2008).

[124] Javier A. Montoya-Zegarra, João P. Papa, Neucimar Jerônimo Leite, Ricardo da Silva Torres, Alexandre X. Falcão, Novel approaches for exclusive and continuous fingerprint classification, in: Advances in Image and Video Technology, Third Pacific Rim Symposium, PSIVT 2009, Tokyo, Japan, January 13-16, 2009, Proceedings, 2009, pp. 386–397.

[125] Rodrigo Nakamura, Daniel Osaku, Alexandre L.M. Levada, Fabio Augusto Cappabianco, Alexandre X. Falcão, João Paulo Papa, OPF-MRF: optimum-path forest and Markov random fields for contextual-based image classification, in: Computer Analysis of Images and Patterns - 15th International Conference, CAIP 2013, York, UK, August 27-29, 2013, Proceedings, Part II, 2013, pp. 233–240.

[126] Rodrigo Nakamura, João Paulo Papa, Leila M. Fonseca, Jefersson Alex dos Santos, Ricardo da Silva Torres, Hyperspectral band selection through Optimum-Path Forest and evolutionary-based algorithms, in: 2012 IEEE International Geoscience and Remote Sensing Symposium, IGARSS 2012, Munich, Germany, July 22-27, 2012, 2012, pp. 3066–3069.

[127] Rodrigo Nakamura, Clayton R. Pereira, João Paulo Papa, Alexandre X. Falcão, Optimum-path forest pruning parameter estimation through harmony search, in: 24th SIBGRAPI Conference on Graphics, Patterns and Images, Sibgrapi 2011, Alagoas, Maceió, Brazil, August 28-31, 2011, 2011, pp. 181–188.

[128] R. Nakamura, L. Pereira, D. Silva, P. Cardozo, C. Pereira, H. Ferasoli, S. Alves, R. Pires, A. Spadotto, J. Papa, Fast robot voice interface through Optimum-Path Forest, in: 2012 IEEE 16th International Conference on Intelligent Engineering Systems (INES), 2012, pp. 67–71.

[129] Rodrigo Y.M. Nakamura, Leila Maria Garcia Fonseca, Jefersson Alex dos Santos, Ricardo da Silva Torres, Xin-She Yang, João P. Papa, Nature-inspired framework for hyperspectral band selection, IEEE Transactions on Geoscience and Remote Sensing 52 (4) (2014) 2126–2137.

[130] Rodrigo Y.M. Nakamura, Luis A.M. Pereira, Kelton A.P. Costa, Douglas Rodrigues, João P. Papa, Xin-She Yang, BBA: a binary bat algorithm for feature selection, in: 25th SIBGRAPI Conference on Graphics, Patterns and Images, SIBGRAPI 2012, Ouro Preto, Brazil, August 22-25, 2012, 2012, pp. 291–297.

[131] Rodrigo Yuji Mizobe Nakamura, Luís Augusto Martins Pereira, Douglas Rodrigues, Kelton Augusto Pontara Costa, João Paulo Papa, Xin-She Yang, 9 - Binary bat algorithm for feature selection, in: Xin-She Yang, Zhihua Cui, Renbin Xiao, Amir Hossein Gandomi, Mehmet Karamanoglu (Eds.), Swarm Intelligence and Bio-Inspired Computation, Elsevier, Oxford, 2013, pp. 225–237.

[132] Navar Medeiros M. Nascimento, Leandro B. Marinho, Solon Alves Peixoto, João Paulo do Vale Madeiro, Victor Hugo C. de Albuquerque, Pedro P. Rebouças Filho, Heart arrhythmia classification based on statistical moments and structural co-occurrence, Circuits, Systems, and Signal Processing 2 (2020) 631–650.

[133] Thiago M. Nunes, André L.V. Coelho, Clodoaldo Ap.M. Lima, João P. Papa, Victor Hugo C. de Albuquerque, EEG signal classification for epilepsy diagnosis via optimum path forest - a systematic assessment, Neurocomputing 136 (2014) 103–123.

[134] Thiago M. Nunes, Victor Hugo C. de Albuquerque, João P. Papa, Cleiton C. Silva, Paulo G. Normando, Elineudo P. Moura, João Manuel R.S. Tavares, Automatic microstructural characterization and classification using artificial intelligence techniques on ultrasound signals, Expert Systems with Applications 40 (8) (2013) 3096–3105.

[135] Roberta B. Oliveira, Aledir S. Pereira, João Manuel R.S. Tavares, Computational diagnosis of skin lesions from dermoscopic images using combined features, Neural Computing & Applications 31 (10) (2019) 6091–6111.

[136] Daniel Osaku, Alexandre L.M. Levada, João P. Papa, On the influence of Markovian models for contextual-based optimum-path forest classification, in: Progress in
Pattern Recognition, Image Analysis, Computer Vision, and Applications - 19th
Iberoamerican Congress, CIARP 2014, Puerto Vallarta, Mexico, November 2-5,
2014, Proceedings, 2014, pp. 462–469.

[137] Daniel Osaku, Alexandre L.M. Levada, João Paulo Papa, A block-based Markov random field model estimation for contextual classification using Optimum-Path Forest,
in: IEEE International Symposium on Circuits and Systems, ISCAS 2016, Montréal,
QC, Canada, May 22-25, 2016, 2016, pp. 994–997.

[138] Daniel Osaku, Rodrigo Nakamura, João Paulo Papa, Alexandre L.M. Levada, Fabio
A.M. Cappabianco, Alexandre X. Falcão, Optimizing contextual-based optimum-
forest classification through swarm intelligence, in: Advanced Concepts for Intelligent
Vision Systems - 15th International Conference, ACIVS 2013, Poznań, Poland, October 28-31, 2013, Proceedings, 2013, pp. 203–214.

[139] Daniel Osaku, Rodrigo Y.M. Nakamura, Luis A.M. Pereira, Rodrigo Jose Pisani,
Alexandre L.M. Levada, Fabio A.M. Cappabianco, Alexandre X. Falcão, João Paulo
Papa, Improving land cover classification through contextual-based optimum-path
forest, Information Sciences 324 (2015) 60–87.

[140] Daniel Osaku, Danillo Roberto Pereira, Alexandre L.M. Levada, João Paulo Papa,
Fine-tuning contextual-based optimum-path forest for land-cover classification, IEEE
Geoscience and Remote Sensing Letters 13 (5) (2016) 735–739.

[141] Andre F. Pagnin, Silvana S. Artioli, João P. Papa, Preliminary diagnosis of ophthalmological diseases through machine learning techniques, Recent Patents on Signal
Processing (Discontinued) 1 (5) (2011) 74–79.

[142] A. Pal, S.K. Pal, Pattern Recognition: Evolution of Methodologies and Data Mining,
World Scientific, 2011, pp. 1–23.

[143] Caio A. Palma, Fábio A.M. Cappabianco, Jaime S. Ide, Paulo A.V. Miranda,
Anisotropic diffusion filtering operation and limitations - magnetic resonance imaging evaluation, IFAC Proceedings Volumes 47 (3) (2014) 3887–3892.

[144] João P. Papa, Fabio A.M. Cappabianco, Alexandre X. Falcão, Optimizing optimum-
path forest classification for huge datasets, in: 20th International Conference on
Pattern Recognition, ICPR 2010, Istanbul, Turkey, 23–26 August 2010, 2010,
pp. 4162–4165.

[145] João Paulo Papa, Victor Hugo C. de Albuquerque, Alexandre X. Falcão, João Manuel
R.S. Tavares, Fast automatic microstructural segmentation of ferrous alloy samples
using optimum-path forest, in: Computational Modeling of Objects Represented in
Images, Second International Symposium, CompIMAGE 2010, Buffalo, NY, USA,
May 5-7, 2010, Proceedings, 2010, pp. 210–220.

[146] J.P. Papa, A.X. Falcão, C.T.N. Suzuki, Supervised pattern classification based on
optimum-path forest, International Journal of Imaging Systems and Technology
19 (2) (June 2009) 120–131.

[147] João P. Papa, Alexandre X. Falcão, A new variant of the optimum-path forest classifier, in: Advances in Visual Computing, 4th International Symposium, ISVC 2008,
Las Vegas, NV, USA, December 1-3, 2008, Proceedings, Part I, 2008, pp. 935–944.

[148] João P. Papa, Alexandre X. Falcão, A learning algorithm for the optimum-path forest
classifier, in: Graph-Based Representations in Pattern Recognition, 7th IAPR-TC-
15 International Workshop, GbRPR 2009, Venice, Italy, May 26-28, 2009, Proceedings, 2009, pp. 195–204.

[149] João P. Papa, Alexandre X. Falcão, On the training patterns pruning for optimum-
path forest, in: Pasquale Foggia, Carlo Sansone, Mario Vento (Eds.), Image Analysis
and Processing – ICIAP 2009, Springer Berlin Heidelberg, Berlin, Heidelberg, 2009,
pp. 259–268.

[150] João P. Papa, Alexandre X. Falcão, Victor Hugo C. de Albuquerque, João Manuel R.S. Tavares, Efficient supervised optimum-path forest classification for large datasets, Pattern Recognition 45 (1) (2012) 512–520.

[151] João Paulo Papa, Alexandre Xavier Falcão, Greice Martins de Freitas, Ana Maria Heuminski de Ávila, Robust pruning of training patterns for optimum-path forest classification applied to satellite-based rainfall occurrence estimation, IEEE Geosciences Remote Sensing Letters 7 (2) (2010) 396–400.

[152] J.P. Papa, A.X. Falcao, A.L.M. Levada, D.C. Correa, D.H.P. Salvadeo, N.D.A. Mascarenhas, Fast and accurate holistic face recognition using Optimum-Path Forest, in: 2009 16th International Conference on Digital Signal Processing, 2009, pp. 1–6.

[153] João P. Papa, A.X. Falcão, Paulo A.V. Miranda, Celso T.N. Suzuki, Nelson D.A. Mascarenhas, Design of robust pattern classifiers based on optimum-path forests, in: 8th International Symposium on Mathematical Morphology, 2007, pp. 337–348.

[154] João P. Papa, Alexandre X. Falcão, Celso T.N. Suzuki, Nelson D.A. Mascarenhas, A discrete approach for supervised pattern recognition, in: Combinatorial Image Analysis, 12th International Workshop, IWCIA 2008, Buffalo, NY, USA, April 7-9, 2008, Proceedings, 2008, pp. 136–147.

[155] J.P. Papa, S.E.N. Fernandes, A.X. Falcão, Optimum-path forest based on k-connectivity: theory and applications, Pattern Recognition Letters 87 (1) (2017) 117–126.

[156] J.P. Papa, M.E.M. Gutierrez, R.Y.M. Nakamura, L.P. Papa, I.B.F. Vicentini, C.A. Vicentini, Automatic classification of fish germ cells through optimum-path forest, in: 2011 Annual International Conference of the IEEE Engineering in Medicine and Biology Society, 2011, pp. 5084–5087.

[157] João Paulo Papa, Aparecido Nilceu Marana, André Augusto Spadotto, Rodrigo Capobianco Guido, Alexandre X. Falcão, Robust and fast vowel recognition using optimum-path forest, in: Proceedings of the IEEE International Conference on Acoustics, Speech, and Signal Processing, ICASSP 2010, ICASSP 2010, 14-19 March 2010, Sheraton Dallas Hotel, Dallas, Texas, USA, 2010, pp. 2190–2193.

[158] João P. Papa, Rodrigo Y.M. Nakamura, Victor Hugo C. de Albuquerque, Alexandre X. Falcão, João Manuel R.S. Tavares, Computer techniques towards the automatic characterization of graphite particles in metallographic images of industrial materials, Expert Systems with Applications 40 (2) (2013) 590–597.

[159] João Paulo Papa, Andre Pagnin, Silvana Artioli Schellini, André Augusto Spadotto, Rodrigo Capobianco Guido, Moacir P. Ponti Jr., Giovani Chiachia, Alexandre X. Falcão, Feature selection through gravitational search algorithm, in: Proceedings of the IEEE International Conference on Acoustics, Speech, and Signal Processing, ICASSP 2011, May 22-27, 2011, Prague Congress Center, Prague, Czech Republic, 2011, pp. 2052–2055.

[160] João P. Papa, Clayton R. Pereira, Victor Hugo C. de Albuquerque, Cleiton C. Silva, Alexandre X. Falcão, João Manuel R.S. Tavares, Precipitates segmentation from scanning electron microscope images through machine learning techniques, in: Combinatorial Image Analysis - 14th International Workshop, IWCIA 2011, Madrid, Spain, May 23-25, 2011, Proceedings, 2011, pp. 456–468.

[161] João Paulo Papa, Anderson Rocha, Image categorization through optimum path forest and visual words, in: 18th IEEE International Conference on Image Processing, ICIP 2011, Brussels, Belgium, September 11-14, 2011, 2011, pp. 3525–3528.

[162] João Paulo Papa, Gustavo Henrique Rosa, Luciene P. Papa, A binary-constrained Geometric Semantic Genetic Programming for feature selection purposes, Pattern Recognition Letters 100 (2017) 59–66.

[163] J.P. Papa, A.A. Spadotto, A.X. Falcao, J.C. Pereira, Optimum path forest classifier applied to laryngeal pathology detection, in: 2008 15th International Conference on Systems, Signals and Image Processing, 2008, pp. 249–252.

[164] Leandro A. Passos, Clayton R. Pereira, Edmar R.S. Rezende, Tiago J. Carvalho, Silke Anna Thereza Weber, Christian Hook, João Paulo Papa, Parkinson disease identification using residual networks and optimum-path forest, in: 2018 IEEE 12th International Symposium on Applied Computational Intelligence and Informatics (SACI), 2018, pp. 000325–000330.

[165] Leandro Aparecido Passos, Claudio Santos, Clayton Reginaldo Pereira, Luis Claudio Sugi Afonso, João Paulo Papa, A hybrid approach for breast mass categorization, in: João Manuel R.S. Tavares, Jorge Natal, Manuel Renato (Eds.), VipIMAGE 2019, Springer International Publishing, 2019, pp. 159–168.

[166] Leandro Passos Júnior, Kelton Costa, João Papa, Fitting multivariate Gaussian distributions with optimum-path forest and its application for anomaly detection, in: 12th International Conference on Applied Computing, 2015.

[167] Leandro Aparecido Passos Júnior, Kelton Augusto Pontara da Costa, Gustavo Henrique de Rosa, João Paulo Papa, Obtenção de neurônios de redes neurais de base radial via agrupamento de dados por floresta de caminhos ótimos, Interciência & Sociedade (2015) 64–74.

[168] Clayton R. Pereira, Rodrigo Nakamura, João Paulo Papa, Kelton A.P. Costa, Intrusion detection system using Optimum-Path Forest, in: IEEE 36th Conference on Local Computer Networks, LCN 2011, Bonn, Germany, October 4-7, 2011, 2011, pp. 183–186.

[169] Clayton R. Pereira, Rodrigo Y.M. Nakamura, Kelton A.P. Costa, João P. Papa, An Optimum-Path Forest framework for intrusion detection in computer networks, Engineering Applications of Artificial Intelligence 25 (6) (2012) 1226–1234.

[170] Clayton R. Pereira, Leandro A. Passos, Ricardo R. Lopes, Silke A.T. Weber, Christian Hook, João Paulo Papa, Parkinson's disease identification using restricted Boltzmann machines, in: Computer Analysis of Images and Patterns - 17th International Conference, CAIP 2017, Ystad, Sweden, August 22-24, 2017, Proceedings, Part II, 2017, pp. 70–80.

[171] Clayton R. Pereira, Danillo Roberto Pereira, Francisco A. da Silva, Christian Hook, Silke A.T. Weber, Luis A.M. Pereira, João Paulo Papa, A step towards the automated diagnosis of Parkinson's disease: analyzing handwriting movements, in: 28th IEEE International Symposium on Computer-Based Medical Systems, CBMS 2015, Sao Carlos, Brazil, June 22-25, 2015, 2015, pp. 171–176.

[172] Clayton R. Pereira, Danillo Roberto Pereira, Francisco A. da Silva, João P. Masieiro, Silke A.T. Weber, Christian Hook, João P. Papa, A new computer vision-based approach to aid the diagnosis of Parkinson's disease, Computer Methods and Programs in Biomedicine 136 (2016) 79–88.

[173] Clayton Roberto Pereira, Danillo Roberto Pereira, João Paulo Papa, Gustavo H. Rosa, Xin-She Yang, Convolutional neural networks applied for Parkinson's disease identification, in: Machine Learning for Health Informatics - State-of-the-Art and Future Challenges, 2016, pp. 377–390.

[174] Clayton R. Pereira, Silke A.T. Weber, Christian Hook, Gustavo H. Rosa, João Paulo Papa, Deep learning-aided Parkinson's disease diagnosis from handwritten dynamics, in: 29th SIBGRAPI Conference on Graphics, Patterns and Images, SIBGRAPI 2016, Sao Paulo, Brazil, October 4-7, 2016, 2016, pp. 340–346.

[175] Danillo Roberto Pereira, Rodrigo Pisani, Rodrigo Nakamura, João Paulo Papa, Land-cover classification through sequential learning-based optimum-path forest, in: 2015 IEEE International Geoscience and Remote Sensing Symposium, IGARSS 2015, Milan, Italy, July 26-31, 2015, 2015, pp. 76–79.

[176] D.R. Pereira, R.J. Pisani, A.N. de Souza, J.P. Papa, An ensemble-based stacked sequential learning algorithm for remote sensing imagery classification, IEEE Journal of Selected Topics in Applied Earth Observations and Remote Sensing 10 (4) (2017) 1525–1541.

[177] Luís A.M. Pereira, Rodrigo Y.M. Nakamura, Guilherme F.S. De Souza, Dagoberto Martins, JoãO P. Papa, Aquatic weed automatic classification using machine learning techniques, Computers and Electronics in Agriculture 87 (2012) 56–63.

[178] Luis A.M. Pereira, João Paulo Papa, Jurandy Almeida, Ricardo da Silva Torres, Willian Paraguassu Amorim, A multiple labeling-based optimum-path forest for video content classification, in: XXVI Conference on Graphics, Patterns and Images, SIBGRAPI 2013, Arequipa, Peru, August 5-8, 2013, 2013, pp. 334–340.

[179] Luís A.M. Pereira, João P. Papa, André L.V. Coelho, Clodoaldo A.M. Lima, Danillo R. Pereira, Victor Hugo C. de Albuquerque, Automatic identification of epileptic EEG signals through binary magnetic optimization algorithms, Neural Computing & Applications (2017).

[180] L.A.M. Pereira, D. Rodrigues, T.N.S. Almeida, C.C.O. Ramos, A.N. Souza, X.-S. Yang, J.P. Papa, A Binary Cuckoo Search and Its Application for Feature Selection, Springer International Publishing, Cham, 2014, pp. 141–154.

[181] Rafael Goncalves Pires, Silas Evandro Nachif Fernandes, João Paulo Papa, Blur parameter identification through optimum-path forest, in: Computer Analysis of Images and Patterns - 17th International Conference, CAIP 2017, Ystad, Sweden, August 22-24, 2017, Proceedings, Part II, 2017, pp. 230–240.

[182] R. Pisani, K. Costa, G. Rosa, D. Pereira, J. Papa, J.M.R.S. Tavares, River sediment yield classification using remote sensing imagery, in: 2016 9th IAPR Workshop on Pattern Recognition in Remote Sensing (PRRS), 2016, pp. 1–6.

[183] Rodrigo Pisani, Paulina Riedel, Kelton A.P. Costa, Rodrigo Nakamura, Clayton R. Pereira, Gustavo H. Rosa, João P. Papa, Automatic landslide recognition through Optimum-Path Forest, in: 2012 IEEE International Geoscience and Remote Sensing Symposium, IGARSS 2012, Munich, Germany, July 22-27, 2012, 2012, pp. 6228–6231.

[184] Rodrigo Pisani, Paulina Riedel, M. Ferreira, M. Marques, R. Mizobe, João P. Papa, Land use image classification through Optimum-Path Forest Clustering, in: 2011 IEEE International Geoscience and Remote Sensing Symposium, IGARSS 2011, Vancouver, BC, Canada, July 24-29, 2011, 2011, pp. 826–829.

[185] Rodrigo Pisani, Paulina Riedel, A. Gomes, R. Mizobe, João P. Papa, Is it possible to make pixel-based radar image classification user-friendly?, in: 2011 IEEE International Geoscience and Remote Sensing Symposium, IGARSS 2011, Vancouver, BC, Canada, July 24-29, 2011, 2011, pp. 4304–4307.

[186] Rodrigo José Pisani, Rodrigo Mizobe, Paulina Setti Riedel, Célia Regina Lopes Zimback, João Paulo Papa, Can we make remote sensing image classification fast enough?, in: Anais XV Simposio Brasileiro de Sensoriamento Remoto, 2011, pp. 2724–2731.

[187] Rodrigo Jose Pisani, Rodrigo Yuji Mizobe Nakamura, Paulina Setti Riedel, Célia Regina Lopes Zimback, Alexandre Xavier Falcão, João Paulo Papa, Toward satellite-based land cover classification through optimum-path forest, IEEE Transactions on Geoscience and Remote Sensing 52 (10) (2014) 6075–6085.

[188] Rodrigo José Pisani, João Paulo Papa, Célia Regina Lopes Zimback, A. Falcao, A. Barbosa, Land use classification using optimum-path forest, in: Proceedings of the 14th Brazilian Symposium on Remote Sensing, 2009, pp. 7063–7070.

[189] N.N. Pise, P. Kulkarni, A survey of semi-supervised learning methods, in: 2008 International Conference on Computational Intelligence and Security, Vol. 2, 2008, pp. 30–34.

[190] Moacir Ponti, Mateus Riva, An incremental linear-time learning algorithm for the Optimum-Path Forest classifier, Information Processing Letters 126 (2017) 1–6.

[191] M.A. Ponti, Relevance image sampling from collection using importance selection on randomized optimum-path trees, in: 2017 Brazilian Conference on Intelligent Systems (BRACIS), 2017, pp. 198–203.

[192] Moacir A. Ponti, Gabriel B. Paranhos da Costa, Fernando P. Santos, Kaue U. Silveira, Supervised and unsupervised relevance sampling in handcrafted and deep learning features obtained from image collections, Applied Soft Computing 80 (2019) 414–424.

[193] Moacir P. Ponti, João Paulo Papa, Alexandre L.M. Levada, A Markov random field model for combining optimum-path forest classifiers using decision graphs and game strategy approach, 2011, pp. 581–590.

[194] Moacir P. Ponti, Isadora Rossi, Ensembles of optimum-path forest classifiers using input data manipulation and undersampling, in: Zhi-Hua Zhou, Fabio Roli, Josef Kittler (Eds.), Multiple Classifier Systems, Springer Berlin Heidelberg, Berlin, Heidelberg, 2013, pp. 236–246.

[195] C.C.O. Ramos, A.N. de Sousa, J.P. Papa, A.X. Falcao, A new approach for nontechnical losses detection based on optimum-path forest, IEEE Transactions on Power Systems 26 (1) (2011) 181–189.

[196] Caio C.O. Ramos, André N. de Souza, Giovani Chiachia, Alexandre X. Falcão, João P. Papa, A novel algorithm for feature selection using Harmony Search and its application for non-technical losses detection, Computers & Electrical Engineering 37 (6) (2011) 886–894.

[197] C.C.O. Ramos, A.N. de Souza, A.X. Falcao, J.P. Papa, New insights on nontechnical losses characterization through evolutionary-based feature selection, IEEE Transactions on Power Delivery 27 (1) (2012) 140–146.

[198] Caio C.O. Ramos, João Paulo Papa, André N. de Souza, Giovani Chiachia, Alexandre X. Falcão, What is the importance of selecting features for non-technical losses identification?, in: International Symposium on Circuits and Systems (ISCAS 2011), May 15-19 2011, Rio de Janeiro, Brazil, 2011, pp. 1045–1048.

[199] C.C.O. Ramos, D. Rodrigues, A.N. de Souza, J.P. Papa, On the study of commercial losses in Brazil: a binary black hole algorithm for theft characterization, IEEE Transactions on Smart Grid PP (99) (2017) 1.

[200] C.C.O. Ramos, A.N. Souza, R.Y.M. Nakamura, J.P. Papa, Electrical consumers data clustering through Optimum-Path Forest, in: 2011 16th International Conference on Intelligent System Applications to Power Systems, 2011, pp. 1–4.

[201] Caio C.O. Ramos, André N. Souza, Joao P. Papa, On the evaluation of different metrics for non-technical losses estimation through optimum-path forest, in: Anais do XVIII Congresso Brasileiro de Automática, 2010, pp. 108–113.

[202] C.C.O. Ramos, A.N. Souza, J.P. Papa, A.X. Falcao, Fast non-technical losses identification through optimum-path forest, in: 2009 15th International Conference on Intelligent System Applications to Power Systems, 2009, pp. 1–5.

[203] Caio C.O. Ramos, André N. Souza, João P. Papa, Alexandre X. Falcão, Learning to identify non-technical losses with optimum-path forest, in: Proceedings of the 17th International Conference on Systems, Signals and Image Processing (IWSSIP 2010), 2010, pp. 154–157.

[204] Caio C.O. Ramos, A.N. Souza, Lucas I. Pereira, Danilo S. Gastaldello, Maria G. Zago, João P. Papa, Técnicas inteligentes aplicadas na identificação de consumidores industriais fraudadores de energia elétrica, in: Latin-American Congress on Electricity Generation and Transmission, Vol. 8, 2009, pp. 281–286.

[205] A. Rauber, D. Merkl, M. Dittenbach, The growing hierarchical self-organizing map: exploratory analysis of high-dimensional data, IEEE Transactions on Neural Networks 13 (6) (Nov 2002) 1331–1341.

[206] P.P. Rebouças Filho, J.W.M. Souza, L.B. Marinho, G.B. Holanda, H.H. Silva, A.A.F. Leite, T.S. Bandeira, A.W.O. Rodrigues, Mobile system to aid in the identification and classification of electrical assets using convolutional neural network, in: 2019 8th Brazilian Conference on Intelligent Systems (BRACIS), 2019, pp. 699–704.

[207] L.C.F. Ribeiro, J.P. Papa, Unsupervised dialogue act classification with optimum-path forest, in: 2018 31st SIBGRAPI Conference on Graphics, Patterns and Images (SIBGRAPI), 2018, pp. 25–32.
[208] Patricia B. Ribeiro, Kelton A.P. da Costa, João Paulo Papa, Roseli A. Francelin Romero, Optimum-path forest applied for breast masses classification, in: 2014 IEEE 27th International Symposium on Computer-Based Medical Systems, New York, NY, USA, May 27-29, 2014, 2014, pp. 52–55.
[209] Patricia B. Ribeiro, Leandro A. Passos Junior, Luis A. da Silva, Kelton A.P. da Costa, João P. Papa, Roseli A.F. Romero, Unsupervised breast masses classification through optimum-path forest, in: 28th IEEE International Symposium on Computer-Based Medical Systems, CBMS 2015, Sao Carlos, Brazil, June 22-25, 2015, 2015, pp. 238–243.
[210] Patricia B. Ribeiro, João P. Papa, Roseli A.F. Romero, An ensemble-based approach for breast mass classification in mammography images, Proceedings - SPIE 10134 (2017) 10134.
[211] Mateus Riva, Moacir Ponti, Teófilo Emídio de Campos, One-class to multi-class model update using the class-incremental optimum-path forest classifier, in: ECAI, 2016.
[212] Leonardo Marques Rocha, Fabio A.M. Cappabianco, Alexandre Xavier Falcão, Data clustering as an optimum-path forest problem with applications in image analysis, International Journal of Imaging Systems and Technology 19 (2) (2009) 50–68.
[213] Leonardo M. Rocha, Alexandre X. Falcão, Luís Geraldo P. Meloni, A robust extension of the mean shift algorithm using optimum-path forest, in: Image Analysis - from Theory to Applications. Proceedings of IWCIA 2008 Special Track on Applications, Buffalo, NY, USA, April 7-9, 2008, 2008, pp. 29–38.
[214] Douglas Rodrigues, Luis A.M. Pereira, T.N.S. Almeida, João Paulo Papa, André N. de Souza, Caio C.O. Ramos, Xin-She Yang, BCS: a Binary Cuckoo Search algorithm for feature selection, in: 2013 IEEE International Symposium on Circuits and Systems (ISCAS2013), Beijing, China, May 19-23, 2013, 2013, pp. 465–468.
[215] Douglas Rodrigues, Luis A.M. Pereira, Rodrigo Y.M. Nakamura, Kelton A.P. Costa, Xin-She Yang, André N. de Souza, João Paulo Papa, A wrapper approach for feature selection based on Bat Algorithm and Optimum-Path Forest, Expert Systems with Applications 41 (5) (2014) 2250–2258.
[216] Douglas Rodrigues, Luis A.M. Pereira, João P. Papa, Caio C.O. Ramos, André N. de Souza, Luciene P. Papa, Optimizing feature selection through binary charged system search, in: Computer Analysis of Images and Patterns - 15th International Conference, CAIP 2013, York, UK, August 27-29, 2013, Proceedings, Part I, 2013, pp. 377–384.
[217] D. Rodrigues, L.A.M. Pereira, J.P. Papa, S.A.T. Weber, A binary krill herd approach for feature selection, in: 2014 22nd International Conference on Pattern Recognition, 2014, pp. 1407–1412.
[218] Douglas Rodrigues, Caio Cesar Oba Ramos, André Nunes de Souza, João Paulo Papa, Black Hole Algorithm for non-technical losses characterization, in: IEEE 6th Latin American Symposium on Circuits & Systems, LASCAS 2015, Montevideo, Uruguay, February 24-27, 2015, 2015, pp. 1–4.
[219] Douglas Rodrigues, Gabriel F.A. Silva, João P. Papa, Aparecido N. Marana, Xin-She Yang, EEG-based person identification through Binary Flower Pollination Algorithm, Expert Systems with Applications 62 (2016) 81–90.
[220] Douglas Rodrigues, André Nunes De Souza, João Paulo Papa, Pruning optimum-path forest classifiers using multi-objective optimization, in: 30th SIBGRAPI Conference on Graphics, Patterns and Images, SIBGRAPI 2017, Niterói, Brazil, October 17-20, 2017, 2017, pp. 127–133.

[221] Douglas Rodrigues, Xin-She Yang, André Nunes de Souza, João Paulo Papa, Binary flower pollination algorithm and its application to feature selection, in: Recent Advances in Swarm Intelligence and Evolutionary Computation, 2015, pp. 85–100.

[222] Marcos V.T. Romero, Adriana S. Iwashita, Luciene P. Papa, André N. de Souza, João P. Papa, Fast optimum-path forest classification on graphics processors, in: VISAPP 2014 - Proceedings of the 9th International Conference on Computer Vision Theory and Applications, Vol. 2, Lisbon, Portugal, 5-8 January, 2014, 2014, pp. 627–631.

[223] G.H. Rosa, K.A.P. Costa, L.A.P. Júnior, J.P. Papa, A.X. Falcão, J.M.R.S. Tavares, On the training of artificial neural networks with radial basis function using optimum-path forest clustering, in: 22nd International Conference on Pattern Recognition, 2014, pp. 1472–1477.

[224] Gustavo H. Rosa, João Paulo Papa, Luciene P. Papa, Feature selection using geometric semantic genetic programming, in: Genetic and Evolutionary Computation Conference, Berlin, Germany, July 15-19, 2017, Companion Material Proceedings, 2017, pp. 253–254.

[225] Priscila T.M. Saito, Willian Paraguassu Amorim, Alexandre X. Falcão, Pedro Jussieu de Rezende, Celso T.N. Suzuki, Jancarlo F. Gomes, Marcelo Henriques de Carvalho, Active semi-supervised learning using optimum-path forest, in: 22nd International Conference on Pattern Recognition, ICPR 2014, Stockholm, Sweden, August 24-28, 2014, 2014, pp. 3798–3803.

[226] Priscila T.M. Saito, Pedro J. de Rezende, Alexandre X. Falcão, Celso T.N. Suzuki, Jancarlo F. Gomes, An active learning paradigm based on a priori data reduction and organization, Expert Systems with Applications 41 (14) (2014) 6086–6097.

[227] Priscila T.M. Saito, Celso T.N. Suzuki, Jancarlo F. Gomes, Pedro Jussieu de Rezende, Alexandre X. Falcão, Robust active learning for the diagnosis of parasites, Pattern Recognition 48 (11) (2015) 3572–3583.

[228] Róger M. Sarmento, Francisco F.X. Vasconcelos, Pedro P. Rebouças Filho, Victor Hugo C. de Albuquerque, An IoT platform for the analysis of brain CT images based on Parzen analysis, Future Generations Computer Systems 105 (2020) 135–147.

[229] S. Sasikala, M. Bharathi, M. Ezhilarasi, Sathiya Senthil, M. Ramasubba Reddy, Particle swarm optimization based fusion of ultrasound echographic and elastographic texture features for improved breast cancer detection, Australasian Physical & Engineering Sciences in Medicine 42 (3) (2019) 677–688.

[230] S. Sasikala, M. Ezhilarasi, S. Arun Kumar, Detection of Breast Cancer Using Fusion of MLO and CC View Features Through a Hybrid Technique Based on Binary Firefly Algorithm and Optimum-Path Forest Classifier, Springer Singapore, Singapore, 2020, pp. 23–40.

[231] Friedhelm Schwenker, Edmondo Trentin, Pattern classification and clustering: a review of partially supervised learning approaches, Pattern Recognition Letters 37 (2014) 4–14.

[232] J. Shi, J. Malik, Normalized cuts and image segmentation, IEEE Transactions on Pattern Analysis and Machine Intelligence 22 (8) (Aug 2000) 888–905.

[233] Luis A. Silva, Kelton A.P. Costa, Patricia B. Ribeiro, Dheny Fernandes, João P. Papa, On the feasibility of optimum-path forest in the context of Internet-of-things-based applications, Recent Patents on Signal Processing (Discontinued) 5 (1) (2015) 52–60.

[234] Luis Alexandre da Silva, Kelton Costa, P. Ribeiro, Gustavo de Rosa, João Papa, Parameter-Setting Free Harmony Search Optimization of Restricted Boltzmann Machines and Its Applications to Spam Detection, 2015, pp. 143–150.

[235] G.J. Sousa, Daniel Carlos Guimarães Pedronette, Alexandre Baldassin, P.I.M. Privatto, M. Gaseta, Ivan Rizzo Guilherme, D. Colombo, Luis Claudio Sugi Afonso, João Paulo Papa, Pattern analysis in drilling reports using optimum-path forest, in: 2018 International Joint Conference on Neural Networks (IJCNN), 2018, pp. 1–8.

[236] A.N. Souza, P. da Costa, P.S. da Silva, C.C.O. Ramos, J.P. Papa, Fault location in underground systems through optimum-path forest, in: 2011 16th International Conference on Intelligent System Applications to Power Systems, 2011, pp. 1–5.

[237] A.N. Souza, C.C.O. Ramos, D.S. Gastaldello, R.Y.M. Nakamura, J.P. Papa, Fast fault diagnosis in power transformers using Optimum-Path Forest, in: 2012 IEEE 16th International Conference on Intelligent Engineering Systems (INES), 2012, pp. 209–212.

[238] Luis Antonio De Souza, Luis Claudio Sugi Afonso, Christoph Palm, João Paulo Papa, Barrett's esophagus identification using optimum-path forest, in: 30th SIBGRAPI Conference on Graphics, Patterns and Images, SIBGRAPI 2017, Niterói, Brazil, October 17-20, 2017, 2017, pp. 308–314.

[239] Roberto Souza, Letícia Rittner, Roberto de Alencar Lotufo, A comparison between k-Optimum Path Forest and k-Nearest Neighbors supervised classifiers, Pattern Recognition Letters 39 (2014) 2–10.

[240] A.A. Spadoto, R.C. Guido, F.L. Carnevali, A.F. Pagnin, A.X. Falcão, J.P. Papa, Improving Parkinson's disease identification through evolutionary-based feature selection, in: 2011 Annual International Conference of the IEEE Engineering in Medicine and Biology Society, 2011, pp. 7857–7860.

[241] A.A. Spadoto, R.C. Guido, J.P. Papa, A.X. Falcão, Parkinson's disease identification through optimum-path forest, in: 2010 Annual International Conference of the IEEE Engineering in Medicine and Biology, 2010, pp. 6087–6090.

[242] A.A. Spadotto, J.C. Pereira, R.C. Guido, J.P. Papa, A.X. Falcao, A.R. Gatto, P.C. Cola, A.O. Schelp, Oropharyngeal dysphagia identification using wavelets and optimum path forest, in: 2008 3rd International Symposium on Communications, Control and Signal Processing, 2008, pp. 735–740.

[243] C.T.N. Suzuki, J.F. Gomes, A.X. Falcao, J.P. Papa, S. Hoshino-Shimizu, Automatic segmentation and classification of human intestinal parasites from microscopy images, IEEE Transactions on Biomedical Engineering 60 (3) (2013) 803–812.

[244] R.D. Trevizan, A.S. Bretas, A. Rossoni, Nontechnical losses detection: a discrete cosine transform and optimum-path forest based approach, in: 2015 North American Power Symposium (NAPS), 2015, pp. 1–6.

[245] R.D. Trevizan, A. Rossoni, A.S. Bretas, D. da Silva Gazzana, R. de Podestá Martin, N.G. Bretas, A.L. Bettiol, A. Carniato, L.F. do Nascimento Passos, Non-technical losses identification using Optimum-Path Forest and state estimation, in: 2015 IEEE Eindhoven PowerTech, 2015, pp. 1–6.

[246] Hjalmar K. Turesson, Sidarta Ribeiro, Danillo R. Pereira, João P. Papa, Victor Hugo C. de Albuquerque, Machine learning algorithms for automatic classification of marmoset vocalizations, PLoS ONE 11 (9) (09 2016) 1–14.

[247] L.J.P. van der Maaten, G.E. Hinton, Visualizing high-dimensional data using t-SNE, Journal of Machine Learning Research 9 (2008) 2579–2605.

[248] Kátia Cristina de Melo Tavares Vieira, Andressa Ágata Fernandes, Karina Martins Silva, Viviane Ribas Pereira, Danillo Roberto Pereira, Ana Paula Alves Favareto, Experimental exposure to gasohol impairs sperm quality with recognition of the classification pattern of exposure groups by machine learning algorithms, Environmental Science and Pollution Research 26 (4) (2019) 3921–3931.

[249] C. Xu, Y. Tang, M. Toyoura, J. Xu, X. Mao, Generating users' desired face image using the conditional generative adversarial network and relevance feedback, IEEE Access 7 (2019) 181458–181468.

[250] Elghzizal Yassir, Khaissidi Ghizlane, Mrabti Mostafa, Chenouni Driss, Towards an automatic and early detection of Parkinson's disease: modeling of a polar coordinates system based on spiral tests, AIP Conference Proceedings 2074 (1) (2019) 020011.

CHAPTER 3

Real-time application of OPF-based classifier in Snort IDS

Luan Utimura[a], Kelton Costa[a], and Rafał Scherer[b]
[a]São Paulo State University, Department of Computing, Bauru, Brazil
[b]Czestochowa University of Technology, Department of Computing, Częstochowa, Poland

3.1 Introduction

With the advent of the internet, humanity was quickly conquered by many facilities that intrinsically transformed the regular life of contemporary organizations. Among the central tendencies of this world–scale infrastructure, the tangibility of the information available in the digital environment, regardless of the location of the user who wishes to access it, stands out. As much as the reach is one of the main characteristics that contributed to the emergence of excellent applications, it is also one of the main reasons why the security of computer systems is now necessary. From the moment an application makes use of the internet to send and receive data, it can allow from the interference of malicious third parties who may compromise the integrity of this information. Therefore the guarantee of security in computer systems is a continuous process in continuous revision.

Among the tools used to shield computer networks, it is worth considering the Intrusion Detection Systems (IDS). Characterized by the functions of monitoring, alerting, and preventing attacks and violations of internal policies, the efficiency of IDSs can be analyzed from three criteria [1]: *(i) accuracy, (ii) performance*, and *(iii) completeness*. Depending on the detection methodology used by the system, some criteria may stand out to the others.

An IDS that performs detection by signature, that is, that searches for known patterns—commonly called *signatures*—in the analyzed data, has a reasonable accuracy rate because it is effective against known attacks. However, its completeness is questionable since it is necessary to update the attack knowledge base [2,3]. On the other hand, an IDS that performs detections for anomalies, that is, that estimates the normal behavior of the monitored system and searches for deviations that potentially represent abnormalities has difficulties in achieving high accuracy rates, due to

Optimum-Path Forest
https://doi.org/10.1016/B978-0-12-822688-9.00011-6

the greater susceptibility to generate false positives. However, since it is not limited to the signatures of known attacks, this methodology is capable of identifying unknown threats and, therefore, has greater completeness to detection by signature [2,3].

It is possible to classify IDSs taking into description the type of monitored environment. In the first developed IDSs, intruder detection was particularly *host*-based; that is, the search for suspicious incidents occurred locally on the machine in question being monitored by the Host-Based Intrusion Detection System (HIDS). However, with the evolution of the area and the popularization of the internet, IDSs concentrated on detecting attacks directed at computer networks, consolidating a state known as Network Intrusion Detection Systems (NIDS) [4].

Although the commercial use of NIDSs based on signature detection methodologies is predominant, several studies in the academic field have attempted to improve anomaly detection methodologies through the application of intelligent machine learning techniques. In these techniques, classification models are generated from the learning of patterns of normal and abnormal behaviors present in a data set. Once incorporated into the IDS, the models become the central mechanism to perform the prediction/classification of any packet/flow of network traffic based on its features.

To Snort, particularly, many contributions have already been and continue to be made in terms of anomaly detection. In [5], an adaptive plugin was developed to improve the accuracy of Snort IDS [6]. Through a hybrid approach, machine learning algorithms were used to reduce the rate of false positives from alarms generated by the tool's base solution. The study proved to be effective in significantly decreasing the rate of false positives through approaches including Support Vector Machine (SVM) with fuzzy logic and SVM with Firefly Algorithm (FA).

In [7], with a more focus on detecting known and unknown Distributed Denial of Service (DDoS) attacks, a plugin with an artificial neural network for Snort-AI [8] was developed. In a controlled environment, the proposed scheme achieved an accuracy of up to 98%, bettering the base solution of Snort itself, that is, without modifications, and other related works.

Despite not being historically incorporated inside Snort like the other traditional machine learning techniques, classifiers based on Optimum-Path Forest (OPF) have also already presented numerous relevant contributions in the field of intrusion detection. In [9], an OPF-based framework was proposed for intrusion detection in computer networks. With three traditional databases in the area, IDS_Bag, KDDCup, and NSL-KDD, the work was evaluated over three steps of experiments. In the first step, when compared to the Bayesian classifier, SVM-RBF, and SOM (Self-Organizing Maps), the OPF presented satisfactory values of accuracy and stood out, to the other techniques, for having been the fastest technique in terms of total training and testing time. In the second step, the authors demonstrated that it is possible to further accelerate the OPF training and testing process, at the rate of a minimal loss of accuracy through the OPF Prunning algorithm. Finally, in the third step, three techniques based on OPF were evaluated for the selection of characteristics in the proposed problem. In this step, the authors showed that it is possible to use a reduced set of features and, even so, improve the recognition rate of the classifier.

In [10], a design model based on MapReduce for the detection of distributed intrusion was proposed for the internet of Things (IoT). In this model, aiming at a multifaceted detection, signature, and anomaly-based intrusion detection agents were used, with the supervised (MOPF) and unsupervised (OPFC) version of OPF in the reduce phase. In a controlled environment, the experimental results showed superior performance in the simultaneous detection of internal and external attacks in IoT, with emphasis on the false alarm rate of the MOPF, which in comparison to SVM, Naive Bayes (NB), and CART (Classification And Regression Tree), was significantly lower.

Although certain are just a few of the works developed in the field in recent years, they show that anomaly-based intrusion detection is still one of the biggest trends in the study of IDSs. Therefore, in this work, the initial proposal is to contextualize the main concepts linked not only to IDSs but also to the intelligent techniques employed. Then, identifying the viable points of contribution to the scientific community, we propose the training, in terms of anomaly-based intrusion detection, of the open-source IDS Snort.

The present work aims to replace the signature-based detection scheme of the latest version of Snort with an anomaly-based detection scheme to classify, in real-time, traffic flows from a network using traditional machine learning techniques and, in an unprecedented way, the OPF classifier.

This chapter is structured as follows: Section 3.2 presents the main concepts and definitions of IDSs. Section 3.3 presents the main concepts and explanations about the machine learning area techniques. Section 3.4 presents the proposed methodology for the development of a plugin with machine learning techniques, capable of classifying network traffic flows in real-time. Section 3.5 presents the experiments and the results obtained in this work. Finally, Section 3.6 presents the final considerations of this work and the next steps to be taken.

3.2 Intrusion detection systems

An IDS is responsible for dynamically monitoring the actions taken in a given environment and also deciding whether specific actions show symptoms of a potential attack or whether they constitute a legitimate use of the environment [4]. Eventually, if malicious actions are detected in the system, the objective is to notify the network administrator through alerts (messages in the terminal, e-mail, etc.).

The IDS, in general, can also be seen as a detector that uses three types of information in its processing: (1) long-term information related to the technique used to detect intrusions, (2) configuration information of the current state of the system, and finally, (3) audit information describing the events that occurred in the order. From these three elements, IDS can filter out unnecessary information and produce a synthetic view containing only the security-related actions taken by users. In this way, a final decision can be made to assess the chances of these actions constituting (or not) a symptom of intrusion into the system [4].

Intrusion detection assumes that it is possible to differentiate the behavior of an attacker from the action of a legitimate user in quantifiable ways [11]. However, there is no exact delimitation that indicates the end of one behavior and the beginning of another. On the other hand, there is a common behavioral region between user profiles, which can make it difficult for IDS to interpret it, which depending on the approach used, can increase the number of false positives (normal users classified as intrusion) or false negatives (attackers classified as normal users).

3.2.1 Detection approaches in IDS

Currently, the most widely used detection approach in IDS is signature-based. IDSs of this nature maintain extensive databases with the signatures of the attacks. Each signature, in practice, is represented by a set of rules that describe both individual packages and groups of packages used in known attacks. In this way, as the IDS analyzes the packets that pass through it, if equivalences are found between the packets and the database signatures, alerts are generated to notify the network administrator. In addition to the inability to detect attacks unknown, an IDS based on signatures can face difficulties related to the performance of the application, depending on the number of signature comparisons made for each package processed [12].

Despite being less used, the anomaly detection approach has attracted attention in recent years in the scientific field. The methodology focuses on identifying variations that exceed certain limits defined in the IDS, which potentially indicate the occurrence of an abnormality, starting from the creation of a behavioral profile considered "normal" of the computer system [2]. As much as this alternative discards the need to maintain a database of known attacks, the difficulty of this approach lies in the search for a well-structured model that represents, in the best possible way, the particularities of the monitored system, reconciling a high accuracy rate and low rate of false positives.

3.2.2 Anomaly detection techniques

The authors of [2] and [13] also define three main categories of anomaly detection techniques: based on statistics based on knowledge and based on machine learning (machine learning). In statistics-based techniques, the activity traffic captured network, and the network captures activity traffic and creates a profile representing stochastic behavior. This profile is based on metrics such as traffic rate, connection rate, the number of packets for each protocol, the number of different IP addresses, among others. The anomaly detection process has two profiles: one corresponding to the current pattern monitored over time, and the other corresponding to the previously trained statistical profile. As events occur on the network, the existing profile is updated, and an anomaly score is estimated by comparing the two behaviors. Representing the degree of irregularity of a given event, if the anomaly score exceeds a preestablished limit, it is the occurrence of an abnormality recorded.

In knowledge-based techniques, the most widely used approach is that of expert systems. Expert systems perform three steps to classify data according to a set of rules.

First, different attributes and classes identified from the training data. Then a set of classification rules, parameters, or procedures are deduced. Finally, the data are classified according to the standards used.

There are also anomaly methods based on specifications, where the desired model is built manually from a human specialist, in terms of a set of rules (specifications) that aim to determine the legitimate behavior of the system. As an alternative to the human specialist, specifications can be developed using formal tools, such as the Finite State Machine (FSM) methodology, which by dealing with sequences of states and the transitions between them, becomes appropriate to model network protocols [14].

Finally, in techniques based on machine learning, the establishment of explicit or implicit models allows learned patterns to be categorized.

A unique feature of these techniques is the need for labeled data to train such behavioral models. Among the main schemes based on machine learning applied to IDSs, we can mention the use of Artificial Neural Networks (ANNs). As it is a flexible approach to changes in the environment, ANNs have already been applied for the creation of user profiles [15], prediction of commands based on sequences of previous commands [16], identification of intrusive behavior of traffic patterns [17], among others.

With the use of Genetic Algorithms (GA), [18] proposed the implementation of a scheme that considers temporal and spatial information of network connections to encode them in terms of the rules of an IDS. Thus, it is understood that the ultimate goal of applying GA is to generate rules that, in a way, are only applicable to anomalous connections. Therefore, these rules are tested on historical connections and used to filter new connections for suspicious network traffic.

3.2.3 Types of IDS

Taking into account the type of system monitored by IDS, it is possible to classify it as [19–23]:

- **NIDS**: is an independent platform that analyzes, examines, and monitors a network's backbone[1] in search of attacks. The positioning of a NIDS is strategic, being typically connected to switches[2] configured with port mirroring.[3] NIDS, therefore, protects an entire network segment.

- **HIDS**: restricted to a particular computer and offers protection by monitoring the operating system and the file system, looking for signs of intrusion. Its analysis includes system calls, application logs, changes to the file system, among other activities.

- **Hybrid of NIDS and HIDS**: focuses on the joint analysis of data from hosts and the network itself, in order to obtain a comprehensive

---

[1] Backbone can be understood as the structure responsible for interconnecting several network elements, allowing data traffic from one network to another.

[2] Switch is a device that performs the redistribution of packets within a network.

[3] Port mirroring is a method of monitoring network traffic where copies of all sent packets are redirected to a specific port.

view of the system. The need to use hybrid systems becomes evident in encrypted networks, where it is necessary to identify correlations between the data that travel and that are decrypted on the hosts.

The authors of [24] also point out the Wireless-based Intrusion Detection Systems (WIDS), Network Behavior Analysis (NBA), and Mixed Intrusion Detection System (MIDS). WIDSs, like NIDSs, capture network traffic but are restricted to analyzing the wireless environment. The NBA, unlike NIDS or WIDS, performs an inspection of network traffic in order to detect threats based solely on the unexpected behavior of this event. Finally, the adoption of multiple technologies results in MIDS, which can contribute to more complete and accurate detections.

3.2.4 Open source IDS

Bearing in mind that the majority of IDS solutions adopted in corporate and domestic environments use primarily signature detection approaches [4], it is essential to maintain databases of attacks in order to keep them updated. Due to the constant renewal of existing attacks and also the appearance of new attacks, such a maintenance process is challenging as it has to adapt, in a timely manner, to such changes in the intrusion detection scenario.

In open-source IDSs, this difficulty is efficiently overcome by the tool community itself, which collectively helps in the construction and updating of diverse and complete databases. Some of the main open source tools available on the market are Snort, Suricata, and Bro IDS, with Snort being the object of study in this chapter. In the next section, some of Snort's strengths are presented.

3.2.4.1 Snort

Snort was created in 1998 by Martin Roesch, Snort is the most popular Intrusion Detection and Prevention System (IDPS) today. Its approach is based on signatures, using rules, and preprocessors to analyze network traffic. The rules provide a simple and flexible mechanism for creating signatures and examining packages. On the other hand, preprocessors allow extensive data manipulation that cannot be done through rules. Preprocessors can perform tasks such as: IP defragmentation, detection of portscan, normalization of web traffic, among others [25].

The main qualities of the tool are [26]:
- *Scalability*: Can be installed in any network environment.
- *Flexibility and Usability*: Multiplatform (Linux, Windows, Mac OS X).

- *Real Time*: Able to deliver information about network traffic events in real time.
- *Deployment flexibility*: Can be customized to operate with different databases, log systems, and third-party tools.
- *Speed in Detection and Responsiveness to Threats*: Along with the firewall and other layers of security infrastructure, Snort is highly effective in detecting and preventing intruders, worms, network vulnerabilities, etc.
- *Modular Detection Mechanism*: The Snort sensors are modular and can monitor several machines from a physical and logical location. Snort can be configured before, after or close to a firewall, acting on different segments of the network, according to the needs of the organization.

3.3 Machine learning

Machine Learning (ML) can be defined in its essence as the extraction of knowledge from databases. ML is a topic composed of the intersection of several other areas, such as statistics, artificial intelligence, and computer science, covering fields such as *predictive analysis* and *statistical learning* [27]. In recent years, ML has enabled the development of applications such as autonomous cars, natural language processing, efficient mechanisms search, intelligent recommendation systems, among others.

The ML application aims to build new algorithms and improve existing ones so that they can learn from databases, building generalizable models capable of making accurate predictions and/or finding patterns, from unknown data [27].

The learning process consists of improving a knowledge system by expanding or rearranging the knowledge base/inference engine [28]. Machine learning comprises computational methods to acquire new knowledge, new skills, and new ways of organizing existing knowledge [29].

Learning problems can vary widely in terms of complexity, from parametric learning (which aims to learn values for specific parameters) to complicated forms of symbolic knowledge (which aims to learn concepts, grammar, functions, and even behaviors) [29].

3.3.1 Learning methods

Regardless of the ML technique chosen to solve a given problem, it is learning linked to its ability to recognize and classify patterns (*pattern recognition* and *pattern classification*, respectively). The creation of classifiers then involves postulating some general form of a model, or form of the classifier, and using training standards to learn or estimate the unknown parameters of the model [30]. In practice, learning can occur in four different ways: supervised learning, unsupervised learning, semisupervised learning, and reinforcement learning.

3.3.2 Algorithms

The supervised machine learning algorithms used in the development of this work for analysis and comparison with the OPF were NB, Decision Tree (DT), Random Forests (RF), SVM and AdaBoost (AB).

3.3.2.1 Optimum-path forest

Created by [31], the classifier based on OPF stands out for its efficiency in the training stage and effectiveness in the testing stage, bringing together in its multiclass approach, speed, and simplicity.

OPF covers the three main learning approaches: supervised, unsupervised and semisupervised, and within the scope of supervised learning, there are three typical cases of binary classification in private spaces two-dimensional: (a) *linearly separable*; (b) *linearly separable by parts*; and (c) *nonseparable classes with arbitrary forms* [32]. The technique itself based on a graph, which depending on the adjacency relationship chosen, can be complete or k-NN, varying in terms of the path cost function and the prototype estimation methodology used. Prototypes that correspond to the samples that best represent their respective classes.

The technique itself aims to segment the space of characteristics, that is, to group samples according to their properties. Therefore, in OPF classifiers with complete graphs, the example characteristic vectors are represented by nodes of a graph where everyone is connected employing edges (Fig. 3.2a). Prototypes chose to compete with each other, winning sample by sample, to start the segmentation process. The prototypes are decided through Minimum Spanning Tree (MST) to select those elements that are in the class boundaries (Fig. 3.1).

In practice, each sample offers a possible nonnegative cost path for the prototype. The choice takes into account the least cost path, according to the path cost function used. At the end of the process, there are several Optimum-Path Trees (OPT) (Fig. 3.2b). The analysis step aims to validate the training of the classifier by calculating the accuracy of the classifications performed on a test set. In this step, an unknown sample presented to the classifier prototypes (Fig. 3.2c), which, in turn, offer paths of various costs

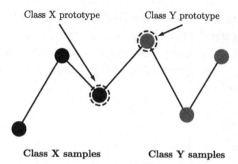

Figure 3.1 Identifying prototypes. *Source: Elaborated by the authors.*

to achieve it. The way that has the lowest cost determines the classification of the sample (Fig. 3.2d).

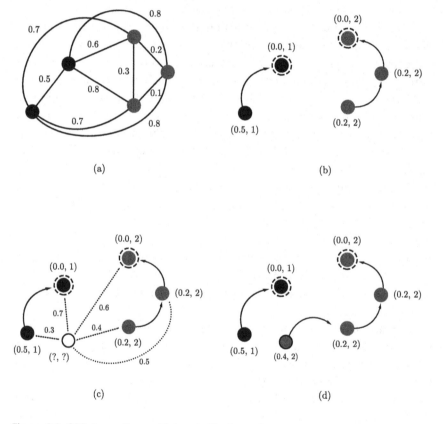

Figure 3.2 OPF stages. *Source: Elaborated by the authors.*

3.3.3 Metrics for effectiveness analysis

Given the diversity of machine learning algorithms that can be applied in the same context to solve problems, it is necessary to use metrics to evaluate and compare their respective performances. In studies that combine the use of these algorithms with the task of detecting intrusions sees those presented.

It is common to use metrics related to the rates of false positives and false negatives obtained in each technique or else in the system itself of classification as a whole, e.g., IDSs. As an example, in [33], it is possible to find a general analysis of the particularities of dealing with data mining and machine learning techniques, within the scope of IDSs, in the search for the reduction of false-positive in these tools.

To better understand the meaning of these rates, it is necessary to bear in mind that, in intrusion detection, benign activities, i.e., normal ones, are considered *negative conditions*. In contrast, malicious activities, i.e., attacks, are considered *positive conditions*. Thus, when an intrusion detection system or a classifier identifies a correctly benign instance as being "normal" (correct classification), it contributes to the *true negative* (TN) rate. Similarly, when a genuinely malicious instance is identified as an "attack," it contributes to the rate of *true positives* (TP).

Following this logic, when a truly benign instance is falsely identified as an "attack," it contributes to the rate of *false positives* (FP). Finally, when a malicious instance is incorrectly identified as being "normal," it contributes to the rate of *false negatives* (FN).

For convenience, these rates are usually presented in the form of a confusion matrix, as shown in Fig. 3.3. From these same rates, it is possible to derive some popular metrics for evaluating models and systems in general:

- **Accuracy:** $\frac{TP+TN}{TP+TN+FP+FN}$. It is the ratio between correctly predicted observations and the total number of observations;
- **Precision:** $\frac{TP}{TP+FP}$. It is the ratio between *positive* predictions correctly predicted and the total of *positive* predicted observations. In other words, taking into account the scope of the IDSs, it is the ratio between the number of correctly predicted attacks and the total number of predicted attacks;
- **Recall:** $\frac{TP}{TP+FN}$. It is the ratio between *positive* observations correctly predicted and the total number of observations in the current class. Again, in the scope of the IDSs, it is the ratio between the number of correctly predicted attacks and the total number of existing attacks.

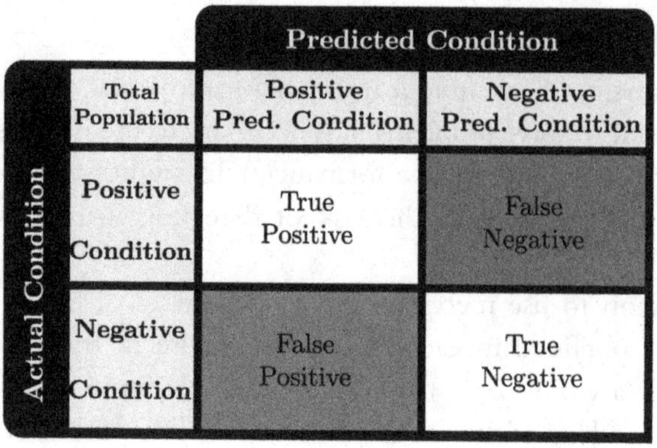

Figure 3.3 Confusion matrix example. *Source: Elaborated by the authors.*

- **F-Score:** $2 \cdot (\frac{\text{Precision} \cdot \text{Recall}}{\text{Precision} + \text{Recall}})$. It is the weighted average of precision and recall. Consequently, it is a metric that takes into account both false-positive and false-negative rates (related to misclassification).

It is noteworthy that the accuracy metric is not always reliable, especially when the data set is unbalanced (as is the case with the intrusion detection problem). For example, given a data set consisting of 95 benign instances and 5 malignant instances, any classifier that classifies all malignant instances as benign would have an accuracy of 95%, which superficially, appears to be a good result. However, as malignant instances represent possible attacks on the network, and this classifier was not able to detect them in the data set; the quality of the model is much lower than that which it appears to be from the perspective of accuracy. In this same example, the *recall*, which aimed at analyzing the classifications made about attacks concerning the correct number of existing attacks, would be 0%.

3.4 Methodology

This section describes the methodology used for the development of this project, addressing the resources, tools, and techniques necessary for this. The general objective of this work is to replace the signature detection scheme of Snort 3, for the classification in time network traffic flows using computational intelligence techniques. Since Snort is unable to interpret labeled databases on its own, it was necessary to divide the project's development into two phases: *preparation* and *execution*.

In the preparation phase, which occurs externally to Snort, the main objective is to perform the preprocessing of the chosen database and the training of classification techniques on this database. Preprocessing the database ensures that it does not have null values, the data is adequately normalized, and the classes are balanced. The training of classification techniques aims at creating their respective machine learning models in a known format that allows, in the *ml_classifiers* plugin (and consequently in Snort 3), the classification of network traffic flows in real-time.

In the execution phase, the main objective is the development of the plugin itself, which will even use the models of classification techniques trained in the preparation phase. If Snort were able to interpret labeled databases, the training of classification techniques would not need to be external to the tool, and it can be done inside the plugin itself. In the next sections, the elements that make up both phases are described in more detail.

3.4.1 CICIDS2017 data set

There is a wide variety of databases available for the evaluation of IDSs. In [34], the authors present an analysis of the main publicly available databases: DARPA (1998–1999), KDD'99 (1998–1999), DEFCON (2000–2002), CAIDA (2002–16), LBNL (2004-05), CDX (2009), Kyoto (2009), Twente (2009), UMASS (2011), ISCX2012 (2012), and ADFA (2013). Among the multiple deficiencies found in the vast majority of these databases, with emphasis on the oldest ones, the authors highlighted as main critical points the dissimilarity between simulated traffic and real traffic, that observed in current computer networks, and the decrease of volume and the diversity of attacks present in these databases.

Given the particularities of a project that involves the use of supervised machine learning techniques, so that it has relevance in the scientific environment, in addition to the points mentioned above, it is extremely important that the chosen database is labeled and properly distinguishes benign traffic malicious traffic so that techniques can learn to recognize such patterns as clearly and unambiguously as possible.

Of the databases mentioned in the work of [34], one of the most suitable is ISCX2012, as it addresses most of the deficiencies discussed above. However, recently, the authors of ISCX2012 published a new database: CICIDS2017 [34]. It is a more updated database that, unlike ISCX2012, has support for the HTTPS protocol (HyperText Transfer Protocol Secure) and provides conveniently in CSV format more than 70 features[4] regarding network traffic flows for learning computational intelligence techniques. The availability of such characteristics was the main factor that led to the choice of this database for the execution of this project.

CICIDS2017 has the full traffic captured over 5 days, totaling 2,830,743 network traffic flows. During the traffic capture process, the benign behavior corresponding to the activity of 25 users on the network is generated, comprising HTTP, HTTPS, FTP, SSH, and other connected protocols to the email service. For malicious behavior, six attack profiles were used: brute force, heartbleed attack, botnet, denial of service and distributed denial of service, web attack, and infiltration attack [34].

The distribution of network traffic flows in the benign and malicious classes is 80.30% and 19.70%, respectively. Therefore it is possible to observe a significant discrepancy between the number of benign and malicious flows, which can impair the learning of supervised techniques. Consequently, it is necessary to balance the database discussed in the following section.

3.4.2 Data set balancing

In this condition where there is a discrepancy in the distribution of the classes involved, the main problem that can be highlighted is that the classifiers tend to achieve good accuracy in the majority class, but on the other hand, inferior accuracy in the minority classes. Consequently, the system's performance as a whole is compromised because there is a bias in the classifiers for the majority class [35]. Two methods are commonly used [36,37] to combat the impact of imbalance between classes in the learning of computational intelligence techniques:

- **Undersampling:** Instances of the majority class are removed at random until the distribution equals that of the minority class;
- **Oversampling:** Instances of the minority class are replicated until the distribution equals that of the majority class.

However, it is worth mentioning that both random methods of *undersampling* and *oversampling* have imperfections worth mentioning. In removal methods, such as *undersampling*, there is a risk of potentially eliminating essential examples from the majority class, while, in *oversampling* methods, the most significant threat is of overtraining the model.

---

[4] Obtained through the CICFlowMeter tool. Available at http://www.netflowmeter.ca/.

In order not to risk losing important information regarding benign flows, the oversampling method was applied to the CICIDS2017 database. Besides, to avoid overtraining the models to be applied later, a specific technique known as Synthetic Minority Oversampling Technique (SMOTE) was used [38], which performs the oversampling of the minority class by creating of synthetic examples, as opposed to oversampling with substitution. In this technique, the oversampling of the minority class takes place by taking each sample of that class and introducing synthetic examples along with the line segments that connect them to any (or all) k-neighbors closest to the minority class [36].

For the implementation of SMOTE and the other computational intelligence techniques, except for OPF (LibOPF [39]), the Python 3 *scikit-learn* [40] was used.

3.4.3 *ml_classifiers* plugin

It was necessary to develop a plugin to extend its capabilities, given that Snort (Snort 2 and Snort 3), until now, does not have a native module to perform intrusion detection with an anomaly-based approach called *ml_classifiers*.[5] As stated in the Snort 3 documentation [41], there are several types of plugins that operate in different parts of the tool's processing pipeline, such as Codecs, Loggers, Inspectors, Mpses, and others.

Once the models of classification techniques previously trained in the preparation phase would be loaded into the plugin, the developed plugin would have to deal directly with the packages being processed by Snort 3, precisely for the creation of the concept of flows hitherto nonexistent, within the tool, for classification using computational intelligence techniques and the extraction of their respective characteristics. Given these circumstances, it was decided to develop an Inspector-type plugin, commonly recommended when it comes to packet inspection, traffic normalization, etc.

Based on the experience of previous studies done on Snort 3 [42], an inspector of the type IT_PROBE was developed. This type has good coverage of network packets and allows, with absolute ease, the extraction of all the necessary characteristics for the creation and manipulation of network traffic flows. In the next sections, we discuss how these flows are created, managed, and finally, classified within *ml_classifiers*.

---

[5] Available in: https://github.com/lnutimura/ml_classifiers.

3.4.3.1 Network traffic flow management

To be able to manage the network traffic flows in *ml_classifiers*, it was necessary to understand beforehand how the flows were created and managed within the CICFlowMeter tool[6] [43,44], responsible for generating the files flow characteristics of the CICIDS2017 database. The reason for this is quite simple. Since these files were used for the training of computational intelligence techniques in the preparation phase, it is necessary to use the same methodology for creating and managing flows in the execution phase because otherwise there would be inconsistencies in the way the vectors flow, characteristics would be assembled during training, outside of Snort and during execution, inside of Snort, potentially resulting in sloppy classifications.

In the methodology used to develop this plugin, every network traffic flow is identified by a unique string called *FlowID*, built from the concatenation of some characteristics of the flow protocol, source, and destination addresses, source, and destination addresses, a destination with which it is associated. An example of *FlowID* would be:

```
Protocol-Source_IP_Address:Source_Port-
Destination_IP_Address:Destination_Port
```

Because the ICMP protocol does not use ports, they are set to 0 in *FlowID*. However, additional, extra information regarding the ICMP header identification field is concatenated. In the previous example, this information corresponds to the value 256.

Whenever a new package is analyzed by Snort 3 and, consequently, by the plugin, it is necessary to check if it belongs to an existing flow or if it is the first package of a new flow to be created. The verification process takes place through the creation of a new *FlowID* (temporary), based on the characteristics of the package under analysis, and the use of this *FlowID* as a search key in a list of flows maintained by the plugin. If there is no correspondence between the newly created*FlowID* and any other*FlowID* present in the list maintained by the plugin, a new flow is created, initialized with the characteristics of the package under analysis, and attached to the flow list with the *FlowID* previously created (before temporary, now permanent).

---

[6] CICFlowMeter is a tool aimed at the generation and analysis of bidirectional network traffic for anomaly-based detection. It has, as one of its main functions, the extraction of network traffic flow characteristics in CSV format from packet capture files (PCAPs).

On the other hand, if there is a match between the *FlowIDs*, the flow identified by the respective *FlowID* is then updated with the characteristics of the package under analysis. This process is represented in Fig. 3.4.

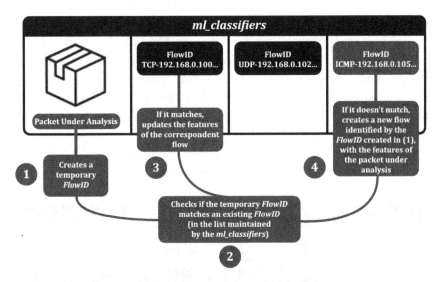

Figure 3.4 Creation and update of network traffic flows. *Source: Elaborated by the authors.*

3.4.3.2 Classification of network traffic flows

Bearing in mind that, up to this point, the network traffic flows are being created and updated by the plugin, so that it can perform the classifications in real time, it is necessary to establish a policy that selects positive flows for the classification process by computational intelligence techniques.

For a connection-oriented protocol, such as TCP, the first approach to this policy would be to select for the classification process, the flows have already reached the final state of this protocol, i.e., that have already closed the connection (using the exchange of packages with the FIN and ACK flags). However, in real network environments, many TCP connections barely reach this state, either due to the occurrence of unexpected events that terminate the connection prematurely or due to the simple extension of the connection. Therefore, it is necessary to use a timeout mechanism that can preemptively dispatch inactive TCP connections for classification techniques. For nonconnection oriented protocols, such as UDP and ICMP, the only alternative is to use this same timeout mechanism, since there is no concept connection status in these protocols. Following the methodology used in the *CICFlowMeter* tool, a limit for the 120-second timeout was established for all protocols. In [44], this limit produced one of the best results in a problem of classification involving two classes, with characteristics obtained by the same tool (*CICFlowMeter*).

The checking of timeouts is done through a thread[7] that, from time to time, checks the activity (or inactivity) of the network traffic flows present in the list maintained by the plugin. When the difference between the timestamp (timestamp) of the thread—which represents the current execution time—and the flow timestamp (or better, from the last package that updated it) is more significant than the preestablished limit for the timeout, it is removed from the list maintained by the plugin and dispatched for the classification techniques. This process is represented in Fig. 3.5.

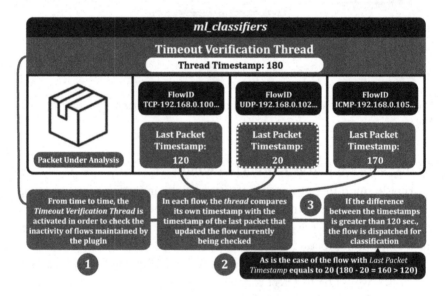

Figure 3.5 Timeouts of network traffic flows. *Source: Elaborated by the authors.*

In this classification phase, all dispatched flows have their characteristics encoded in the form of a vector that, in practice, has 77 features, with information related to the flow—bidirectional—and also to the *forward* (from origin to destination) and *backward* (from target to source) directions.

---

[7] Thread, in computing, is a mechanism used to perform subtasks of a program concurrently.

Depending on the plugin's configuration, this feature vector can be passed on to different classification techniques, as discussed in the next section.

3.4.3.3 Plugin configuration

Through the Snort 3 configuration files, it is possible to create and provide the access to several plugin startup parameters. For the *ml_classifiers*, a single key was created so that it is possible to choose the classification technique to be used.

Thus in the configuration file (*snort.lua*), one can choose the technique as follows:

```
ml_classifiers = {key = <dt|rf|ab|bnb|gnb|svc|opf>}
```

where `dt` is Decision Tree, `rf` is Random Forests, `ab` is AdaBoost, `bnb` is Bernoulli Naive Bayes, `gnb` is Gaussian Naive Bayes, `svc` is Support Vector Machine, and `opf` is Optimum-Path Forest. Once the classifier is chosen, all the classifications made by it will be displayed in real time on the terminal running Snort 3 with the *ml_classifiers*.

3.5 Experiments and results

This section describes the experiments carried out to evaluate this work and presents and discusses the results obtained. The experiments divided into two stages. In the first, the classification techniques evaluated in the *preparation* phase, outside Snort, in the second, the classification techniques evaluated in the *execution* step, within Snort. For the experiments' execution, a computer with the Debian 9 operating system (64 bits), Intel i7-4790 processor of 3.60GHz, GeForce GTX 970 video card, and 16GB of 1333MHz DDR3 RAM used.

In the first stage, training and testing of all classification techniques were carried out on a reduced version of the CICIDS2017 database (2.5%), with a proportion of 2/3 and 1/3 for the training and test sets, respectively. The training set, composed initially of 47,366 network traffic flows, now has 75,952 samples after applying the SMOTE balancing algorithm, with an approximate 50% proportion for both classes present in CICIDS2017. The test set, consisting of 23,330 network traffic flows, has an estimated proportion of 80.32% samples of the benign class (normal) and 19.68% samples of the malicious class (attack).

All classifiers underwent 15 training rounds to ensure greater consistency in each classification technique's results, after which the respective means and standard deviations of the results obtained extracted. Furthermore, for all classification techniques, except for the OPF,[8] the training and test set data were normalized to the [0, 1] range, using the *MinMaxScaler* estimator from the *scikit-learn* library.

In the second step, a comparison made between the modified Snort 3 with the *ml_classifiers* and the unmodified Snort 3 in a test environment to identify possible attack scenarios where the modified solution excels concerning the base solution of Snort 3, and vice versa. In *plugin ml_classifiers*, the machine learning techniques that presented the best results in the first stage of the experiments considered, namely: AB, OPF, RF, DT, and SVM.

In the next sections, the results obtained in the first and second stages of the experiments presented.

3.5.1 First stage of experiments

This section presents the individual training and test results of each classification technique shown in the CICIDS2017 database. Subsequently, the different results compared with each other, and some considerations made regarding the classifiers' performances.

3.5.1.1 Naive Bayes

For NB, the default settings of the *scikit-learn* library were used for *BernoulliNB* and *GaussianNB*, as there were not many parameters to calibrate. From this configuration, the results shown in Tables 3.1, 3.2, 3.3, and 3.4 are obtained.

Table 3.1 Results of Bernoulli NB.

	Accuracy (%)	Precision (%)	Recall (%)	F-Score (%)	Fit Time (s)	Test Time (s)
Mean	67.17	35.20	80.07	48.90	0.06	0.02
Standard Deviation	0.31	0.42	0.44	0.42	0.00	0.00

Source: Elaborated by the authors.

From the tables, it is possible to notice that both techniques did not present a satisfactory performance in the classification of network traffic

---

[8] Since the function of calculating the distance between samples is, by default, the log-Euclidean distance, it is recommended not to normalize the features of the problem.

Table 3.2 Results of Gaussian NB.

	Accuracy (%)	Precision (%)	Recall (%)	F-Score (%)	Fit Time (s)	Test Time (s)
Mean	64.64	36.55	96.91	52.74	0.08	0.02
Standard Deviation	10.22	6.72	0.28	7.09	0.01	0.00

Source: Elaborated by the authors.

Table 3.3 Confusion Matrix of Bernoulli NB (15th round of training).

	Positive	Negative	Total
Positive	3622 (15.53%)	921 (3.95%)	4543
Negative	6853 (29.37%)	11934 (51.15%)	18787
Total	10475	12855	23330

Source: Elaborated by the authors.

Table 3.4 Confusion Matrix of Gaussian NB (15th round of training).

	Positive	Negative	Total
Positive	4404 (18.88%)	139 (0.60%)	4543
Negative	6139 (26.31%)	12648 (54.21%)	18787
Total	10543	12787	23330

Source: Elaborated by the authors.

flows. As an example, the results obtained with the Bernoulli NB, it is possible to observe that although this technique has correctly classified a considerable number of attacks (80.07% of average *recall*). On the other hand, it presented an expressive rate of false positives (29.37%). It erroneously classified as belonging to the attack class a significant amount of normal flows, resulting in an average precision of 35.20%.

In the results obtained with Gaussian NB, it is possible to observe that the technique presented a behavior similar to that of Bernoulli NB. Although it correctly classified almost all attack streams in the test suite (96.91% *recall* average), on the other hand, it erroneously classified many normal streams as belonging to the attack class, resulting in a rate of false positives of 26.31% and an average accuracy of 36.55%.

3.5.1.2 Decision tree

For DT (*DecisionTreeClassifier*), the *scikit-learn*'s *GridSearchCV* technique was applied to determine the maximum depth of the tree (*max_depth*), the minimum number of samples needed to split an internal node (*min_sam-*

ples_split), the minimum number of samples needed to be on a leaf node (*min_samples_leaf*), and the maximum number of features to take into account in the search for the best division (*max_features*), as shown in Table 3.5. From this configuration, the results presented in Tables 3.6 and 3.7 are obtained.

Table 3.5 Hyperparameters of DT.

Hyperparameter	Explored Values	Optimum Value
max_depth	{None, 3}	None
min_samples_split	$\lceil \{0.1, 1.0, 10.0\} \cdot n\_samples \rceil$	0.1
min_samples_leaf	$\lceil \{0.1, 0.2, 0.3, 0.4, 0.5\} \cdot n\_samples \rceil$	0.1
max_features	$\lfloor \{0.1, 0.5, 1.0\} \cdot n\_samples \rfloor$	1.0

Source: Elaborated by the authors.

Table 3.6 Results of DT.

	Accuracy (%)	Precision (%)	Recall (%)	F-Score (%)	Fit Time (s)	Test Time (s)
Mean	92.73	73.40	98.76	84.21	75.16	0.00
Standard Deviation	0.25	0.85	0.22	0.49	2.01	0.00

Source: Elaborated by the authors.

Table 3.7 Confusion Matrix of DT (15th round of training).

	Positive	Negative	Total
Positive	4487 (19.23%)	56 (0.24%)	**4543**
Negative	1648 (7.06%)	17139 (73.46%)	**18787**
Total	**6135**	**17195**	**23330**

Source: Elaborated by the authors.

In general, the technique presented a balance concerning the classification of network traffic flows of both classes involved. Both the normal flows and the attack flows were mostly classified correctly, showing not only a high average accuracy (92.73%) but also reasonable values of precision (73.40%), and *recall* (98.76%) average, indicating that the rates of false positives (7.06%) and false negatives (0.24%) moderate.

3.5.1.3 Random forests

For RF (*RandomForestClassifier*), the *scikit-learn*'s *GridSearchCV* technique was applied to determine the number of estimators (*n_estimators*), the maximum depth of each tree (*max_depth*), the minimum number of samples needed to split an internal node (*min_samples_split*), the minimum number of samples needed to be on a leaf node (*min_samples_leaf*), and the maximum number of features to take into account when searching for the best division (*max_features*), as shown in Table 3.8. From this configuration, the results presented in Tables 3.9 and 3.10 are obtained.

Table 3.8 Hyperparameters of RF.

Hyperparameter	Explored Values	Optimum Value
n_estimators	$\{10, 50, 100\}$	100
max_depth	$\{$None, 3$\}$	None
min_samples_split	$\lceil \{0.1, 0.2, \dots, 0.9, 1.0\} \cdot n\_samples \rceil$	0.1
min_samples_leaf	$\lceil \{0.1, 0.2, 0.3, 0.4, 0.5\} \cdot n\_samples \rceil$	0.1
max_features	$\lfloor \{0.1, 0.5, 1.0\} \cdot n\_samples \rfloor$	0.5

Source: Elaborated by the authors.

Table 3.9 Results of RF.

	Accuracy (%)	Precision (%)	Recall (%)	F-Score (%)	Fit Time (s)	Test Time (s)
Mean	93.44	76.18	96.93	85.30	2109.07	0.08
Standard Deviation	0.50	1.58	0.45	0.88	37.22	0.02

Source: Elaborated by the authors.

Table 3.10 Confusion Matrix of RF (15th round of training).

	Positive	Negative	Total
Positive	4402 (18.87%)	141 (0.60%)	**4543**
Negative	1282 (5.50%)	17505 (75.03%)	**18787**
Total	**5684**	**17646**	**23330**

Source: Elaborated by the authors.

From the tables, it is possible to see that the technique was satisfactorily effective in classifying network traffic flows, presenting significant values of average accuracy (93.44%), average precision (76.18%), average *recall* (96.93%), and consequently, the average *f-score* (85.30%), resulting from the relatively low rates of false positives (5.50%) and false negatives (0.60%) obtained from the classifications carried out.

3.5.1.4 Support vector machine

For SVM (*SVC*), the following configuration was used:
- **Function *kernel*:** RBF;
- **Maximum Iterations:** 1000;
- **Cost:** 100.

In particular, for the Cost (C) parameter, the *scikit-learn's GridSearchCV* technique was applied to find the best performance value in the classification of network traffic flows, as shown in Table 3.11. From this configuration, the results presented in Tables 3.12 and 3.13 are obtained.

Table 3.11 Hyperparameters of SVM.

Hyperparameter	Explored Values	Optimum Value
C	{0.1, 1.0, 10.0, 100.0}	100.0

Source: Elaborated by the authors.

Table 3.12 Results of SVM.

	Accuracy (%)	Precision (%)	Recall (%)	F-Score (%)	Fit Time (s)	Test Time (s)
Mean	96.93	87.92	97.83	92.61	689.82	7.72
Standard Deviation	0.12	0.59	0.27	0.26	11.41	0.12

Source: Elaborated by the authors.

Table 3.13 Confusion Matrix of SVM (15th round of training).

	Positive	Negative	Total
Positive	4454 (19.09%)	89 (0.38%)	**4543**
Negative	637 (2.73%)	18150 (77.80%)	**18787**
Total	**5091**	**18239**	**23330**

Source: Elaborated by the authors.

In general, the technique had a satisfactory performance in the classification of network traffic flows, correctly classifying the vast majority of flows in both classes involved, presenting a high average accuracy (96.93%) and also significant values of precision average (87.92%) and average *recall* (97.83%). Note that the technique made more errors in the classification of normal flows than in the ranking of attack flows, presenting a false positive rate of 2.73% and a false negative rate of 0.38%.

3.5.1.5 Optimum-path forest

For OPF (*Supervised OPF*), the default settings of the LibOPF library were used, with the function of calculating the distance between the samples being the log-Euclidean distance. From this configuration, the results presented in Tables 3.14 and 3.15 are obtained.

From the tables, it is possible to see that the technique was satisfactorily effective in classifying network traffic flows, with high values of average accuracy (98.02%), average precision (93.07%), average *recall* (97.13%).

Table 3.14 Results of OPF.

	Accuracy (%)	Precision (%)	Recall (%)	F-Score (%)	Fit Time (s)	Test Time (s)
Mean	98.02	93.07	97.13	95.06	482.83	172.91
Standard Deviation	0.07	0.32	0.28	0.18	0.00	0.00

Source: Elaborated by the authors.

Table 3.15 Confusion Matrix of OPF (15th round of training).

	Positive	Negative	Total
Positive	4441 (19.04%)	102 (0.44%)	4543
Negative	345 (1.48%)	18442 (79.05%)	18787
Total	4786	18544	23330

Source: Elaborated by the authors.

Consequently, the average *f-score* (95.06%), resulting from the low rates of false positives (1.48%) and false negatives (0.44%) obtained from the classifications performed.

3.5.1.6 AdaBoost

For AB (*AdaBoostClassifier*), the following configuration was used:
1. **Base estimator:** Decision Tree;
2. **Algorithm:** SAMME.R [45].

The *scikit-learn's GridSearchCV* technique was applied to determine the number of estimators (*n_estimators*) and the learning rate (*learning_rate*), as shown in Table 3.16. From this configuration, the results presented in Tables 3.17 and 3.18 are obtained.

Table 3.16 Hyperparameters of AB.

Hyperparameter	Explored Values	Optimum Value
n_estimators	{10, 50, 100}	100
learning_rate	{0.01, 0.05, 0.1, 1.0}	1.0

Source: Elaborated by the authors.

From the tables, it is possible to observe that the technique is extremely effective and balanced with regard to the classification of network traffic flows, presenting an accuracy (99.30%), precision (97.15%), *recall* (99.36%), and *f-score* (98.24%) satisfactory averages. In general, there were few classification errors; see false-positive (0.63%) and false-negative (0.12%) rates.

Table 3.17 Results of AB.

	Accuracy (%)	Precision (%)	Recall (%)	F-Score (%)	Fit Time (s)	Test Time (s)
Mean	99.30	97.15	99.36	98.24	224.04	0.46
Standard Deviation	0.05	0.17	0.13	7.77	777.08	0.00

Source: Elaborated by the authors.

Table 3.18 Confusion Matrix of AB (15th round of training).

	Positive	Negative	Total
Positive	4514 (19.35%)	29 (0.12%)	**4543**
Negative	148 (0.63%)	18639 (79.89%)	**18787**
Total	**4662**	**18668**	**23330**

Source: Elaborated by the authors.

3.5.1.7 Comparison of classification techniques

Given the results obtained individually in each classification technique (Sections 3.5.1.1, 3.5.1.2, 3.5.1.3, 3.5.1.4, 3.5.1.5, and 3.5.1.6), it is possible to compare them in terms of the metrics presented previously, as shown in Table 3.19. Table 3.19 highlights in bold the two best classification techniques, in terms of *f-score*, taking into account the Wilcoxon test [46] with a significance of 0.05.

Table 3.19 Comparative of the classification techniques.

Technique	Accuracy (%)	Precision (%)	Recall (%)	F-Score (%)	Fit Time (s)	Test Time (s)
Bernoulli NB	67.17 ± 0.31	35.20 ± 0.42	80.07 ± 0.44	48.90 ± 0.42	0.06 ± 0.00	0.02 ± 0.00
Gaussian NB	64.64 ± 10.22	36.55 ± 6.72	96.91 ± 0.28	52.74 ± 7.09	0.08 ± 0.01	0.02 ± 0.00
DT	92.73 ± 0.25	73.40 ± 0.85	98.76 ± 0.22	84.21 ± 0.49	75.16 ± 2.01	0.00 ± 0.00
RF	93.44 ± 0.50	76.18 ± 1.58	96.93 ± 0.45	85.30 ± 0.88	2109.07 ± 37.22	0.08 ± 0.02
SVM	96.93 ± 0.12	87.92 ± 0.59	97.83 ± 0.27	92.61 ± 0.26	689.82 ± 11.41	7.72 ± 0.12
OPF	**98.02 ± 0.07**	**93.07 ± 0.32**	**97.13 ± 0.28**	**95.06 ± 0.18**	**482.83 ± 0.00**	**172.91 ± 0.00**
AB	**99.30 ± 0.05**	**97.15 ± 0.17**	**99.36 ± 0.13**	**98.24 ± 0.12**	**224.04 ± 7.77**	**0.46 ± 0.00**

Source: Elaborated by the authors.

In general, taking into account the accuracy, precision, *recall* and *f-score*, it is clear that the most consistent techniques in the first stage of the experiments were the AB and OPF, whereas on the other hand, the least consistent techniques were the two variations of NB: Bernoulli and Gaussian (Table 3.19).

In the case of the AB, according to the results obtained, it is the most suitable technique for the classification of network traffic flows in a closed environment, see not only the accuracy, and mainly, the *f-score* obtained, but also the lowest false-positive and false-negative rates observed (Table 3.18). The OPF, just like the AB, also stands out, since it made few errors in the classification of network traffic flows, and above all, presented a high *f-score* demonstrating effectiveness in the correct classification of attack flows.

On the other side, the Bernoulli NB and Gaussian NB did not stand out in the classification of network traffic flows, being the two techniques that most missed during the tests conducted in the first stage of the experiments. The Bernoulli NB, for example, despite correctly classifying a significant amount of attack flows present in the test set, was the technique that most erroneously classified the normal flows, presenting a total of false positives of 6,853, that is, approximately 29.37% of normal flows were classified incorrectly (Table 3.3).

Despite having made fewer errors in the classification of normal flows compared to the Bernoulli NB, the Gaussian NB was the second technique with the highest number of false positives, 6,139, indicating that approximately 26.31% of normal flows were classified incorrectly (Table 3.4).

Given the number of features and the fact that certain subsets of features are more relevant for detecting certain attacks [34], the inconsistency of NB may be related to the very assumption of the technique that all the characteristics used are independent of each other, something that in the real world is hardly true.

On the other hand, regarding the consistency of AB and RF, a possible justification for the balance of these techniques may be related to the fact that both use a committee of estimators to obtain more accurate results and also of criteria should be used to moderate the impurities and entropies of the respective models, something that does not exist in NB.

Interestingly, despite not using classifier committees like the techniques mentioned above, the OPF and the SVM proved to be superior to RF, with notoriously high *f-scores*, of 95.06% and 92.61%, respectively. In the past [9], these techniques have proved their worth by effectively processing two of the most classic databases of the intrusion detection area, the KDD Cup and the NSL-KDD.

In a more weighted spectrum of the metrics used, there is the DT. As expected, the DT's performance was lower than that of the techniques that used it in the form of a committee to obtain better results (RF and AB). The results presented by it were superior in terms of all metrics to those offered by the two variations of NB.

In the first stage of the experiments, the Bernoulli NB, the Gaussian NB, and the DT were the techniques with the shortest training time to the other testing times for each classification technique. The RF were by far the techniques with the longest training time. Concerning the test times, the techniques with the longest test time observed the OPF, and in general, there were no significant differences between the other classification techniques in this regard, taking into account the number of samples tested and also the fact that this step performs in an intrusion detection *offline* environment. In a real-time intrusion detection environment, the tendency is for the test time issue to become even more irrelevant, since the amount of classified network traffic flows over time is substantially less.

In the second stage of the experiments, the purpose is to compare the techniques that stood out in the first stage. The AB and the OPF with the methods that showed average performance such as RF, the DT, and the SVM to verify their respective performances in a real-time intrusion detection environment, and to test the generalization capacity of the respective machine learning models.

3.5.2 Second stage of experiments

In this section, the results obtained with Snort 3 in its modified version—with the techniques AB, OPF, RF, DT, SVM—and in its unmodified version, that is, with the signature-based detection approach, are presented in the task of real-time classification of network traffic flow in a test environment. In this stage, a different network infrastructure was used than the one that originated the CICIDS2017 database, precisely to evaluate the machine learning models' generalization capacity.

In this testing environment, benign traffic is mostly generated from the desktop computer (Windows 10), *smartphone* (iOS 13), and the server (Debian 9), due to the use of different applications, services, and protocols commonly observed in computer networks, as shown in Table 3.20.

The traffic related to the attacks carried out in the test environment, in turn, is generated by a virtualized machine with the Kali Linux[9] operating system, responsible for executing DoS attacks (Slowloris, SlowHTTPTest, and Hulk), *Port Scan* (Nmap), and SSH Brute Force (Patator) on the *web* server. Compared to the test environment's infrastructure that originated

---

[9] Kali Linux is a Linux distribution, derived from Debian, designed for digital forensic analysis and penetration tests.

Table 3.20 Test environment applications, services and protocols.

Application/Service	Protocol	Application/Service	Protocol
Google Chrome (Browser *web*)	HTTP e HTTPS	Client/Server SSH	SSH
Spotify (Audio *Streaming*)	TCP/UDP	Client/Server DHCP	DHCP
Skype e *Discord* (VoIP)	TCP/UDP	Time and Server Synchronization	NTP
Email client (*Gmail*-iOS 13)	IMAP, POP3, SMTP		

Source: Elaborated by the authors.

the CICIDS2017 database, the infrastructure of this stage of the experiments is significantly smaller, in terms of the number of *hosts*, and simpler, in terms of the degree of complexity of the network. For these reasons, the attacks based on *botnets* (distributed) and those whose settings and procedures were not made available by the authors of CICIDS2017 have not been replicated. Still, DoS, *Port Scan,* and Brute Force SSH are topics frequently explored in the area of computer network security [47–52].

The server, the main target of the virtual machine with Kali Linux and serving *web* pages with Apache, is also responsible for executing Snort 3, and consequently, for monitoring all network traffic flows during the second stage of the experiments.

The attacks conducted in this second stage of the experiments presented in greater detail and the results obtained with Snort 3 discussed, both in its modified version with machine learning techniques and in its unmodified version, this, that is, using the signature-based detection approach.[10]

3.5.2.1 DoS slowloris

Slowloris is a DoS attack program that allows an attacker to overload a target server by opening and maintaining several simultaneous HTTP connections between the attacker and the target [53]. For this experiment's execution, a version of the tool made available in a public repository of GitHub.[11] The command line used to execute the attack directed at the server (192.168.0.5) and port 80:

```
$ ./slowloris.py 192.168.0.5 -p 80 -v
```

[10] In the unmodified version of Snort 3, the community rules file used. Available in: https://www.snort.org/downloads/community/snort3-community-rules.tar.gz.

[11] Available in: https://github.com/gkbrk/slowloris.

where −p determines the target port and −v the verbose mode. The results regarding the detection of the attack with Snort 3 were:

Table 3.21 Results of DoS Slowloris detection.

	Snort 3 + AB	Snort 3 + OPF	Snort 3 + RF	Snort 3 + DT	Snort 3 + SVM	Snort 3
Detected	Yes	Yes	No	Yes	No	No
Avg Classification Time[a]	0.0107	0.1671	–	0.0001	–	–

[a] It refers to the average time that machine learning techniques took to classify all network traffic flows related to the attack.
Source: Elaborated by the authors.

In the results presented in Table 3.21, considered that the attack was *detected* successfully if at least one network traffic flow referring to the attack was classified correctly in the case of machine learning or if at least one alert was generated by Snort 3 unmodified on the execution of the attack (180 seconds).

Given the results obtained about the detections performed, it is possible to observe that the only approaches capable of detecting DoS Slowloris were Snort 3 with AB, OPF, and DT. The Snort 3 with RF, SVM, and the unmodified Snort 3 were unable to detect the attack.

Note that were many false alarms in the approaches with AB and DT, classified erroneously, the vast majority of interactions made with the router and other devices. This phenomenon is repeated throughout the other experiments.

3.5.2.2 DoS SlowHTTPTest

SlowHTTPTest is a highly configurable tool that simulates DoS attacks at the application level by extending HTTP connections differently. For the execution of this experiment, a version of the tool was made available in a public repository of GitHub.[12] The command line used to execute the attack directed at the server (192.168.0.5) and port 80:

```
$ slowhttptest −c 50 −H −g −o slowhttp −i 10 \
−r 200 −t GET −u http://192.168.0.5:80 −x 24
```

where −c determines the number of connections, −H the test mode *slow headers*, −g and −o the reporting options, −i the interval between tracking data in seconds, −r the number of connections per second, −t the verb to

---

[12] Available in: https://github.com/shekyan/slowhttptest.

use for requests, −u the URL target, and −x the maximum length of each random name/value pair of tracking data by *tick*. The results regarding the detection of the attack with Snort 3 were:

Table 3.22 DoS SlowHTTPTest detection results.

	Snort 3 + AB	Snort 3 + OPF	Snort 3 + RF	Snort 3 + DT	Snort 3 + SVM	Snort 3
Detected	No	Yes	No	Yes	No	No
Avg Classification Time[a]	–	0.1692	–	0.0001	–	–

[a] It refers to the average time that machine learning techniques took to classify all network traffic flows related to the attack.
Source: Elaborated by the authors.

Given the results obtained about the detections performed, as shown in Table 3.22, observed that they were very close to those obtained with the execution of DoS Slowloris, precisely because they are conceptually similar techniques. This time, Snort 3 with AB was unable to detect the attack (like RF), the SVM and the unmodified Snort 3. Such a phenomenon may represent a possible AB *overfitting* with certain types of attacks, since although similar, it was not able to detect the SlowHTTPTest as it did with the Slowloris DoS.

3.5.2.3 DoS hulk

Hulk is a tool developed for research purposes that conducts DoS attacks. It is designed to generate volumes of unique and obfuscated traffic on a *web* server, bypassing the *cache* mechanisms, and thus reaching the server's direct feature set [54]. For the execution of this experiment, a version of the tool made available in a public repository of GitHub.[13] The command line used to execute the attack directed at the server (192.168.0.5) and port 80:

```
$ python hulk.py http://192.168.0.5:80
```

The results regarding the detection of the attack with Snort 3 were:

Table 3.23 DoS Hulk detection results.

	Snort 3 + AB	Snort 3 + OPF	Snort 3 + RF	Snort 3 + DT	Snort 3 + SVM	Snort 3
Detected	No	Yes	No	Yes	Yes	Yes
Avg Classification Time[a]	–	0.1423	–	0.0001	0.0018	–

[a] It refers to the average time that machine learning techniques took to classify all network traffic flows related to the attack.
Source: Elaborated by the authors.

[13] Available in: https://github.com/grafov/hulk.

Given the results obtained about the detections performed, as shown in Table 3.23, observed that they were very close to those obtained with the execution of the DoS SlowHTTPTest. This time, Snort 3 with SVM and unmodified Snort 3 could also detect the DoS Hulk. Unlike DoS Slowloris and SlowHTTPTest, the DoS Hulk is much easier to mitigate and present in more significant quantities in the CICIDS2017 database. Such factors certainly contributed to detecting this attack by the SVM and the unmodified Snort 3.

3.5.2.4 Port scan

Port Scanning is one of the most popular techniques used by attackers to discover exploitable services on a *host* and a network. With *port scanning*, an attacker can find much information about a target system, such as which services are running, which users have these services, whether anonymous authentication is supported, if certain network services require authentication, among others [55]. For this experiment's execution, the free and open-source utility Nmap,[14] designed for network discovery and security auditing. The command line used to execute the attack directed at the server (192.168.0.5):

$$\$ \ nmap \ -sS \ -sV \ -Pn \ -O \ 192.168.0.5$$

where −sS determines the scanning technique (TCP SYN), −sV indicates which open ports will be scanned for service/version information, −Pn indicates that all *hosts* will be treated as online, and −O enables detection of the operating system. The results regarding the detection of the attack with Snort 3 were:

Table 3.24 *Port Scan*Detection results.

	Snort 3 + AB	Snort 3 + OPF	Snort 3 + RF	Snort 3 + DT	Snort 3 + SVM	Snort 3
Detected	Yes	Yes	Yes	Yes	No	Yes
Avg Classification Time[a]	0.0109	0.5754	0.0053	0.0001	–	–

[a] It refers to the average time that machine learning techniques took to classify all network traffic flows related to the attack.

Source: Elaborated by the authors.

Given the results obtained about the detections made in Table 3.24, observed that all machine learning techniques except the SVM and the unmodified Snort 3 detect the attack by *Port Scan*. As it is one of the attacks

[14] Available in: https://nmap.org/.

with the highest number of instances in the CICIDS2017 database and because it is one of the most classic attacks used by attackers, machine learning techniques can expect to quickly identify the pattern of *port scanning*, and that Snort 3, by itself, has the signature of this attack and possible variations in its community rules file.

3.5.2.5 SSH brute force

Brute force or exhaustive search is one of the oldest *hacking* techniques in history, in addition to being considered one of the most straightforward automated attacks that exist, as it requires little knowledge and minimal intervention from the attacker.

The attack consists of making countless authentication attempts using a database or a dictionary of usernames and passwords until there is a match between the [56]. For the execution of this experiment, the tool Patator,[15] a multipurpose *brute-forcer*, with modular *design,*[16] and adaptable use for executing an SSH Brute Force attack. The command line used to execute the attack directed at the server (192.168.0.5) and port 22:

```
$ ./patator.py ssh_login host=192.168.0.5 \
user=lnutimura password=FILE0 \
0=/root/Desktop/wordlist-master/passlist.txt \
-x ignore:mesg='Authentication failed.'
```

Where ssh_login specifies the module to be used, host the target machine, user the user names to be tested (in this case, only one, lnutimura), the passwords to be tested (in this case, several passwords, specified in the passlist .txt file), and −x ignore a parameter to ignore authentication failure messages. The results regarding the detection of the attack with Snort 3 were:

Table 3.25 Results of SSH Brute Force detection.

	Snort 3 + AB	Snort 3 + OPF	Snort 3 + RF	Snort 3 + DT	Snort 3 + SVM	Snort 3
Detected	Yes	No	No	Yes	No	No
Avg Classification Time[a]	0.0106	–	–	0.0001	–	–

[a] It refers to the average time that machine learning techniques took to classify all network traffic flows related to the attack.

Source: Elaborated by the authors.

[15] Available in: https://github.com/lanjelot/patator.

[16] Modules for executing different brute force attacks: for FTP, SSH, SMTP, POP protocols.

Given the results obtained about the detections performed, as shown in Table 3.25, it is observed that this time, only Snort 3 with AB and DT were able to detect the SSH Brute Force attack. These two techniques most presented false alarms in the second phase of the experiments. As it is an attack that is not very present in CICIDS2017 compared to the DoS Hulk or the *Port Scan*, it expects that most techniques will find some difficulty in detecting it.

Therefore understand that if the objective is to detect DoS, *Port Scan*, and SSH Brute Force attacks, it is much more efficient and effective to choose the use of Snort 3 combined with machine learning techniques for this purpose, considering that in several scenarios, they were able to detect attacks in which Snort 3, without modifications, was not capable. At first, of all approaches, the only one that could detect all attacks was Snort 3 with DT, with a significant amount of false alarms, as mentioned earlier.

However, although Snort 3 with OPF failed to detect the SSH Brute Force attack, it was by far the most consistent approach with its results, since it only classified as attacks the flows that were - indeed - attacks, without presenting false alarms during the execution of the second stage of the experiments.

A strength of the anomaly-based intrusion detection approach is that, unlike the signature-based approach (or rules), it was unnecessary to configure Snort 3 with *ml_classifiers* to monitor precisely the infrastructure for this step. That is, parameters related to this test environment's infrastructure not configured in Snort 3 and *plugin* so that machine learning techniques could detect the attacks of this stage of the experiments, requiring only their training based on CICIDS2017 data.

Finally, despite unmodified Snort 3 being unable to detect attacks like DoS Slowloris, DoS SlowHTTPTest, and Brute Force SSH with the community rules file, the signature detection approach or rule is still essential for the maintenance and protection of computer networks. In the vast majority of cases where signature-based IDS configured correctly, taking into account the particularities of the network planned to monitored, they are usually less susceptible to false alerts than anomaly-based approaches. However, nothing prevents hybrid IDSs from being deployed in computer network projects. In a hybrid configuration of Snort 3, the signature-based method could use to contain static threats, which easily mitigated, on the other hand, the anomaly-based approach could focus on a more threat containment complex, dynamic. A classification model could be more appropriate in this scenario, as observed in the experiments conducted during this stage.

3.6 Final considerations

In the evolutionary stage, in which the technology is currently a device's ability to connect to the internet, is seen as an indispensable essential for it to be considered relevant in the context of technological innovations. As a consequence of this phenomenon, which says a lot about the way technology touches people's daily lives, it is clear that computer networks are in a state of constant renewal, not only to support the adhesion of new devices but also to guarantee the safety and integrity of all the components that make up your architectures.

However, the growth of computer networks goes in the opposite direction to their security, since as they become more heterogeneous, their attack surfaces, that is, their amplitude of penetrability, increase. In intrusion detection, known attacks are usually contained—with some effectiveness—through signature-based approaches, used in the vast majority of network intrusion detection systems, such as Snort. On the other hand, unknown attacks—increasingly relevant given the frequency with which they appear over the years—are contained through anomaly-based approaches, usually using machine learning techniques.

Given the challenge of dealing with unknown attacks, and consequently, adapting existing tools to contain these attacks, this work proposed replacing the signature-based detection scheme of the latest version of Snort (Snort 3) with a security scheme. Anomaly-based detection enables real-time classification of network traffic flows through the use of machine learning techniques, which up to the present moment, do not exist in IDS. To this end, a *plugin* was developed for the task in question, called *ml_classifiers*.

For the evaluation of the methodology proposed, the experiments were divided into two stages: First, the training of Bernoulli NB, Gaussian NB, DT, RF, SVM, OPF, and AB on the CICIDS2017 database. Once trained, the idea is that afterward the best techniques would be incorporated into *ml_classifiers* to use them for the real-time classification of network traffic flows in a testing environment. From the partial results obtained (Table 3.19) at first, it concluded that the best techniques for the classification of network traffic flows were AB and the OPF, with an average accuracy of 99.30% and 98.02% and average *f-scores* of 98.24% and 95.06%, respectively.

In the second stage, a comparison was made between the modified Snort 3 with the AB, OPF, RF, DT, SVM, and the unmodified Snort 3 with the community rules archive for detecting DoS Slowloris, DoS SlowHTTPTest, DoS Hulk, *Port Scan,* and SSH Brute Force attacks. From the partial results obtained, it concluded that, in general, Snort 3 with *ml_classifiers* was more efficient and effective than unmodified Snort 3 in detecting these attacks, with emphasis on the OPF for being the only technique capable of consistently detecting the vast majority of attacks, demonstrating a greater power of generalization and applicability in comparison to the other methods.

Therefore understand that it is opportune to study methodologies and approaches that employ machine learning techniques for the detection of known and unknown attacks on computer networks. Furthermore, according to the final considerations of Section 3.5.2.5, see that the development of hybrid IDSs is increasingly becoming a solid alternative for detecting attacks on computer networks. The signature-based approach can be used to detect attacks that are easy to mitigate. The anomaly-based approach can be used to detect more complex, dynamic attacks using classification models, as they were proposed and employed in this work.

3.6.1 Future works

As future work, we planned to explore methodologies for optimizing the hyperparameters of machine learning techniques. In addition to this optimization process, we also scheduled to include other attacks for the real-time assessment of *ml_classifiers*, as well as introducing an additional step for the selection of network traffic flow features.

Finally, another point to be considered is the restructuring of the *ml_classifiers* code so that it is possible to combine it, more harmoniously, with the Snort 3 signature-based detection scheme, making it genuinely hybrid.

Acknowledgments

The authors are grateful to the Brazilian National Council for Research and Development (CNPq) via grant No. 429003/2018-8.

References

[1] Phillip A. Porras, Alfonso Valdes, Live traffic analysis of TCP/IP gateways, in: NDSS, 1998.

[2] Pedro Garcia-Teodoro, J. Diaz-Verdejo, Gabriel Maciá-Fernández, Enrique Vázquez, Anomaly-based network intrusion detection: techniques, systems and challenges, Computers & Security 28 (1–2) (2009) 18–28.

[3] Shadi Aljawarneh, Monther Aldwairi, Muneer Bani Yassein, Anomaly-based intrusion detection system through feature selection analysis and building hybrid efficient model, Journal of Computational Science (ISSN 1877-7503) 25 (2018) 152–160, https://doi.org/10.1016/j.jocs.2017.03.006, http://www.sciencedirect.com/science/article/pii/S1877750316305099.

[4] Hervé Debar, Marc Dacier, Andreas Wespi, Towards a taxonomy of intrusion-detection systems, Computer Networks 31 (8) (1999) 805–822.

[5] Syed Ali Raza Shah, Biju Issac, Performance comparison of intrusion detection systems and application of machine learning to Snort system, Future Generations Computer Systems 80 (2018) 157–170.

[6] Martin Roesch, et al., Snort: lightweight intrusion detection for networks, in: Lisa, Vol. 99, 1999, pp. 229–238.

[7] Alan Saied, Richard E. Overill, Tomasz Radzik, Detection of known and unknown DDoS attacks using Artificial Neural Networks, Neurocomputing 172 (2016) 385–393.

[8] Charles Bedón, Alan Saied, Snort-AI (Version 2.4.3) "Open Source Project", http://snort-ai.sourceforge.net/index.php, 2009.

[9] Clayton R. Pereira, Rodrigo Y.M. Nakamura, Kelton A.P. Costa, João P. Papa, An Optimum-Path Forest framework for intrusion detection in computer networks, Engineering Applications of Artificial Intelligence 25 (6) (2012) 1226–1234.

[10] Mansour Sheikhan, Hamid Bostani, A hybrid intrusion detection architecture for Internet of things, in: 2016 8th International Symposium on Telecommunications (IST), IEEE, 2016, pp. 601–606.

[11] William Stallings, Network Security Essentials: Applications and Standards, 4/e, Pearson Education India, 2000.

[12] James F. Kurose, Keith W. Ross, Computer Networking: A Top-down Approach, Vol. 4, Addison Wesley, Boston, USA, 2009.

[13] Elike Hodo, Xavier J.A. Bellekens, Andrew W. Hamilton, Christos Tachtatzis, Robert C. Atkinson, Shallow and deep networks intrusion detection system: a taxonomy and survey, CoRR, arXiv:1701.02145, http://arxiv.org/abs/1701.02145, 2017.

[14] Juan M. Estevez-Tapiador, Pedro Garcia-Teodoro, Jesus E. Diaz-Verdejo, Stochastic protocol modeling for anomaly based network intrusion detection, in: Information Assurance, 2003. IWIAS 2003. Proceedings. First IEEE International Workshop on, IEEE, 2003, pp. 3–12.

[15] Kevin Fox, A neural network approach wowards intrusion detection, Tech. Rep., 1990.

[16] Hervé Debar, Marc Dacier, S. Lampart, An Experimentation Workbench for Intrusion Detection Systems, IBM TJ Watson Research Center, 1998.

[17] A. Cansian, Edson dos Santos Moreira, André Carlos Ponce de Leon Carvalho, J.M. Bonifácio Junior, Network Intrusion Detection Using Neural Networks, 1997.

[18] Wei Li, Using genetic algorithm for network intrusion detection, Proceedings of the United States Department of Energy Cyber Security Group 1 (2004) 1–8.

[19] Khattab M. Alheeti, Intrusion detection system and artificial intelligent, in: Intrusion Detection Systems, InTech, 2011.

[20] Tao Song, Calvin Ko, Jim Alves-Foss, Cui Zhang, Karl Levitt, Formal reasoning about intrusion detection systems, in: International Workshop on Recent Advances in Intrusion Detection, Springer, 2004, pp. 278–295.

[21] Aurobindo Sundaram, An introduction to intrusion detection, Crossroads 2 (4) (1996) 3–7.

[22] Tim Crothers, Implementing Intrusion Detection Systems: A Hands-on Guide for Securing the Network, Wiley, 2003.

[23] Przemyslaw Kazienko, Piotr Dorosz, Intrusion detection systems (IDS) Part 2- classification; methods; techniques, WindowsSecurity.com, 2004.

[24] Hung-Jen Liao, Chun-Hung Richard Lin, Ying-Chih Lin, Kuang-Yuan Tung, Intrusion detection system: a comprehensive review, Journal of Network and Computer Applications 36 (1) (2013) 16–24.

[25] Stephen Northcutt, Judy Novak, Network Intrusion Detection, Sams Publishing, 2002.

[26] TacticalFlex, Snort vs suricata, https://tacticalflex.zendesk.com/hc/en-us/articles/360010678893-Snort-vs-Suricata, 2019.

[27] Kapil Bakshi, Kiran Bakshi, Considerations for artificial intelligence and machine learning: approaches and use cases, in: 2018 IEEE Aerospace Conference, IEEE, 2018, pp. 1–9.

[28] Stuart J. Russell, Peter Norvig, Artificial Intelligence: A Modern Approach, Pearson Education Limited, Malaysia, 2016.

[29] Enn Tyugu, Artificial intelligence in cyber defense, in: Cyber Conflict (ICCC), 2011 3rd International Conference on, IEEE, 2011, pp. 1–11.

[30] Richard O. Duda, Peter E. Hart, David G. Stork, Pattern Classification, John Wiley & Sons, 2012.

[31] Joao P. Papa, Alexandre X. Falcao, Celso T.N. Suzuki, Supervised pattern classification based on optimum-path forest, International Journal of Imaging Systems and Technology 19 (2) (2009) 120–131.

[32] Joao Paulo Papa, Alexandre Xavier Falcao, Optimum-Path Forest: A Novel and Powerful Framework for Supervised Graph-Based Pattern Recognition Techniques, Institute of Computing University of Campinas, 2010, pp. 41–48.

[33] Tadeusz Pietraszek, Axel Tanner, Data mining and machine learning—towards reducing false positives in intrusion detection, Information Security Technical Report 10 (3) (2005) 169–183.

[34] Iman Sharafaldin, Arash Habibi Lashkari, Ali A. Ghorbani, Toward Generating a New Intrusion Detection Dataset and Intrusion Traffic Characterization, 2018.

[35] Vaishali Ganganwar, An overview of classification algorithms for imbalanced datasets, International Journal of Emerging Technology and Advanced Engineering 2 (4) (2012) 42–47.

[36] Nitesh V. Chawla, Data mining for imbalanced datasets: an overview, in: Data Mining and Knowledge Discovery Handbook, Springer, 2009, pp. 875–886.

[37] Bee Wah Yap, Khatijahhusna Abd Rani, Hezlin Aryani Abd Rahman, Simon Fong, Zuraida Khairudin, Nik Nik Abdullah, An application of oversampling, undersampling, bagging and boosting in handling imbalanced datasets, in: Proceedings of the First International Conference on Advanced Data and Information Engineering (DaEng-2013), Springer, 2014, pp. 13–22.

[38] Nitesh V. Chawla, Kevin W. Bowyer, Lawrence O. Hall, W. Philip Kegelmeyer, SMOTE: synthetic minority over-sampling technique, Journal of Artificial Intelligence Research 16 (2002) 321–357.

[39] João Paulo Papa, Celso Tetsuo Nagase Suzuki, Alexandre Xavier Falcão, LibOPF: a library for the design of optimum-path forest classifiers, Software version 2, 2009.

[40] Fabian Pedregosa, Gaël Varoquaux, Alexandre Gramfort, Vincent Michel, Bertrand Thirion, Olivier Grisel, Mathieu Blondel, Peter Prettenhofer, Ron Weiss, Vincent Dubourg, et al., Scikit-learn: machine learning in Python, Journal of Machine Learning Research 12 (Oct) (2011) 2825–2830.

[41] Snort, Snort 3 user manual, https://snort.org/downloads/snortplus/snort_manual.pdf, 2019.

[42] Luan N. Utimura, Kelton A. Costa, Aplicação e Análise Comparativa do Desempenho de Classificadores de Padrões para o Sistema de Detecção de Intrusão Snort, in: Anais do XXXVI Simpósio Brasileiro de Redes de Computadores e Sistemas Distribuídos, SBC, Porto Alegre, RS, Brasil, 2018, ISSN 2177-9384, https://ojs.sbc.org.br/index.php/sbrc/article/view/2426.

[43] Gerard Draper-Gil, Arash Habibi Lashkari, Mohammad Saiful Islam Mamun, Ali A. Ghorbani, Characterization of encrypted and vpn traffic using time-related, in: Proceedings of the 2nd International Conference on Information Systems Security and Privacy (ICISSP), 2016, pp. 407–414.

[44] Arash Habibi Lashkari, Gerard Draper-Gil, Mohammad Saiful Islam Mamun, Ali A. Ghorbani, Characterization of Tor traffic using time based features, in: ICISSP, 2017, pp. 253–262.

[45] Trevor Hastie, Saharon Rosset, Ji Zhu, Hui Zou, Multi-class adaboost, Statistics and Its Interface 2 (3) (2009) 349–360.

[46] Frank Wilcoxon, Individual comparisons of grouped data by ranking methods, Journal of Economic Entomology 39 (2) (1946) 269–270.

[47] Mutalifu Kuerban, Yun Tian, Qing Yang, Yafei Jia, Brandon Huebert, David Poss, FlowSec: DOS attack mitigation strategy on SDN controller, in: 2016 IEEE International Conference on Networking, Architecture and Storage (NAS), IEEE, 2016, pp. 1–2.

[48] Satyendra Kumar Patel, Abhilash Sonker, Internet protocol identification number based ideal stealth port scan detection using snort, in: 2016 8th International Conference on Computational Intelligence and Communication Networks (CICN), IEEE, 2016, pp. 422–427.

[49] Heng Zhang, Yifei Qi, Huan Zhou, Jian Zhang, Jing Sun, Testing and defending methods against DoS attack in state estimation, Asian Journal of Control 19 (4) (2017) 1295–1305.

[50] Gokul Kannan Sadasivam, Chittaranjan Hota, Bhojan Anand, Honeynet data analysis and distributed SSH brute-force attacks, in: Towards Extensible and Adaptable Methods in Computing, Springer, 2018, pp. 107–118.

[51] Joshua Faust, Distributed analysis of SSH brute force and dictionary based attacks, in: Culminating Projects in Information Assurance, Vol. 56, 2018, https://repository.stcloudstate.edu/msia_etds/56.

[52] Mohammad Almseidin, Mouhammd Al-Kasassbeh, Szilveszter Kovacs, Detecting slow port scan using fuzzy rule interpolation, in: 2019 2nd International Conference on New Trends in Computing Sciences (ICTCS), IEEE, 2019, pp. 1–6.

[53] CloudFlare, Slowloris DDoS attack, https://www.cloudflare.com/learning/ddos/ddos-attack-tools/slowloris/, 2017.

[54] Barry Shteiman, HULK - HTTP unbearable load king, https://packetstormsecurity.com/files/112856/HULK-Http-Unbearable-Load-King.html, 2012.

[55] Roger Christopher, Port scanning techniques and the defense against them, https://www.sans.org/reading-room/whitepapers/auditing/port-scanning-techniques-defense-70, 2001.

[56] Ivan Vanney, Brute force against SSH and FTP services: attacking and defending SSH and FTP, https://linuxhint.com/bruteforce_ssh_ftp/, 2019.

CHAPTER 4

Optimum-path forest and active learning approaches for content-based medical image retrieval

Rafael S. Bressan, Pedro H. Bugatti, and Priscila T.M. Saito

Department of Computing, Federal University of Technology – Parana, Cornelio Procopio, Brazil

4.1 Introduction

The volume of medical imaging data has been growing in recent years due to scientific advances in data acquisition and storage devices. Considering this growth, approaches for automatic retrieval and classification [1–10] have become necessary to manipulate and organize such data. Content-based image retrieval techniques (CBIR) are proposed to perform such tasks. The CBIR process aims to recover images based on the similarity (or dissimilarity) between a query image and an image data set.

Similarity calculations are based in low-level features (color, texture and/or shape) extracted from the images [11]. To obtain more precise results, in addition to the set of features, the CBIR process depends on the interaction of the specialist and the dissimilarity function (or distance function). The relevance feedback (RF) process can be applied to capture the specialist's intention in a granular way. It allows the specialist to label retrieved images as relevant or irrelevant in relation to a given iteration, refining the retrieving process, and returning the more similar images according to the query image [12]. The RF process can be done until the expert is satisfied with the returned images.

Even though there are several RF methods in the literature [13–16], to the best of our knowledge, the specialist usually defines the degree of relevance and irrelevance. At each query refinement, these methods generally return the most relevant images. However, these returned images may not contribute to the learning process of an image classification model. Therefore, to suppress these issues, an active learning (AL) approach can be integrated into the CBIR process.

Optimum-Path Forest
https://doi.org/10.1016/B978-0-12-822688-9.00012-8

Active learning is based on selecting more informative samples for the learning process, allowing a small set of unlabeled samples to be selected for specialist annotations in a given iteration [17]. After selection, the annotated set is used for training a classifier. Different approaches were proposed [18,19] to select the most informative samples. Although well known and widely used in different domains, many of them are unfeasible, specifically for the medical context and its inherent constraints (e.g., related to dealing with large data sets, required interactive response times, and minimal specialist interaction in the learning process).

Considering these characteristics, in the subsequent sections we propose the use of optimum-path forest and active learning approaches dedicated to RF in the CBIR process, based on the criteria of uncertainty and diversity. Our proposal is applied in the medical context, specifically involving the diagnosis of pigmented lesions on the skin.

4.2 Methodology

The proposed approach explores active learning strategies for the content-based skin lesion image retrieval. The first iteration is based on the classic RF loop (e.g., the specialist indicates the relevant and irrelevant images according to a given query image). The images retrieved in this stage are based on a similarity metric and the samples closest to each clustering centroid. In the other iterations, our approach uses an active learning process to select the most informative images to the learning process. Unlike the works in the literature, our approach obtains the informative images that present the best balance between not only the similarity regarding the query image, but also certain degrees of diversity and uncertainty. To do so, it finds images from distinct classes and difficult to differentiate (e.g., images at the boundaries of two different/overlapped classes).

As an example, in Fig. 4.1, we can see two retrieved images, melanoma and benign keratosis-like lesions, respectively, that will be presented to the specialist for annotation. The images are from different and informative (uncertain) classes, rather than just images closer to the query image. They show a high degree of similarity in relation to their lesions (highlighted by dashed lines) and other tissues. Our approach is able to balance the learning process with the subset of images that better contribute to the classifier, allowing to achieve higher accuracies in fewer iterations. Consequently, the quality of the retrieved images w.r.t. the CBIR process will improve. This is because the classifier is trained with the most informative (similar and uncertain) samples for its learning.

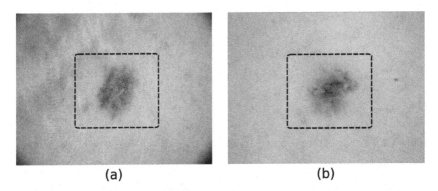

(a)   (b)

Figure 4.1 Examples of informative (uncertain) samples from two different classes of the data set HAM10000 [20]: (a) Melanoma and (b) Benign keratosis-like lesions. It is possible to notice that both images (regions of interest from different classes) present a high similarity degree regarding their lesions (highlighted by dashed lines) and other tissues.

Fig. 4.2 illustrates the pipeline of the proposed approach. In Step 1, given a query image and an image data set, we selected the best descriptor (i.e., the best feature extractor and distance function pair). After this choice, the features are extracted from the image data set and the query image. In Step 2, we obtain the images most similar to the query image, according to the traditional CBIR approach. Then we grouped the set of images in k clusters to select the images closest to their centroids. Next, the selected images are presented to the specialist for annotation (as relevant or irrelevant). These annotated images are used for the initial training, generating the first instance of the learning model (Step 3).

In Step 4, through our active learning strategy (see Section 4.2.1), the learning model selects the most informative images to enhance itself, and boost the similarity query. For this, our approach is based on the uncertainty and similarity w.r.t. the query image, allowing the selection of the most informative images. Next, in Step 5, the selected images are shown to the specialist, and he/she just need to confirm their labels. Thus the annotation effort is only to correct labels of misclassified images.

After the annotation by the specialist, the images are added to the previous training set and the classifier is re-trained, generating a new instance of the learning model. Steps 3–5 are repeated until the specialist is satisfied with the results obtained by the proposed learning process. When satisfied,

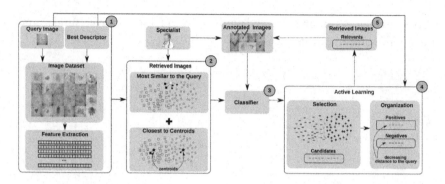

Figure 4.2 Pipeline of the proposed approach.

the trained model can be applied to an unlabeled set and we can obtain a final list ordered by relevance regarding the query image.

4.2.1 Active learning strategy

We also propose a new active learning strategy that selects a small set of informative images. To do so, it explores the classifier's knowledge obtained from the most informative samples, improving the image retrieval process. Initially, we check if there is a total number of desired samples in the analyzed set. We need to do this, because it is an iterative approach in which a set of images is selected at each iteration. Thus the trained model classifies this set of images and we obtain the list of the most informative images (candidates), according to the proposed selection criteria.

Considering the proposed selection strategy, we initially created a L_C list to store the candidate images to be displayed to the specialist; and two learning lists that will store the images organized by labels (i.e., a list for relevant images L_1 and another for irrelevant ones L_0). Then each image in the set, classified by the current learning model, is analyzed to assess which are the most informative candidates. Our strategy considers that the images corresponding to the nearest neighbors with different labels are candidates. Therefore when analyzing each image, we verify its nearest neighbor image. If it is from a different class, both images will be stored in L_C.

If the selection criterion (previous condition) is satisfied (i.e., the set L_C is not empty), two auxiliary lists L_R and L_I are created, containing the relevant and irrelevant images of L_C, respectively. The images from the auxiliary lists are ordered by the distance from the query. Then the images from the two lists are concatenated to compose the list of candidates.

If the previous criterion is not satisfied, we propose another strategy for selecting images. For each list L_0 and L_1, we locate and store its center of mass. Each list is then ordered, in a descending order, according to the distances from its center of mass. Then we can get a list of candidates L_C by concatenating an image from each list L_0 and L_1, respectively, until the desired number of images is obtained.

4.3 Experiments

In order to corroborate the generalization and allow the replication of our approach, we used the public medical image data set called "Human Against Machine" (HAM10000) [20]. The data set consists of 10015 dermoscopic images from different populations, acquired and stored by different modalities. The data set is divided into 7 classes, which can be seen in Fig. 4.3 that includes representative samples of the main diagnostic categories in the field of pigmented skin lesions. The samples were annotated and validated by specialists and by clinical examinations, such as histopathology and by in-vivo confocal microscopy. Table 4.1 shows the total number of images in each class of the HAM10000 data set.

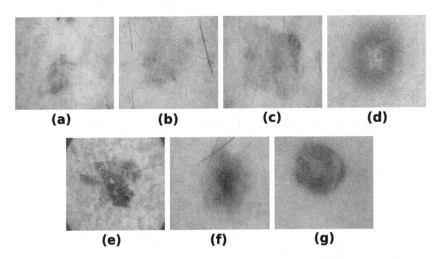

Figure 4.3 Example images from each class: (a) Actinic keratoses and intraepithelial carcinoma, (b) basal cell carcinoma, (c) benign keratosis-like lesions, (d) dermatofibroma, (e) melanoma, (f) melanocytic nevi, and (g) vascular lesions.

From this data set, we extracted color, texture and shape-based features, detailed in Table 4.2, using different feature extractors. Each type of feature

Table 4.1 Description of the HAM10000 data set.

Classes	Images
Melanocytic nevi	6705
Melanoma	1113
Benign keratosis-like lesions	1099
Basal cell carcinoma	514
Actinic keratoses and intraepithelial carcinoma	327
Vascular lesions	142
Dermatofibroma	115

was compared with several distance functions, in order to obtain the best descriptor (a feature extractor joined with a distance function) to the image data set. To do so, seven different distance functions were considered: L_1, L_2, L_∞, X_2, Canberra, Jeffrey Divergence (JD), and dLog [21].

Table 4.2 Properties of each feature extractor applied to the image data set.

Feature Extractor	Category	Features
ACC [22]	Color	768
BIC [23]	Color	128
CEDD [24]	Color	144
FCTH [25]	Color and Texture	192
Gabor [26]	Texture	60
GCH [27]	Color	66
Haralick [28]	Texture	14
Haralick color [28]	Texture	32
JCD (CEDD + FCTH)	Color and Texture	168
LBP [29]	Texture	256
LCH [30]	Color	264
Moments [31]	Texture	4
PHOG [32]	Shape	40
RCS [33]	Color	77
Surf [34]	Texture	70
Tamura [35]	Texture	18
Zernike [36]	Shape	72

Learning strategies with RF in CBIR have been extensively studied to improve the semantic gap issue [11]. In order to show the efficacy of our approach we presented comparisons with widely and well-known RF techniques, such as: Query Point Movement strategy (QPM) [16] and Query

Expansion (QEX) [15]. QPM is based on the concept of moving the query center, throughout the iterations, toward more dense and relevant regions of the query space according to the expert's intention. QEX promotes the expansion of the query, aggregating to it new query centers.

Moreover, to improve the learning efficiency of the RF process, active learning approaches have been explored. For this, different selection criteria have been developed [18,19], and also applied in different classification tasks and domains. For instance, it is possible to select the most diverse and uncertain samples, which can be near the decision boundary of a classifier [18,19]. They can be the most difficult samples, consequently, providing greater benefit to the model. In [18], the authors proposed an active learning method (SVM-AL) that selects samples closest to the classification boundary of the SVM classifier. There are also some latter research efforts [18,37,38]. However, they require the optimization of an objective function, resulting in high computational complexity. Then, in the present paper, we also presented comparisons with the well-known and pioneering SVM-AL proposed by [18], which is closer to our proposed approach, since it fuses the active learning paradigm into the CBIR process.

Our approach can be instantiated considering any supervised classifier or clustering technique. For the sake of simplicity, in our experiments, we used kmeans and Optimum-Path Forest (OPF) for clustering [39] and OPF for supervised classification [40] processes.

To evaluate our proposed approach, we generated Precision and Recall (P&R) graphs [41]. As a rule of thumb, the closer the P&R curve to the top of the graphic, the better is the technique. To build the P&R graphs, we performed several similarity queries based on the k-nearest neighbor operator and randomly choosing the query images from the image data set. The number of images retrieved by each similarity search was defined as $k = 30$ (based on a daily medical practice routine). When a given image class contains less samples than 30, the value of k is set according to the number of samples of such class. To summarize the results, we employed the mean average precision (MAP), as defined in [41].

4.3.1 Results and discussion

Initially, we performed an analysis of the best descriptors for the pigmented skin lesion image data set. Table 4.3 presents the best distance function for each feature extractor, and the best descriptor is highlighted in bold. The best descriptor was the Auto Color Correlogram (ACC) extractor using the distance function Canberra. Then this descriptor was considered in the experiments to compare our proposed approach against the state-of-the-art ones.

Table 4.3 Best distance function for each feature extractor. Highlight in bold indicates the best descriptor.

Feature Extractor	Distance Function
ACC	**Canberra**
BIC	Canberra
CEDD	Canberra
FCTH	Canberra
Gabor	Canberra
GCH	Canberra
Haralick	dLog
HaralickColor	Canberra
JCD (CEDD + FCTH)	Canberra
LBP	Canberra
LCH	Canberra
Moments	L_2
PHOG	Canberra
RCS	L_∞
Surf	JD
Tamura	Canberra
Zernike	JD

Fig. 4.4 shows the results comparing our proposed approach (ourAL) with the QEX, QPM, and SVM-AL approaches from the first to eighth learning iteration. Analyzing the results obtained in all learning iterations, our proposal presented greater precision when compared with QEX, QPM, and SVM-AL. For instance, in Fig. 4.4 (a), our approach reached precision gains of up to 67.19% at a recall level of 10% against SVM-AL. In this same scenario, we achieved gains of 2.51% and 4.88% when compared to QEX and QPM, respectively.

When analyzing the second and third iterations, Figs. 4.4(b) and (c), our proposed approach obtained precision gains of 4.55% and 18.46% when compared with QEX in the second iteration and SVM-AL in the third iteration, respectively at a recall level of 10%. In the fourth iteration, considering 50% of recall (Fig. 4.4(d)), our approach achieved precision gains of up to 7.07%, 6.33%, and 11,67% when compared to QEX, QPM, and SVM-AL, respectively.

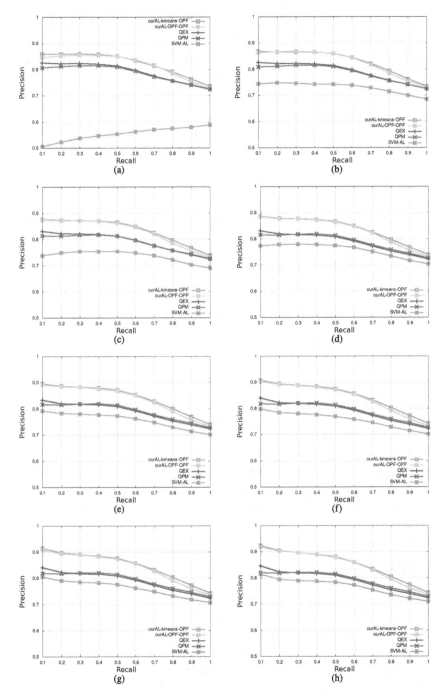

Figure 4.4 P&R curves obtained by each approach over the data set, considering the: (a) first, (b) second, (c) third, (d) fourth, (e) fifth, (f) sixth, (g) seventh, and (h) eighth learning iterations.

The same behavior can be observed in the other iterations (Figs. 4.4(e)–(h)). As the learning progresses, our model presents the most informative images to be classified (see Fig. 4.3). Generally, real scenarios have intrinsic interclass similarity, which leads to a harder separation between relevant and irrelevant images, and also requires a fine-grained annotation process. However, the experiments testify that our approach can cope with these issues. It achieved the best results in comparison with the other approaches.

It is also worth to mention that although the results using kmeans and OPF clustering statistically ties, OPF does not require to know the number of clusters in advance as kmeans. Besides, kmeans can also get trapped in local optima, which is mitigated by OPF.

Summarizing the results, Table 4.4 presents the overall MAP obtained by each approach, throughout the (1st to 8th) learning iterations. According to our extensive experimental evaluation, ourAL presented the best precisions for all iterations.

Table 4.4 Overall MAP throughout the (1st to 8th) iterations. Bold data correspond to the best results.

ourAL-kmeans-OPF	ourAL-OPF-OPF	QEX	QPM	SVM-AL
85.06	**84.61**	78.85	78.76	72.61

Through our approach, it was also possible to minimize the computational time of the learning process, once it reduces the specialist's involvement in the analysis and annotation process (reducing up to 88%). This reduction occurs because the specialist does not need to annotate (correct) the labels of all samples, as required by the literature works. Our approach enables to obtain a more robust classifier (i.e., it has fewer misclassifications, as can be seen from the presented results, see Table 4.4), as more informative samples are selected for its learning.

4.4 Conclusion

In this chapter, we proposed an approach that aggregates AL and RF methods in the field of medical imaging. Moreover, we also presented an active learning strategy that selects the most informative (most uncertain and similar) samples. The integration of AL to CBIR was successful and mitigated several inconveniences, regarding the effectiveness and efficiency of such domain. This is because our strategy is not based only on similarity. It selects a small set of images containing degrees of diversity and uncertainty.

The experiments corroborated that the proposed approach overcomes the other state-of-the-art approaches. As future work, we intend to propose other AL strategies added to RF, providing more informative samples to improve even more the quality of the retrieved images.

4.5 Funding and acknowledgments

This work has been supported by National Council for Scientific and Technological Development – CNPq; Coordination for the Improvement of Higher Education Personnel – CAPES; Fundação Araucária; SETI; and UTFPR.

References

[1] C. Yan, L. Li, C. Zhang, B. Liu, Y. Zhang, Q. Dai, Cross-modality bridging and knowledge transferring for image understanding, IEEE Transactions on Multimedia PP (2019) 1–10.

[2] C. Yan, Y. Tu, X. Wang, Y. Zhang, X. Hao, Y. Zhang, Q. Dai, Stat: spatial-temporal attention mechanism for video captioning, IEEE Transactions on Multimedia (2019).

[3] C. Yan, H. Xie, J. Chen, Z. Zha, X. Hao, Y. Zhang, Q. Dai, A fast uyghur text detector for complex background images, IEEE Transactions on Multimedia 20 (12) (2018) 3389–3398.

[4] T. Turki, Z. Wei, Boosting support vector machines for cancer discrimination tasks, Computers in Biology and Medicine 101 (2018) 236–249.

[5] I. Fondón, A. Sarmiento, A.I. García, M. Silvestre, C. Eloy, A. Polónia, P. Aguiar, Automatic classification of tissue malignancy for breast carcinoma diagnosis, Computers in Biology and Medicine 96 (2018) 41–51.

[6] S. Liu, J. Zeng, H. Gong, H. Yang, J. Zhai, Y. Cao, J. Liu, Y. Luo, Y. Li, L. Maguire, X. Ding, Quantitative analysis of breast cancer diagnosis using a probabilistic modelling approach, Computers in Biology and Medicine 92 (2018) 168–175.

[7] J. Chen, U. Scholz, R. Zhou, M. Lange, Lailaps-qsm: a restful api and Java library for semantic query suggestions, PLoS Computational Biology 14 (3) (2018) 1–10.

[8] A. Kihm, L. Kaestner, C. Wagner, S. Quint, Classification of red blood cell shapes in flow using outlier tolerant machine learning, PLoS Computational Biology 14 (6) (2018) 1–15.

[9] G.H.B. Miranda, J.C. Felipe, Computer-aided diagnosis system based on fuzzy logic for breast cancer categorization, Computers in Biology and Medicine 64 (2015) 334–346.

[10] J.M. Tenório, A.D. Hummel, F.M. Cohrs, V.L. Sdepanian, I.T. Pisa, H. de Fátima Marin, Artificial intelligence techniques applied to the development of a decision-support system for diagnosing celiac disease, International Journal of Medical Informatics 80 (11) (2011) 793–802.

[11] P. Malode, S.V. Gumaste, A review paper on content based image retrieval, International Journal of Research in Engineering and Technology 20 (2015) 883–885.

[12] D.C.N.W. Uluwitige, S. Geva, G. Zuccon, V. Chandran, T. Chappell, Effective user relevance feedback for image retrieval with image signatures, in: Australasian Document Computing Symposium, ACM, 2016, pp. 49–56.

[13] L. Feng, S. Liu, Y. Xiao, Q. Hong, B. Wu, A novel CBIR system with WLLTSA and ULRGA, Neurocomputing 147 (2015) 509–522.

[14] X.-Y. Wang, Y.-W. Li, H.-Y. Yang, J.-W. Chen, An image retrieval scheme with relevance feedback using feature reconstruction and svm reclassification, Neurocomputing 127 (2014) 214–230.

[15] C. Carpineto, G. Romano, A survey of automatic query expansion in information retrieval, ACM Computing Surveys 44 (1) (2012) 1:1–1:50.

[16] D. Liu, K.A. Hua, K. Vu, N. Yu, Fast query point movement techniques for large cbir systems, IEEE Transactions on Knowledge and Data Engineering 21 (5) (2009) 729–743.

[17] B. Settles, Active learning literature survey, Tech. Rep., Computer Sciences Technical Report 1648, University of Wisconsin–Madison, 2009.

[18] J. Kremer, K. Steenstrup Pedersen, C. Igel, Active learning with support vector machines, Wiley Interdisciplinary Reviews: Data Mining and Knowledge Discovery 4 (4) (2014) 313–326.

[19] M. Wang, X.-S. Hua, Active learning in multimedia annotation and retrieval: a survey, ACM Transactions on Intelligent Systems and Technology 2 (2) (2011) 10:1–10:21.

[20] P. Tschandl, C. Rosendahl, H. Kittler, The ham10000 dataset, a large collection of multi-source dermatoscopic images of common pigmented skin lesions, Scientific Data 5 (2018) 180161.

[21] H. Samet, Foundations of Multidimensional and Metric Data Structures, Elsevier, Amsterdam, 2006.

[22] J. Huang, S.R. Kumar, M. Mitra, W.-J. Zhu, R. Zabih, Image indexing using color correlograms, in: Computer Vision and Pattern Recognition, 1997. Proceedings., 1997 IEEE Computer Society Conference on, IEEE, 1997, pp. 762–768.

[23] R.O. Stehling, M.A. Nascimento, A.X. Falcão, A compact and efficient image retrieval approach based on border/interior pixel classification, in: Intl. Conf. on Information and Knowledge Management, 2002, pp. 102–109.

[24] S.A. Chatzichristofis, Y.S. Boutalis, Cedd: color and edge directivity descriptor: a compact descriptor for image indexing and retrieval, in: International Conference on Computer Vision Systems, Springer, 2008, pp. 312–322.

[25] S.A. Chatzichristofis, Y.S. Boutalis, Fcth: fuzzy color and texture histogram-a low level feature for accurate image retrieval, in: Image Analysis for Multimedia Interactive Services, 2008. WIAMIS'08. Ninth International Workshop on, IEEE, 2008, pp. 191–196.

[26] D. Zhang, A. Wong, M. Indrawan, G. Lu, Content-based image retrieval using Gabor texture features, IEEE Transactions on Pattern Analysis and Machine Intelligence (2000) 13–15.

[27] M.A. Stricker, M. Orengo, Similarity of color images, in: Storage and Retrieval for Image and Video Databases III, Vol. 2420, International Society for Optics and Photonics, 1995, pp. 381–392.

[28] R.M. Haralick, K. Shanmugam, I. Dinstein, Textural features for image classification, IEEE Transactions on Systems, Man and Cybernetics SMC-3 (6) (1973) 610–621.

[29] Z. Guo, L. Zhang, D. Zhang, Rotation invariant texture classification using LBP variance (LBPV) with global matching, Pattern Recognition 43 (3) (2010) 706–719.

[30] J.R. Smith, S.-F. Chang, Local color and texture extraction and spatial query, in: Proceedings of 3rd IEEE International Conference on Image Processing, Vol. 3, IEEE, 1996, pp. 1011–1014.

[31] M. Sugiyama, Chapter 2 - random variables and probability distributions, in: M. Sugiyama (Ed.), Introduction to Statistical Machine Learning, Morgan Kaufmann, 2016, pp. 11–24.

[32] A. Bosch, A. Zisserman, X. Munoz, Representing shape with a spatial pyramid kernel, in: Proceedings of the 6th ACM International Conference on Image and Video Retrieval, ACM, 2007, pp. 401–408.

[33] H.-P. Kriegel, E. Schubert, A. Zimek, Evaluation of multiple clustering solutions, in: MultiClust@ ECML/PKDD, Citeseer, 2011, pp. 55–66.

[34] H. Bay, A. Ess, T. Tuytelaars, L. Van Gool, Speeded-up robust features (surf), Computer Vision and Image Understanding 110 (3) (2008) 346–359.

[35] H. Tamura, S. Mori, T. Yamawaki, Textural features corresponding to visual perception, IEEE Transactions on Systems, Man and Cybernetics 8 (6) (1978) 460–473.

[36] A. Khotanzad, Y.H. Hong, Invariant image recognition by Zernike moments, IEEE Transactions on Pattern Analysis and Machine Intelligence 12 (5) (1990) 489–497.

[37] S.C.H. Hoi, M.R. Lyu, A semi-supervised active learning framework for image retrieval, in: IEEE Computer Society Conference on Computer Vision and Pattern Recognition, Vol. 2, 2005, pp. 302–309.

[38] L. Wang, K.L. Chan, Z. Zhang, Bootstrapping svm active learning by incorporating unlabelled images for image retrieval, in: IEEE Computer Society Conf. on Computer Vision and Pattern Recognition, Vol. 1, 2003, p. I.

[39] L.M. Rocha, F.A. Cappabianco, A.X. Falcão, Data clustering as an optimum-path forest problem with applications in image analysis, International Journal of Imaging Systems and Technology 19 (2) (2009) 50–68.

[40] J.P. Papa, A.X. Falcao, C.T. Suzuki, Supervised pattern classification based on optimum-path forest, International Journal of Imaging Systems and Technology 19 (2) (2009) 120–131.

[41] R. Baeza-Yates, B. Ribeiro-Neto, Modern Information Retrieval: The Concepts and Technology Behind Search, 2nd edition, Addison-Wesley Publishing Company, USA, 2011.

CHAPTER 5

Hybrid and modified OPFs for intrusion detection systems and large-scale problems

Mansour Sheikhan[a] and Hamid Bostani[b,c]
[a]Department of Electrical Engineering, South Tehran Branch, Islamic Azad University, Tehran, Iran
[b]Young Researchers and Elite Club, South Tehran Branch, Islamic Azad University, Tehran, Iran
[c]Digital Security Group, Radboud University, Nijmegen, The Netherlands

5.1 Introduction

Rapid growth of computer networks makes security as a critical necessity. Intrusion detection systems (IDSs) are known as important tools for providing required level of security. They analyze network traffic using gathered input data and detect anomalies or attacks. Based on the analysis methods, there are three types of IDS: (a) anomaly detectors; (b) misuse detectors; and (c) specification-based systems [1]. A statistical or machine learning-based model can be used for the anomaly detection [2]. In the misuse detectors, attack patterns are modeled and kept in the attacks' signature database. These signatures are employed for collected data matching. User guidance is needed in the specification-based IDSs to develop a model of normal behavior.

Over the past years, different techniques of machine learning models have been employed in IDSs to achieve high detection rate (DR), low false alarm rate (FAR), and low computational complexity [3]. These models are classified into three categories: (a) unsupervised; (b) supervised; and (c) semisupervised. The unsupervised learning models use the likelihood of data points for clustering without employing class-labeled data. The supervised learning models use labeled data in the training phase. The semisupervised learning models use both unlabeled and labeled data in the training phase [4].

Optimum-path forest (OPF) is a machine learning algorithm that has been introduced in supervised and unsupervised forms [5,6]. This graph-based model reduces a classification problem into partitioning the vertices of an undirected fully connected weighted graph [7]. This graph is based on the samples and their distances in the data set. Indeed, the derived graph of the input data set will be partitioned to some optimum-path trees (OPTs) rooted at the key samples (called prototypes) to represent each class in the classification or the clustering problems. This model that is a fast and parameter-independent classifier has been successfully used in the following applications: probability density function (pdf) estimation [8], classification of remote sensing images [9,10], learning patterns in nonstationary environments [11], remote sensing image segmentation [12], multilabel semisupervised classification [13], loss identification in electrical power systems [14], embedded applications [15], ECG arrhythmia classification [16], classification of large data sets [17], content-based image retrieval (CBIR) [18,19], segmentation of medical image [20,21], sedimentary petrography [22], spoken emotion recognition [23], and EEG signal classification [24].

Similarly, OPF has been used in IDSs, as well. For example, Pereira et al. [25] introduced an OPF-based IDS equipped with a pruning algorithm to select samples of the training set to speed up the classification. This system was faster than a support vector machine (SVM) with radial-basis kernel function (called SVM-RBF) and a self-organizing map (SOM) neural network while offering similar accuracy. Costa et al. [8] proposed a nature-inspired approach to estimate the pdf used for an OPF-based data clustering. They employed this approach for the intrusion detection in computer networks. Sheikhan and Bostani [26] reduced the number of input features by using a hybrid feature selection algorithm and then employed a modified OPF (MOPF) to detect simultaneously both insider and cyber attacks in Internet of things (IoT). Recently, some of the outstanding OPF-based IDSs used in IoT have been reviewed by Costa et al. [27]. In fact, they reviewed about 100 works on the machine learning-based IDSs with focus on the IoT environments.

To improve the speed of OPF and make it efficient for the large-scale problems, several studies have been reported. For example, Papa et al. [17] proposed a supervised learning method based on the reduced-size training data sets. Iwashita et al. [28] derived a formulation to relate the minimum spanning tree (MST) with the minimum spanning forest (MSF) generated by the OPF. Saito et al. [29] employed a data preorganization method to balance the sample selection from all classes and the uncertain samples for training. Amorim and Carvalho [7] proposed a modified version of supervised OPF by changing its training phase. This method estimated the prototypes in the dense area of samples. Bostani et al. [30] developed a fast supervised OPF using the coreset concept to overcome the high computational complexity of OPF over the massive data sets. Papa et al. [31] considered the supervised OPF classifier with k-neighborhood (OPF$_k$). They proposed two different training and classification algorithms to speed up OPF$_k$. Bostani and Sheikhan [32] proposed a modified OPF based on Markov cluster process algorithm and tested it on different public data sets such as Spambase.

In this chapter, in order to show the efficiency of OPF in the intrusion detection systems and also in the large-scale problems, we introduce five hybrid and modified OPFs as follows: (a) a modified OPF using unsupervised learning and social network concept; (b) a hybrid IDS using unsupervised OPF based on MapReduce approach; (c) a hybrid IDS using a modified OPF (MOPF) and selected input features; (d) a modified OPF using Markov cluster process algorithm; and (e) a modified OPF based on the coreset concept. Furthermore, the MOPF-based IDS is improved in the last section as a contribution by using an outperformed clustering algorithm.

5.2 Modified OPF-based IDS using unsupervised learning and social network concept

This model consists of the following three modules: (a) partitioning; (b) pruning; and (c) detecting. To solve the problem of scalability in large data sets, k-means clustering (i.e., an unsupervised learning method) is used in the first module. So, the training set is partitioned into k clusters that are used as the training and evaluation sets of OPF in the detecting module. To speed up OPF, the centrality and the prestige concepts (introduced in the social network analysis) are used in the pruning module. Hence, the training set of OPF is pruned by selecting the most informative samples. The OPFs are trained in the detecting module by different training and evaluation sets which have been projected in the first module [33].

It is noted that the pattern recognition process using OPF is generally composed of two phases: (a) training and (b) classification. The prototypes are determined using the training set for each class in the first phase. In the second phase, all of the arcs that connect an unlabeled sample to all samples in the OPF are considered in the classification of that unlabeled sample. In addition, a learning phase is usually used for accuracy improvement of OPF. This phase is run by using the classification errors on the evaluation set (for more details, refer to [5]).

On the other hand, both OPF and the social network are based on the graph theory; so the betweenness centrality (BC) [34] and the proximity prestige (PR) [35] (as two measures in the social network analysis for identification of important actors [36]) are used for pruning the training set of OPF and improving its performance. The BC measure shows the importance of an actor (in terms of connecting other actors) and is calculated using Eq. (5.1) [35]:

$$BC\left(x_{k}\right) = \sum_{x_{i} \neq x_{j} \neq x_{k}, x_{i}, x_{j}, x_{k} \in M} \frac{b_{x_{i}x_{j}}\left(x_{k}\right)}{b_{x_{i}x_{j}}} \qquad (5.1)$$

in which $b_{x_{i}x_{j}}\left(x_{k}\right)$ is the number of the shortest paths between nodes x_{i} and x_{j} that contains node x_{k}, $b_{x_{i}x_{j}}$ is the number of the shortest paths between nodes x_{i} and x_{j}, and M is the node set. The PR in a directed graph is also calculated using Eq. (5.2) [35]:

$$PR\left(x_{i}\right) = \frac{\frac{I_{i}}{n-1}}{\frac{\sum_{j=1}^{I_{i}} d(y_{j}, x_{i})}{I_{i}}} = \frac{I_{i}^{2}}{(n-1)\sum_{j=1}^{I_{i}} d\left(y_{j}, x_{i}\right)} \qquad (5.2)$$

in which I_{i} is the number of all actors in the influence domain of actor x_{i}, y_{j} is an actor in the influence domain of actor x_{i}, $d\left(y_{j}, x_{i}\right)$ is the distance between these nodes, and n is the total number of nodes.

The framework of this modified OPF-based IDS is shown in Fig. 5.1.

As shown in Fig. 5.1, these steps are followed in this framework: (a) preprocessing; (b) partitioning; (c) pruning; and (d) detecting. In the first step, the values of features are normalized to avoid data imbalance. In the second step, the training set is partitioned into k clusters using k-means clustering to address the problem of scalability in large data sets. This step includes two parts in Fig. 5.1. As shown in Part 2 of this step, the IDS determines the preference group of the training samples associated with a new sample and the corresponding OPF is selected for classification. In the third step, one of BC or PR metrics is used for pruning based on the evaluated performance. In the fourth step, an OPF model is projected for each pruned training/evaluation set.

In this new version of OPF (called AOPF), the distance between the unlabeled sample and the root of each sample in the training set is also considered as an important factor for improving the performance of a traditional OPF [33]. To evaluate the performance of partitioning and pruning modules in this model, the results of applying AOPF+P (partitioning),

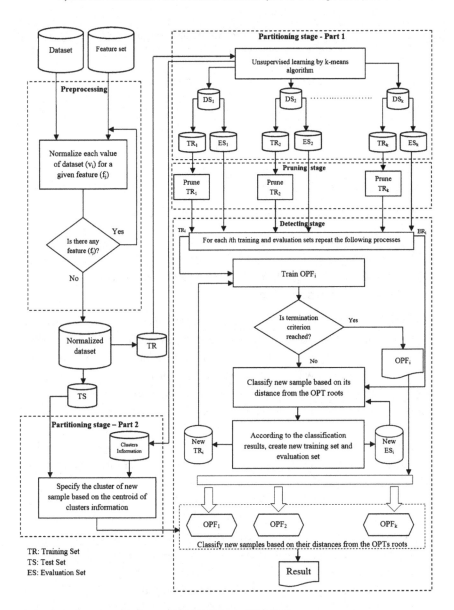

Figure 5.1 Framework of a modified OPF-based IDS [33].

AOPF+Pr (pruning), and AOPF+P+Pr (called MOPF) are compared with the traditional OPF when NSL-KDD intrusion detection data set [37] is used (Table 5.1).

Table 5.1 Performance comparison of
the investigated models in terms of DR
and FAR [33].

Model	DR (%)	FAR (%)
Traditional OPF	90.30	4.19
AOPF	96.13	10.55
AOPF+P	93.83	1.96
AOPF+Pr	96.27	9.23
MOPF	96.20	1.44

As seen in Table 5.1, MOPF can achieve the best performance when considering both DR and FAR.

5.3 Hybrid IDS using unsupervised OPF based on MapReduce approach

One of the novel paradigms in the computer networks is IoT in which resource-constrained objects connect to the unreliable Internet via IPv6 network and IPv6 over low-power wireless personal area networks (6LoW-PANs). Notably, 6LoWPAN is the main attempt to make the concept of real IoT. The requirements of IoT security are as follows [38]: (a) data confidentiality and authentication and (b) privacy and trust among users and things. So, IDSs are needed for detecting attacks in the IoT besides the standard security mechanisms. Several IDSs have been proposed for wireless sensor networks (WSNs); however, most of them are not applicable in 6LoWPAN.

In this section, a hybrid IDS is introduced for detecting sinkhole and selective-forwarding attacks (as the severe DoS attacks in 6LoWPAN) [39]. This IDS consists of a centralized anomaly-based module located in the root of 6LoWPAN and some specification-based agents located in the router nodes. Each specification-based agent works as a local IDS, which sends its analysis results to the root. The anomaly-based module, as a global IDS, uses unsupervised OPF for projecting clustering models based on the MapReduce architecture [40] for detecting anomalous behaviors. Based on the local and global results of these two modules, the root makes a general decision about the occurred anomalies in the network by using a voting mechanism.

It is noted that OPF-based clustering (OPFC) was introduced by Rocha et al. [6]. In the OPFC, each sample in the data set is represented by a node in the k-nearest neighbors graph (G_{k-nn}) that is connected with its k best neighbors in a given feature space. When G_{k-nn} is created, one sample is found at each maximum pdf as a root of cluster. Then an OPT is created from each root to every node in the cluster such that each OPT node is strongly connected to its root as compared to other obtained roots in the G_{k-nn}.

On the other hand, MapReduce is a solution for big data problems [40]. In this approach, a big data set is split to smaller data sets that are stored on different machines. These machines process these smaller data sets in parallel, and finally, the results will be integrated. The framework of this hybrid IDS is shown in Fig. 5.2.

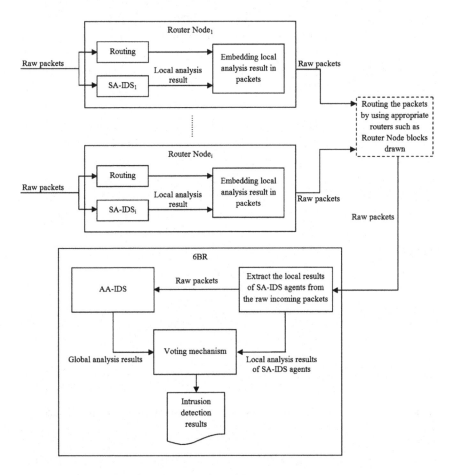

Figure 5.2 Framework of a hybrid OPF-based IDS [39].

This model consists of an anomaly agent-based IDS (AA-IDS) and some specification agent-based IDSs (SA-IDSs). As seen in Fig. 5.2, each router node monitors the input/output traffic independently to identify the potential malicious nodes by using SA-IDS. Then the analysis results are sent to the 6BR (i.e., a single root node in the destination-oriented directed acyclic graph/DODAG). In the 6BR, the AA-IDS projects some OPFC-based models to detect anomalies. Then a final decision is made based on the local results reported by SA-IDS agents and the global results reported by the AA-IDS agent.

The detection of intrusion and identification of malicious nodes in this system are performed in three stages: (a) identifying the malicious nodes; (b) anomaly detection in the 6BR; and (c) decision making on the anomaly detection based on a voting mechanism. The first stage is performed by identifying the suspicious nodes launching sinkhole attack (that results in the route updating misbehavior) and selective-forwarding attack (that results in the data forwarding misbehavior). The general architecture of anomaly detection in the 6BR that is based on MapReduce approach is shown in Fig. 5.3. As seen in Fig. 5.3, the root node (i.e., the 6BR) extracts traffic-related features (f_i) from the received raw packets and creates a new sample for the source nodes. $SrcID_i$ in Fig. 5.3 represents the ID of i-th source node. Then it sends the sample's information with key-value pair format to a node (i.e., the reducer). The reducer node projects a clustering model by using its samples which are received from the mapper node. So, the reducer node returns a new key-value pair with $\langle SID, Label\rangle$ format (in response to the incoming key-value pair) to the root node. The label in Fig. 5.3 is normal/anomalous.

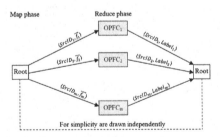

Figure 5.3 Architecture of an anomaly detection system based on MapReduce approach [39].

Some IDSs for 6LoWPANs and IP-based WSNs are compared in Table 5.2. As seen in Table 5.2, the introduced model in this section detects

Table 5.2 Comparison of some IDSs for IoT [39].

Method	Highlights	Requirements	
		Additional control messages	Monitor nodes
SVELTE [41]	Hybrid detection (a host-based IDS that employs the routing protocol's network information)	✓	✗
Specification-based IDS for routing protocol (IP-based WSNs) [42]	Specification-based detection (a finite-state machine design for detecting routing protocol-based attacks)	✗	✓
Denial of service (DoS) attack detection in 6LoWPAN [43]	Signature-based detection (DoS detection architecture that integrates an IDS into the network framework developed in European business-based Internet of things and services [EBBITS] project)	✗	✓
Decentralized intrusion detection in WSNs [44]	Specification-based detection (IDSs are distributed on the WSN for decentralized detection)	✗	✓
The introduced IDS in this section	Hybrid detection	✗	✗

intrusions without employing additional control messages and monitor nodes.

5.4 Hybrid IDS using modified OPF and selected features

The hybrid IDS that is introduced in this section has three main differences as compared to the IDS presented in the previous section of this chapter for the IoT environments: (a) This IDS consists of anomaly-based and misuse-based modules to detect simultaneously both insider and cyber attacks in IoT (instead of a specification-based module used in the previous section); (b) the proposed misuse-based detection module employs the MOPF (introduced in Section 5.2 of this chapter); and (c) a hybrid feature selection (FS) algorithm based on the mutual information and the binary gravitational search algorithm (MI-BGSA) [45] is used in the misuse-based intrusion detection module to reduce the number of input features of the Internet-traffic samples.

With the aim of multifaceted detection of internal and external attacks of IoT, this IDS detects simultaneously both malicious behavior of 6LoW-PAN and the Internet (or LANs) sides. The functional block diagram of this hybrid IDS is shown in Fig. 5.4.

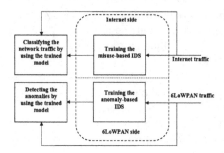

Figure 5.4 Functional block diagram of the MOPF-based IDS for IoT [26].

As seen in Fig. 5.4, this MOPF-based IDS includes two modules: (a) Internet-side module (called the misuse detection module) that classifies the Internet (or LAN) traffic, and consequently detects cyber attacks and (b) 6LoWPAN-side module (called the anomaly detection module) that identifies the insider attacks (e.g., sinkhole and selective-forwarding). For anomaly detection in the 6LoWPAN-side, a sample is created for each source node by extracting four traffic-related features at each time-slot: (a) packet receiving rate; (b) packet dropping rate; (c) average latency; and (d) maximum hop-count. Then an OPFC-based clustering model is projected for each source node.

Similar to the model introduced in the previous section, the MapReduce approach is employed to speed up anomaly detection (Fig. 5.5). As seen in Fig. 5.5, the root node in the anomaly detection module (i.e., the 6BR) sends the sample's information with key-value pair format to a reducer that works with a special key. This format includes source ID as the key and feature vector as the value. Then the reducer node projects a clustering model by using its samples, which are received from the mapper node. This scenario is repeated for the misuse detection module.

To improve the performance of MOPF, an optimal subset of NSL-KDD features are selected using MI-BGSA approach [45]. The MI-BGSA is a population-based heuristic search based on BGSA and MI. This approach employs the BGSA as a global search method to find the optimal subset of

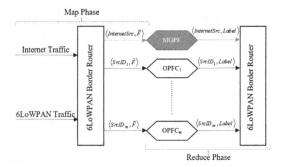

Figure 5.5 Architecture of a hybrid OPF-based IDS based on MapReduce approach [26].

Table 5.3 Performance comparison of MOPF and three classifiers in the misuse detection module of the hybrid IDS [26].

Classifier type (used in misuse-based IDS)	DR (%)	FAR (%)
SVM	95.05	2.10
NB	81.00	9.37
CART	97.15	2.75
MOPF	97.88	1.96

features as a wrapper-based feature selection method. Moreover, with the aim of improving the quality of selected features, the MI is used as a local search for finding the best features among all selected features. To evaluate the performance of MOPF in detecting cyber attacks, this module was replaced with other classifiers such as SVM, classification and regression tree (CART), and naïve Bayes (NB) (Table 5.3). As seen in Table 5.3, the MOPF classifier achieves better DR and FAR as compared to other investigated classifiers.

5.5 Modified OPF using Markov cluster process algorithm

Identifying the optimal prototypes among training samples is an important process in the training phase of an OPF. These prototypes are obtained using an MST in a traditional OPF. Generation of MST is a time-consuming process in the large graphs and leads to OPF inefficiency for the large-scale problems. The training phase of traditional OPFs is modified by using Markov cluster (MCL) algorithm in this section to overcome the problem of scalability, and consequently speeding up OPF in the large-scale applications. The MCL was originally proposed for clustering the vertices of a graph [46]. In other words, MCL algorithm can partition the undirected fully connected weighted graph (which is used in OPF) into some clusters to find the prototypes among them. The MCL algorithm is based on the random walks. The idea of using random walks for graph clustering was raised firstly on the community detection in social networks. Simulating random walks on a graph is performed by MCL algorithm. Notably, the process of Markov chain in MCL algorithm refers to the stochastic flow where in this process the probability for traveling from node u to node t only depends on u and the given corresponding edge (between u and t) and it does not depend on its previous route. It means that the probabilities for the next time step only depend on the current probabilities.

For using the MCL algorithm, a transition matrix should be formed based on the adjacency matrix of a graph. This process is performed by column normalizing of the original adjacency matrix. It is noted that the transition matrix is a probability matrix; so the sum of elements in each column will be one. The MCL algorithm computes the stochastic flow through a network by alternating dissipation and reinforcement steps in order to approximate the partitions [47]. Each node has an initial amount of flow. Then a percentage of flow travels form a node to its neighbors in each MCL's operation. The MCL algorithm employs two operators (i.e., expansion and inflation) to find the cluster structure. The expansion (or power) operator is represented by the usual transition matrix product and is used for the flow expansion in graph. The different regions of a graph can be connected to each other by using this operator. The inflation operator is represented by the entrywise Hadamard–Schur product combined with a diagonal scaling and is used for strengthening/weakening of the current [46]. Suppose $M \in IR^{k \times l}$; $M \geq 0$ and r as a probability matrix and a real nonnegative number, respectively. The matrix resulting from rescaling each of the columns of M with power coefficient r, which is called $\Gamma_r M$, is calculated using Eq. (5.3) [46]:

$$\Gamma_r M = \frac{\left(M_{pq}\right)^r}{\sum_{i=1}^{k}\left(M_{iq}\right)^r}; \quad 1 \leq p \leq k, \ 1 \leq q \leq l \tag{5.3}$$

where Γ_r is called the inflation operator. It is noted that to provide the ability to stay in the same place for a walker in his next step, self-loop should be added to each vertex of the graph.

The steps of MCL algorithm are as follows:

Step 1:   Create a transition matrix using the adjacency matrix of the given graph by normalizing the adjacency matrix.

Step 2: Expand the transition matrix by applying the expansion operator (by taking it to the eth power, where e is an input power parameter).

Step 3: Inflate the resulting matrix by applying the inflation operator (by taking inflation with parameter r, where r is the inflation parameter).

Step 4: Repeat Steps 2 and 3 until the stopping criterion is met (convergence).

The convergence (or steady state) occurs when the transition matrix is a "doubly idempotent" matrix (idempotent under both expansion and inflation operators) [46]. It is noted that in the steady state, all values in a single column of transition matrix are equal (homogeneous). This kind of matrix is shown by M_{mcl}^{∞}. The resulting matrix is used for clustering. The vertices of a graph are divided to two groups: (a) the attractors which attract other vertices and (b) the attracted vertices. These vertices are belonged to the same cluster. It is noted that in the steady matrix, some vertices which have at least one positive value within their corresponding row are attractors. Moreover, at each attractor's row, the vertices which have positive values will be attracted by the corresponding attractor.

In this section, the identification of prototypes in the training phase of OPF is modified by using the MCL algorithm for overcoming the problem of high computational load of generating MST in the big data applications. For this purpose, the training samples of OPF are partitioned to some clusters based on the MCL algorithm. The natural operation of MCL algorithm is based on finding a key sample (attractor) who attracts other related samples; so the obtained key sample is an appropriate candidate to be selected as a prototype. To create an OPT, which is rooted to the obtained prototype, just the samples will be used that are attracted by that prototype. This strategy can lead to generate more accurate OPTs in addition to overcoming the costly process of identifying prototypes. The framework of MCL-based OPF model is depicted in Fig. 5.6.

According to Fig. 5.6, these steps are followed in this model:

Step 1: The training set is split into k training subsets based on the class labels. It is noted that k is the number of classes in the given classification problem.

Step 2: These subsets are partitioned into some clusters by applying the MCL algorithm to each training subset. As discussed previously, each obtained cluster in the MCL algorithm consists of an attractor and other samples that are attracted by the attractor. Then an OPT rooted at the cluster's attractor (as the prototype) is generated by using the samples

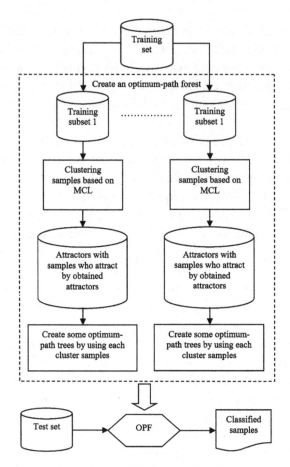

Figure 5.6 Framework of the MCL-based OPF model [32]. (Reproduced with permission from IEEE, License Number: 4963690292342.)

in each obtained cluster. Obviously, the main OPF is consisted of these obtained OPTs.

Step 3: The new unlabeled samples are classified in this step (similar to the classification phase of a traditional OPF). The performance of the MCL-based OPF model and the traditional OPF is compared using Spambase public data set [48] in terms of accuracy and prototype identification time (Table 5.4).

It is noted that most processes of the training phase (except of the identification process of prototypes) and all processes of the classification phase of MCL-based OPF and traditional OPF are exactly same; therefore, the prototype identification time of models was considered for evaluating the

Table 5.4 Performance comparison of MCL-based OPF and traditional OPF [32]. (Reproduced with permission from IEEE, License Number: 4963690292342.)

Data set	Model	Accuracy rate (%)	Prototype identification time (s)
Spambase	Traditional OPF	73.67	576.07
	MCL-based OPF	72.28	20.53

speed of them in Table 5.4. Moreover, three-fold cross-validation is applied for computing the accuracy of models. In other words, each data set is split into three approximately equal subsets. In each validation, two subsets are used for training the models and another subset is used for testing the generated OPFs. As seen in Table 5.4, modifying the identification process of prototypes has led to considerable improvement of prototype identification time in the MCL-based OPF model as compared to the traditional OPF. However, the accuracy rate of traditional OPF is slightly better than the proposed model.

5.6 Modified OPF based on coreset concept

As mentioned earlier, for a massive data set which includes hundreds of thousands samples, the computational complexity of OPF grows fast, which makes it an impractical method. Constructing a coreset over the massive data sets results in reducing the computational complexity. In fact, the coreset is a small weighted set that can approximate the characteristics of the original data set for an optimization problem. One of the main challenges of clustering problems is the high computational complexity of the clustering algorithms (e.g., k-median and k-means) when applied to the massive data sets. There are different studies that use the coreset for overcoming this dilemma. In this way, Frahling and Sohler [49] introduced an effective grid-based coreset for the k-means clustering to speed up the traditional k-means algorithm. In another study, Chen [50] proposed an approximation method for k-median and k-means clustering algorithms based on a ring-based coreset method. Accordingly, Lucic et al. [51] introduced a general coreset technique based on the Bergman divergence [52] that has been used for a wide range of clustering algorithms.

It is noted that a clustering problem using k-median or k-means algorithms can be viewed as an optimization problem in which the optimum centers (and their partitions) should be found as optimization variables to maximize an objective function over the partitions and their centers. On the other hand, the partitioning process in OPF is similar to the k-median clustering in which OPF finds the optimum partitions (i.e., OPTs) that provide the optimum paths from the nonprototype samples to the closest prototypes. So, a coreset-based technique is proposed in this section to speed up OPF and overcome the high computational complexity of it over massive data sets.

To introduce the coreset, suppose a clustering problem that is based on the partitioning methods [53] (e.g., k-median and k-means) in which (X, d) is a metric space and d represents the distance (e.g., Euclidean distance) defined over m-dimensional points of X. If the distance between point $p \in X$ and the center set $C \subseteq X$ is defined using Eq. (5.4):

$$D(C, p) = \min_{q \in C} d(q, p) \tag{5.4}$$

then the clustering algorithm can be considered as an optimization problem with the objective function introduced in Eq. (5.5):

$$Cost(C, P) = \sum_{p \in P} D(C, p) \tag{5.5}$$

where $P \subseteq X$ and $C \subseteq X$ represent the original input point set and the center set, respectively. For this kind of problems, the weighted subset $S \subseteq P$ is a (k, ε)-coreset of P if [50]:

$$|Cost(C, P) - Cost(C, S)| \leq \varepsilon. Cost(C, P) \tag{5.6}$$

in which ε is the error of the coreset approximation.

The main idea behind the introduced system in this section is that the coreset for OPF is a union of obtained coresets for the OPTs of OPF. Based on this idea, the complete-weighted graph G is partitioned into k OPTs (partitions) where k is the number of prototypes. Then by using these points in each partition P_i; $1 \leq i \leq k$, the proper coreset is found based on a technique that will be discussed later in this section. According to this initial approach, the OPF should be completely implemented for achieving the point set of each P_i. However, obtaining the coreset based on this approach is time-consuming for the massive data sets. In fact, the goal of optimization problem in OPF is finding a proper set of OPTs and the coreset can be used in this context with the aim of speeding up this process. On the other hand, the OPTs are required for the coreset construction in this approach; so, this kind of coreset construction cannot be applied as a proper method to the mentioned optimization problem. This problem can be solved by using an incremental coreset construction algorithm, which performs in some iterations. In this approach, OPF will be constructed incrementally. It means that OPTs and consequently their coresets will be constructed incrementally, as well. Notably, the obtained coreset in this algorithm is a weighted subset of the full data set.

According to this approach, the prototypes and OPTs will be called as the centers and the clusters in k-clustering problems, respectively. If a point p belongs to an OPT that the prototype s_i is its root, we can say that p belongs to a cluster that s_i is its center, or the nearest center of p is s_i. The main idea of this approach is that the Euclidean space (which includes all the training points) should be partitioned into some rings around each center. As depicted in Fig. 5.7a; suppose two centers named s_1 and s_2. The algorithm in each iteration just works with the points that belong to the corresponding rings of the current iteration. For example, as shown in Fig. 5.7b, the algorithm specifies all the points that are in the first ring of each center at the first iteration. Then the OPF should be constructed on these points for the reason of determining the nearest center of each point. In fact, each point in OPF belongs to a special OPT; so, the cluster and the nearest center (the cluster center) of every point can be specified based on the OPF. Obviously, the required time for constructing the OPF model is short, because a subset of total points is used for OPF construction. Then, by using a sector-based coreset technique, the proper coreset will be found for each cluster with the consideration of the obtained OPF structure as shown in Fig. 5.7c. A union of these coresets is the final coreset in this iteration. Now, as shown in Fig. 5.7d, by keeping the points of the obtained coreset and removing other points of OPF, the OPF will be extended to a new set of points located in the second ring of the centers. According to the extended OPF, the proper clusters and the nearest centers of these new points will be determined. Again, a coreset of new points is constructed for each cluster with the consideration of the extended OPF structure as shown in Fig. 5.7e. Furthermore, the final coreset of the current iteration is a union of the obtained coresets. As seen in Figs. 5.7f and 5.7g, this process will be repeated for other rings. Finally, the main coreset will be specified by unioning of the obtained coreset in each iteration.

Notably, the optimum-path cost of all the points in the last OPF is determined (Fig. 5.8a); so, extending OPF is not much time-consuming because a new subset of the total points is used for extending the OPF. As seen in Fig. 5.8b, just the optimum-path of these new points should be

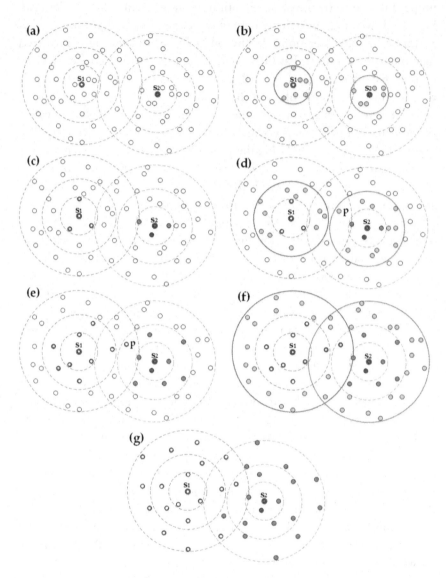

Figure 5.7 Incremental coreset construction for a simple example in which the proper coreset is constructed through steps (b) to (g): (a) two rings with the centers s_1 and s_2, (b) first iteration, (c) finding proper coreset for each cluster, (d) extending OPF to a new set of points in the second ring of the centers, (e) constructing a coreset of new points for each cluster, (f) repeating step (d) for other rings, (g) repeating step (e) for other rings [30]. (Reproduced with permission from IEEE, License Number: 4963741046400.)

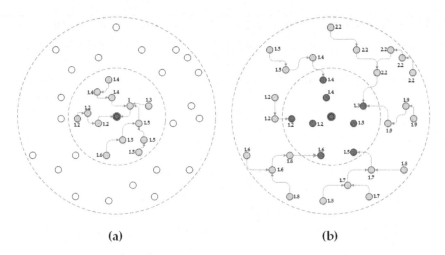

(a)   (b)

Figure 5.8 A simple example of the extending process of OPF: (a) optimum-path cost of the existing points in the latest OPF, (b) optimum-path of the new points in the extending process [30]. (Reproduced with permission from IEEE, License Number: 4963741046400.)

determined in the extending process based on the optimum–path cost of the existing points in the last OPF. So, for determining the optimum–path of a point p in the current iteration, specifying a point in the last OPF located on the way of the optimum–path of p is enough. In other words, the details of the optimum–path is not important, because the label of p can be specified easily by using just the root of this path that every point in the last OPF knows this information.

The pseudocode reported as Algorithm 5.1 describes the incremental coreset construction algorithm for obtaining a coreset for OPF. In Algorithm 5.1, $S^* = \{s_i | 1 \leq i \leq k\} \subset Z_1$ is the optimum set of prototypes, which will be determined before the coreset construction based on the generated MST on G. It is noted that the process of identifying the prototypes is an initial process of the training phase of OPF. However, for simplicity, it is assumed that this process has been performed in a separate process. As shown in Algorithm 5.1, the coreset will be constructed incrementally for providing a proper coreset. Generally, the proposed technique includes two main steps: (a) partitioning and (b) sampling based on the regular coreset (Step 18 of Algorithm 5.1).

Algorithm 5.1 Incremental coreset construction algorithm for obtaining a coreset for OPF [30]. (Reproduced with permission from IEEE, License Number: 4963741046400.)

Input: Z_1 as the training set is a set of n points (samples) in $\mathbb{R}^d$ where d is the dimension of points. $S^* \subset Z_1$ is the optimum set of prototypes or key samples and m is the number of rings.

Output: P_{core} is the coreset of Z_1.

Steps:

1:   Set $R = \max_{\forall s_i \in S^*} \left(\max_{p \in Z_1 \setminus S^*} d(p, s_i) \right)$ where R is the distance of the furthest point from prototypes and $d(.,.)$ is the Euclidean distance between every two points;

2:   Set $r = R/m$ that is the radius of each ring.

3:   Initialize $j = 1$;

4:   Initialize $OPF = \{\}$ where OPF keeps the structure of OPF model;

5:   **while** $j \leq m$

6:     **for each** $s_i \in S^*$

7:       Set $C_j^i = \begin{cases} \underset{\forall p \in Z_1 \setminus S^*}{argmin}\ d(p, s_i) < r; & j = 1 \\ (j-1).r \leq \underset{\forall p \in Z_1 \setminus S^*}{argmin}\ d(p, s_i) < j.r; & 1 < j < m \\ (j-1).r \leq \underset{\forall p \in Z_1 \setminus S^*}{argmin}\ d(p, s_i) \leq j.r; & j = m \end{cases}$;

8:     **end for each**

9:     Set $\widehat{Z}_1 = \cup_{1 \leq i \leq k} C_j^i$;

10:    **if** $j = 1$

11:      Create an optimum-path forest model on $\widehat{Z}_1$ and set OPF by the resulting model of this algorithm;

12:    **else**

13:      Remove all the points in OPF except P_{core};

14:      Extend the OPF on $\widehat{Z}_1$ by keeping the path cost of each $p \in P_{core}$ in the last OPF;

15:    **end if**

16:    **for each** $s_i \in S^*$

17:      Set P_i by all the points in OPF that belong to an OPT in OPF that s_i is the roots of them (OPT_{s_i});

18:      Create a coreset named P_{i-core} by using the regular sampling modules on $P_i \cap C_j^i$;

19:      Set $P_{core} = P_{core} \cup P_{i-core}$

20:    **end for each**

21:    Set $j = j + 1$;

22: **end while**

23: **return** P_{core};

5.6.1 Partitioning step

Suppose R is the distance of the furthest point from prototypes that was computed in Step 1 of Algorithm 5.1. As seen in Fig. 5.7a, at the first time, the Euclidean space should be partitioned into some rings $Ring_j^i$ with radius

$r = R/m$ that are centered at each $s_i \in S^*$. Notice m is the number of rings for each s_i and $1 \le j \le m$. Then, as Step 7 of Algorithm 5.1 shows, for each $s_i \in S^*$ all the points that are within the range of $Ring_1^i$ (as the first ring of s_i) should be determined based on their Euclidean distance to s_i and the radius of $Ring_1^i$ in the first iteration. Then they should be added to C_1^i as a ring set which corresponds to the $Ring_1^i$. Because of possible overlapping among the rings, a point may be located in different rings. But it is not important, because the algorithm works by a union of them. Let $\widehat{Z}_1$ is the union of the obtained points (Step 9 of Algorithm 5.1). Next, as seen in Step 11 of Algorithm 5.1, for determining the OPT (or partition) that the points of $\widehat{Z}_1$ belong to it, an OPF model should be constructed on $\widehat{Z}_1$ (notably, the main idea implies that a coreset should be constructed for each OPT). Obviously, $\widehat{Z}_1$ is a subset of Z_1, so the required time for constructing the OPF model on $\widehat{Z}_1$ is much shorter than the required time for constructing the OPF model on Z_1. Moreover, the partition P_i which corresponds to the OPT_{s_i} includes all the points of OPT_{s_i}. Next, as seen in Steps 17 to 19 of Algorithm 5.1, for the point set $P_i \cap C_1^i$ of OPT_{s_i} (all the points that are in the range of $Ring_1^i$ and belong to the OPT_{s_i}), a coreset P_{i-core} will be constructed based on the sampling step. The final coreset P_{core} is the union of P_{i-core} where $1 \le i \le k$. Now, by keeping all the points P_{core} of OPF and removing other samples, the OPF model will be extended by the new point set $\widehat{Z}_1$ (Steps 13 and 14 of Algorithm 5.1). The remaining process is the same as the first iteration. It is noted that in this iteration the coreset will be constructed just for the points of each OPT_{s_i} that are in the $Ring_2^i$ (the second ring of prototype s_i). Furthermore, by keeping the cost of all the points of OPF, which were not participated in the coreset construction, they will be used in the extending process of OPF. Other iterations will be performed same as the second iteration until $j > m$.

5.6.2 Sampling step

As mentioned earlier, the proper coreset should be found for each ring with the consideration of the obtained OPF structure. Therefore, a novel sector-based coreset technique is introduced that can increase the possibility of selecting samples from different regions of every ring. Fig. 5.9 shows this sectorialization process. As depicted in Fig. 5.9, the size of sectors will be greater by getting away from the center of ring. This geometric characteristic results in selecting more informative samples from the closer regions. Notably, these samples are more important as compared to other samples in OPF, because they are likely the parents or the ancestors of a

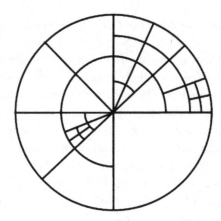

Figure 5.9 A simple example of the sectoralization process [30]. (Reproduced with permission from IEEE, License Number: 4963741046400.)

large amount of the further samples. In the sectoralization process, for each prototype s_i, all the remaining input points must be transformed from the cartesian coordinates to the spherical coordinates where s_i is the origin of the new spherical coordinate system. Suppose that the input points are in 2-dimensional space. In the initial step, the $s_i = (x_s, y_s)$ should be selected as the origin; so, the position of each remaining point $p = (x_p, y_p)$ will be changed by a simple linear transformation $p' = (x_p + x_s, y_p + y_s)$. Then the coordinate of p' will be transformed to the polar coordinate $p'' = (r, \theta)$ where $r = \sqrt{x^2 + y^2}$ and $\theta = tan^{-1}(y/x)$. As seen in Fig. 5.9, at the first step of this process, the current ring is portioned into four sectors based on dividing θ by four. Then for each sector t, if the size of the inside points is lower than or equal to a predefined threshold α, a point that has maximum betweenness centrality [34] will be selected as a representative point with the consideration of the obtained OPF. Otherwise, t will be partitioned into four subsectors by dividing r and θ by two. Now, a partitioning should be performed again based on the mentioned discussion for each subsector. This process will be repeated until the representative points are provided for all the obtained sectors.

The performance of the coreset-based OPF and the traditional OPF is evaluated on a sample benchmark data set named HTRU2 with 17898 samples, 8 features, and two classes [48]. For evaluating the performance, 1000, 500, and 1000 samples were selected randomly from the HTRU2 as the training, the evaluation, and the test sets, respectively. In the OPF construction phases, the performance of the coreset-based OPF in terms of

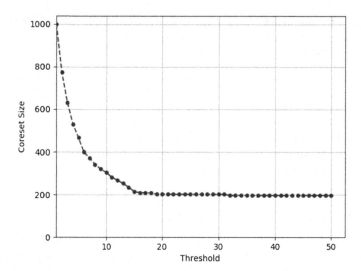

Figure 5.10 Effect of the threshold value on the coreset size [30]. (Reproduced with permission from IEEE, License Number: 4963741046400.)

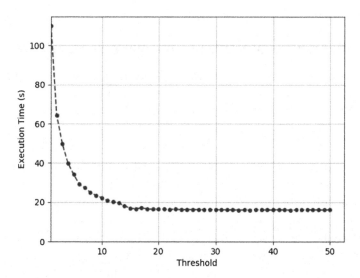

Figure 5.11 Effect of the threshold value on the execution time [30]. (Reproduced with permission from IEEE, License Number: 4963741046400.)

the number of selected samples (the coreset size) and the execution time in 50 various thresholds α are depicted in Figs. 5.10 and 5.11, respectively.

As seen in these figures, the coreset size and the execution time are decreased considerably by increasing α. The performance comparison of

Table 5.5 Performance comparison of the coreset-based OPF and the traditional OPF [30]. (Reproduced with permission from IEEE, License Number: 4963741046400.)

Evaluation term	Method	
	Traditional OPF	Coreset-based OPF
Number of samples	1000	197
Execution time of construction (s)	40.40	16.14
Approximation error	Not-Applicable	1.82
Execution time of classification (s)	7.36	6.44
Accuracy of classification (%)	88	88

the traditional OPF and the coreset-based OPF is reported in Table 5.5 (when $\alpha = 50$). As seen in Table 5.5, by using the coreset approach in the construction phase of OPF, the number of samples and the execution time are reduced by 80% and 60%, respectively. Moreover, the execution time of the classification phase of OPF is improved by 12.5% without accuracy reduction.

5.7 Enhancement of MOPF using k-medoids algorithm

In this section, the k-medoids clustering algorithm is used rather than the k-means in the partitioning module in order to improve the performance of MOPF in terms of DR and FAR. There are various kinds of clustering algorithms (i.e., partitioning, hierarchical, density-based, and grid-based methods). The k-means and the k-medoids are two simple and effective partitioning methods, which are widely used in the clustering problems. The k-means and the k-medoids algorithms are both iterative and partitional algorithms that try to minimize the squared error/distances between the center and data points of each cluster. However, a data point of each cluster named "medoid" is chosen in k-medoids algorithm as a center of that cluster while in the k-means algorithm, the mean of data points of a cluster is selected as the center [54]. This strategy have caused the k-medoids algorithm more robust against noise and outlier in comparison with the k-means algorithm [54]. Notably, a medoid is a reference point of a cluster whose average dissimilarity to all the remaining data points of that cluster is minimal.

Fig. 5.12 shows the performance comparison of AOPF + P (using the k-medoids algorithm) and AOPF + P (using the k-means algorithm) models over the obtained training and test sets of [33]. As seen in Fig. 5.12, using

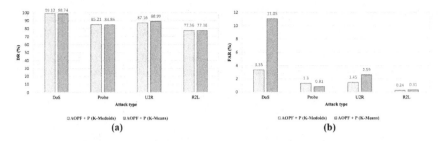

Figure 5.12 Performance comparison of AOPF + P (using the k-medoids algorithm) and AOPF + P (using the k-means algorithm): (a) DR, (b) FAR.

the k-medoids algorithm in the partitioning module have led to improve the performance of intrusion detection model, especially in terms of FAR. For example, the FAR of DoS attack in AOPF + P (using the k-medoids algorithm) is improved considerably (i.e., 7.70%).

References

[1] N. Stakhanova, S. Basu, J. Wong, On the symbiosis of specification-based and anomaly-based detection, Computers & Security 29 (2) (2010) 253–268.

[2] V. Golmah, An efficient hybrid intrusion detection system based on C5.0 and SVM, International Journal of Database Theory and Application 7 (2) (2014) 59–70.

[3] M. Zamani, Machine Learning Techniques for Intrusion Detection, Department of Computer Science, University of New Mexico, USA, 2013.

[4] S.X. Wu, W. Banzhaf, The use of computational intelligence in intrusion detection systems: a review, Applied Soft Computing 10 (1) (2010) 1–35.

[5] J.P. Papa, A.X. Falcão, C.T.N. Suzuki, Supervised pattern classification based on optimum-path forest, International Journal of Imaging Systems and Technology 19 (2) (2009) 120–131.

[6] L.M. Rocha, F.A.M. Cappabianco, A.X. Falcão, Data clustering as an optimum-path forest problem with applications in image analysis, International Journal of Imaging Systems and Technology 19 (2009) 50–68.

[7] W.P. Amorim, M.H. Carvalho, Supervised learning using local analysis in an optimal-path forest, in: Proceedings of the 25th Conference on Graphics, Patterns and Images, Ouro Preto, Brazil, 2012, pp. 330–335.

[8] K.A.P. Costa, L.A.M. Pereira, R.Y.M. Nakamura, C.R. Pereira, J.P. Papa, A.X. Falcão, A nature-inspired approach to speed up optimum-path forest clustering and its application to intrusion detection in computer networks, Information Sciences 294 (2015) 95–108.

[9] J.A. Santos, A.T. Silva, R.D.S. Torres, A.X. Falcão, L.P. Magalhães, R.A.C. Lamparelli, Interactive classification of remote sensing images by using optimum-path forest and genetic programming, in: Proceedings of the International Conference on Computer Analysis of Images and Patterns, Seville, Spain, 2011, pp. 300–307.

[10] D. Osaku, R.Y.M. Nakamura, L.A.M. Pereira, R.J. Pisani, A.L.M. Levada, F.A.M. Cappabianco, A.X. Falcão, J.P. Papa, Improving land cover classification through contextual-based optimum-path forest, Information Sciences 324 (2015) 60–87.

[11] A.S. Iwashita, V.H.C. Albuquerque, J.P. Papa, Learning concept drift with ensembles of optimum-path forest-based classifiers, Future Generation Computer Systems 95 (2019) 198–211.

[12] S. Chen, T. Sun, F. Yang, H. Sun, Y. Guan, An improved optimum-path forest clustering algorithm for remote sensing image segmentation, Computers & Geosciences 112 (2018) 38–46.

[13] W.P. Amorim, A.X. Falcão, J.P. Papa, Multi-label semi-supervised classification through optimum-path forest, Information Sciences 465 (2018) 86–104.

[14] L.A.P. Júnior, C.C.O. Ramos, D. Rodrigues, D.R. Pereira, J.P. Papa, Unsupervised non-technical losses identification through optimum-path forest, Electric Power Systems Research 140 (2016) 413–423.

[15] W.F.S. Diniz, V. Fremont, I. Fantoni, E.G.O. Nóbrega, An FPGA-based architecture for embedded systems performance acceleration applied to optimum-path forest classifier, Microprocessors and Microsystems 52 (2017) 261–271.

[16] E.J.S. Luz, T.M. Nunes, V.H.C. Albuquerque, J.P. Papa, D. Menotti, ECG arrhythmia classification based on optimum-path forest, Expert Systems with Applications 40 (9) (2013) 3561–3573.

[17] J.P. Papa, A.X. Falcão, V.H.C. Albuquerque, J.M.R.S. Tavares, Efficient supervised optimum-path forest classification for large datasets, Pattern Recognition 45 (1) (2012) 512–520.

[18] A.T. Silva, A.X. Falcão, L.P. Magalhães, Active learning paradigms for CBIR systems based on optimum-path forest classification, Pattern Recognition 44 (12) (2011) 2971–2978.

[19] A.T. Silva, J.A. Santos, A.X. Falcão, R.S. Torres, L.P. Magalhães, Incorporating multiple distance spaces in optimum-path forest classification to improve feedback-based learning, Computer Vision and Image Understanding 116 (4) (2012) 510–523.

[20] F.A.M. Cappabianco, A.X. Falcão, C.L. Yasuda, J.K. Udupa, Brain tissue MR-image segmentation via optimum-path forest clustering, Computer Vision and Image Understanding 116 (10) (2012) 1047–1059.

[21] P.P.R. Filho, A.C.S. Barros, J.S. Almeida, J.P.C. Rodrigues, V.H.C. Albuquerque, A new effective and powerful medical image segmentation algorithm based on optimum path snakes, Applied Soft Computing 76 (2019) 649–670.

[22] I.M. Filho, T.V. Spina, A.X. Falcão, A.C. Vidal, Segmentation of sandstone thin section images with separation of touching grains using optimum path forest operators, Computers & Geosciences 57 (2013) 146–157.

[23] A.I. Iliev, M.S. Scordilis, J.P. Papa, A.X. Falcão, Spoken emotion recognition through optimum-path forest classification using glottal features, Computer Speech & Language 24 (3) (2010) 445–460.

[24] T.M. Nunes, A.L.V. Coelho, C.A.M. Lima, J.P. Papa, V.H.C. Albuquerque, EEG signal classification for epilepsy diagnosis via optimum path forest–a systematic assessment, Neurocomputing 136 (2014) 103–123.

[25] C.R. Pereira, R.Y.M. Nakamura, K.A.P. Costa, J.P. Papa, An optimum-path forest framework for intrusion detection in computer networks, Engineering Applications of Artificial Intelligence 25 (2012) 1226–1234.

[26] M. Sheikhan, H. Bostani, A security mechanism for detecting intrusions in Internet of things using selected features based on MI-BGSA, International Journal of Information & Communication Technology Research 9 (2) (2017) 53–62.

[27] K.A.P. Costa, J.P. Papa, C.O. Lisboa, R. Munoz, V.H.C. Albuquerque, Internet of things: a survey on machine learning-based intrusion detection approaches, Computer Networks 151 (2019) 147–157.

[28] A.S. Iwashita, J.P. Papa, A.N. Souza, A.X. Falcão, R.A. Lotufo, V.M. Oliveira, V.H.C. Albuquerque, J.M.R.S. Tavare, A path- and label-cost propagation approach to speed

up the training of the optimum-path forest classifier, Pattern Recognition Letters 40 (2014) 121–127.

[29] P.T.M. Saito, C.T.N. Suzuki, J.F. Gomes, P.J. Rezende, A.X. Falcão, Robust active learning for the diagnosis of parasites, Pattern Recognition 48 (2015) 3572–3583.

[30] H. Bostani, M. Sheikhan, B. Mahboobi, Developing a fast supervised optimum-path forest based on corset, in: Proceedings of the 19th International Symposium on Artificial Intelligence and Signal Processing, Shiraz, Iran, 2017, IEEEXplore https://doi.org/10.1109/AISP.2017.8324076.

[31] J.P. Papa, S.E.N. Fernandes, A.X. Falcão, Optimum-path forest based on k-connectivity: theory and applications, Pattern Recognition Letters 87 (2017) 117–126.

[32] H. Bostani, M. Sheikhan, Modification of optimum-path forest using Markov cluster process algorithm, in: Proceedings of the 2nd International Conference on Signal Processing and Intelligent Systems, Tehran, Iran, 2016, IEEEXplore, https://doi.org/10.1109/ICSPIS.2016.7869874.

[33] H. Bostani, M. Sheikhan, Modification of supervised OPF-based intrusion detection systems using unsupervised learning and social network concept, Pattern Recognition 62 (2017) 56–72.

[34] A. Rusinowska, R. Berghammer, H.D. Swart, M. Grabisch, Social networks: prestige, centrality, and influence, in: Relational and Algebraic Methods in Computer Science, Springer, 2011, pp. 22–39.

[35] K. Musiał, P. Kazienko, P. Bródka, User position measures in social networks, in: Proceedings of the 3rd Workshop on Social Network Mining and Analysis, New York, USA, 2009.

[36] S. Wasserman, K. Faust, Social Network Analysis: Methods and Applications, Cambridge University Press, New York, 1994.

[37] M. Tavallaee, E. Bagheri, L. Wei, A. Ghorbani, NSL-KDD Data Set, available on http://nsl.cs.unb.ca/NSL-KDD.

[38] S. Sicari, A. Rizzardi, L.A. Grieco, A. Coen-Porisini, Security, privacy and trust in Internet of things: the road ahead, Computer Networks 76 (2015) 146–164.

[39] H. Bostani, M. Sheikhan, Hybrid of anomaly-based and specification-based IDS for Internet of things using unsupervised OPF based on MapReduce approach, Computer Communications 98 (2017) 52–71.

[40] J. Dean, S. Ghemawat, MapReduce: simplified data processing on large clusters, in: Proceeding of the 6th Symposium on Operating Systems Design and Implementation, San Francisco, USA, 2004.

[41] S. Raza, L. Wallgren, T. Voigt, SVELTE: real-time intrusion detection in the Internet of things, Ad Hoc Networks 11 (2013) 2661–2674.

[42] A. Le, J. Loo, Y. Luo, Specification-based IDS for securing RPL from topology attacks, in: Proceedings of the Wireless Days, Niagara Falls, Canada, 2011.

[43] P. Kasinathan, C. Pastrone, M.A. Spirito, M. Vinkovits, Denial-of-service detection in 6LoWPAN based Internet of things, in: Proceedings of the 9th International Conference on Wireless and Mobile Computing, Networking and Communications, Lyon, France, 2013.

[44] A.P.R. Silva, M.H.T. Martins, B.P.S. Rocha, A.A.F. Loureiro, L.B. Ruiz, H.C. Wong, Decentralized intrusion detection in wireless sensor networks, in: Proceedings of the 1st ACM International Workshop on Quality of Service & Security in Wireless and Mobile Networks, Montreal, Canada, 2005.

[45] H. Bostani, M. Sheikhan, Hybrid of binary gravitational search algorithm and mutual information for feature selection in intrusion detection systems, Soft Computing 21 (2017) 2307–2324.

[46] S.M. van Dongen, Graph Clustering by Flow Simulation, Ph.D. Thesis, Universiteit Utrecht, Utrecht, The Netherlands, 2000.

[47] S.V. Dongen, C. Abreu–Goodger, Using MCL to extract clusters from networks, Bacterial Molecular Networks 804 (2011) 281–295.

[48] D.J. Newman, S. Hettich, C.L. Blake, C.J. Merz, UCI Repository of Machine Learning Databases, Irvine, CA, 1998, available on http://archive.ics.uci.edu/ml/datasets.html.

[49] G. Frahling, C. Sohler, Coresets in dynamic geometric data streams, in: Proceedings of the 37th Annual ACM Symposium on Theory of Computing, Baltimore, USA, 2005.

[50] K. Chen, On coresets for k-median and k-means clustering in metric and Euclidean spaces and their applications, SIAM Journal on Computing 39 (3) (2009) 923–947.

[51] M. Lucic, O. Bachem, A. Krause, Strong coresets for hard and soft Bregman clustering with applications to exponential family mixtures, in: Proceedings of the 19th International Conference on Artificial Intelligence and Statistics, Cadiz, Spain, 2016.

[52] L.M. Bregman, The relaxation method of finding the common point of convex sets and its application to the solution of problems in convex programming, U.S.S.R. Computational Mathematics and Mathematical Physics 7 (3) (1967) 200–217.

[53] L. Rokach, O. Maimon, Clustering methods, in: O. Meimon, L. Rokach (Eds.), Data Mining and Knowledge Discovery Handbook, Springer, New York, 2005, pp. 321–352.

[54] T.S. Madhulatha, Comparison between k-means and k-medoids clustering algorithms, in: Proceedings of the International Conference on Advances in Computing and Information Technology, Chennai, India, 2011.

CHAPTER 6

Detecting atherosclerotic plaque calcifications of the carotid artery through optimum-path forest

Danilo Samuel Jodas[a], **Mateus Roder**[a], **Rafael Pires**[a],
Marcos Cleison Silva Santana[a], **Luis A. de Souza Jr.**[b], and
Leandro Aparecido Passos[a]
[a]Department of Computing, São Paulo State University, Bauru, Brazil
[b]Department of Computing, São Carlos Federal University, São Carlos, Brazil

6.1 Introduction

Cardiovascular diseases are hazardous to human health since they damage the heart and vascular system functioning. Their underlying pathologies' immediate diagnosis is critical to avoid the progress of severe conditions such as heart attacks, transient ischemic attacks, or even strokes. According to the World Health Organization, cardiovascular diseases continuously increase and take approximately 17.9 million people's lives each year [1]. Moreover, 85% of all cardiovascular diseases' mortality is caused by heart attacks [1]. Therefore, public policies and efficient diagnostic tools are remarkably necessary to rapidly control the premature fatality and ensure adequate treatment planning according to the patients' condition.

Among a variety of cardiovascular diseases, the well-known atherosclerosis is responsible for reducing the blood flow through the artery and leading to severe conditions such as amaurosis fugax, transient ischemic attacks, and strokes [17,45,51]. Atherosclerotic lesions in the carotid arteries represent an imminent risk for a cerebrovascular accident since they narrow the artery and block the blood flow toward the brain. In such cases, treatment by medications or even surgical intervention is highly required to prevent future strokes.

The composition of an atherosclerotic lesion regards lipid core, fibrous tissue, smooth muscle cells, intraplaque hemorrhage, and calcifications. Such lesions are classified according to the American Heart Association lesion type classification [48], which provides histological examinations divided into categories based on the composition of the plaques, thereby providing efficient progress' evaluation protocol for disease's advance in several images' modalities. Based on such classification, many studies were capable of indicating the hazards related to advanced stages of the disease, when thrombus and calcified debris are present in the lesion, being the last the focus of interest in several studies. The role of calcified atherosclerosis is still under discussion, and its influence in the plaque stability is somehow unknown so far. However, densely calcified plaques are reported as an indicator of the disease burden in some studies [7,22,36].

Cardiovascular and carotid artery related diseases are commonly diagnosed by invasive or noninvasive procedures that help physicians determine patients' health status. Among such methods, ultrasound, computed tomography angiography (CTA), and magnetic resonance imaging (MRI) represent the gold standard to identify the narrowing of the examined artery and the atherosclerosis composition [28,49]. In this context, the ultrasound denotes an inexpensive, noninvasive, and simple imaging modality. However, the image quality provided by the technique is significantly low, noisy, and often affected by acoustic shadows, thereby making the diagnostic of possible lesions somehow challenging and unreliable, since the quality of the images has a vital role in distinguishing the different components of the lesion. MRI examination raises attention due to the possible combination of distinct MRI image modalities such as Proton-Density Weighted, T1-Weighted, and Time of Flight imaging techniques, thus distinguishing different tissues within the atherosclerotic lesions [9,12,42]. CTA exams provide high-resolution images and a clear distinction of calcified regions, making such imaging examination remarkably attractive for proper diagnostic in late-stage atherosclerotic lesions [25,44].

Even though the diagnosis performed by specialists and physicians is essential in the treatment of carotid artery diseases, they present several drawbacks usually related to medical issues, such as elevated time demand, intervariability from several experts' diagnostics, and human mistakes due to fatigue, among others. Therefore analysis through computational algorithms plays a crucial role and has been commonly employed to identify and quantify atherosclerotic plaques components. In this context, Jodas et al. [21], for instance, presented a comprehensive review of several image processing techniques and supervised classification-based approaches to automatically delineate atherosclerotic boundary plaques and classify the composition of the lesion.

Image processing and analysis gathered significant attention concerning disease detection in medical images, namely the boundary segmentation of different structures related to pathological conditions. In the context of cardiovascular diseases, one can highlight the lumen and artery wall delineation as the first step for the subsequent atherosclerotic lesion identification, from which several handcrafted features can be extracted for further assessment [5,6,19,23,43,50]. Regarding the latter stage, machine learning models emerge as a powerful instrument to support quick diagnostics and avoid in advance severe health circumstances, providing precise quantitative results compared to an expert's judgment. In this research line, typical solutions based on machine learning models include the prediction of the plaque rupture [10,24] and the atherosclerosis characterization [8,15].

Regarding machine learning models, the Optimum-Path Forest (OPF) [29,30] emerges as a powerful, deterministic, and parameterless graph-based framework developed for supervised and unsupervised learning tasks in different domains of application, such as energy losses detection [38] and feature selection [40], to cite a few. In the context of medical applications, OPF-based algorithms have been successfully used for pattern analysis of several diseases either in a supervised or unsupervised fashion. Ribeiro et al. [39] employed the unsupervised OPF in breast masses data to separated malignant nodes from benign ones. Souza et al. [46] carried out the comparison between the supervised OPF and Support Vector Machines in the context of Barrett's esophagus classification, being OPF the classifier that presented the best results. Passos et al. [33] used the supervised OPF for classifying Parkinson's disease by using a set of features extracted from images through a ResNet50, obtaining paramount results as well.

Moreover, OPF has also been employed to improve other machine learning-based approaches such as radial basis function neural networks [41] and the brainstorm optimization algorithm [2], for instance. Besides, OPF's intrinsic features have been successfully employed to model a sort of solutions to deal with anomaly detection [18,34], probabilistic classification [16], data imbalance [32], fuzzy logic [47], among others. The outstanding results obtained from the applications mentioned above are encouraging to use the OPF algorithms in atherosclerotic lesions assessment.

Therefore the main contributions of this chapter are three-fold:

- detect calcified regions on atherosclerotic lesion through OPF-based approaches;
- compare the standard OPF classifier against four variants, i.e., Probabilistic OPF [16], Fuzzy OPF [47], OPF-AD [18,34], and OPF_{knn} [31], as well as the well-known radial-basis function Support Vector Machines [11], to the task mentioned above;

- to foster the literature regarding both cardiovascular disease detection and OPF-based approaches.

The remainder of this chapter is presented as follows. Section 6.2 introduces the main concepts regarding calcified atherosclerotic lesion detection through CAD-based approaches and OPF-based classifiers. Further, Section 6.3 exposes the methodology employed in work, comprising a description of the data set and the experimental setup. Finally, Sections 6.4 and 6.5 present the experimental results and conclusions, respectively.

6.2 Theoretical background

This section presents the main concepts regarding calcified atherosclerotic lesion detection through CAD systems, as well as a brief description of the standard OPF classifier and the variants employed in this work.

6.2.1 Computer-aided diagnosis of atherosclerotic lesions

Computer-Aided Diagnosis (CAD) systems have gained attention as essential support for a rapid clinical decision of particular diseases. A medical-decision system relies on data obtained from laboratory exams or features extracted from medical imaging to predict the patients' health condition. In this context, special attention is given to machine learning algorithms, namely the supervised classification procedure, which aims at assigning similar samples to a particular category that follows a specific data distribution. In clinical diagnosis, it may be used to assign the presence or absence of individual pathologies in laboratory examinations. Further, features extracted from the segmented regions may be used to classify the objects inside the images.

In the context of cardiovascular diseases, machine learning-based approaches have been reported in numerous literature studies. Amin et al. [4], for instance, proposed a pipeline to predict heart diseases using a grid search feature selection and seven machine learning models. Mohan et al. [26] presented a similar study with a hybrid approach based on the random forest classifier and linear model. Alaa et al. [3] used a large data set composed of 423,604 participants to predict the risk of cardiovascular diseases. The authors proposed a framework named AutoPrognosis to optimize the data preprocessing and machine learning models through ensemble modeling.

Despite the importance of the mentioned methods, an in-depth study of the underlying factors that lead to cardiovascular diseases is highly demanded. In this context, Holzapfel et al. [20] carried out research to assess atherosclerosis composition for structural assessment of the plaque. Besides, calcified atherosclerosis detection has been reported in a few studies of the literature employing machine learning algorithms for medical assistance diagnosis. Zhao et al. [53], for instance, presented the detection of calcified and noncalcified plaque components in coronary arteries through support vector machines and random forest classifiers trained on features extracted from CTA images. The authors proposed the extraction and combination of statistical intensities, texture features, and gradient information from several small circular regions with a fixed radius inside the coronary artery region. Acharya et al. [37] presented an approach to classify calcified and noncalcified atherosclerotic lesions in CTA images of the coronary arteries. The authors used the Gabor transformation to obtain textural details in different directions of the image's pixels. Also, the authors used a set of entropy-based features that are assumed to be more disordered in calcified plaques in comparison to noncalcified or normal arteries at specific orientations of the Gabor transform domain.

The studies mentioned above employed well-known machine learning models for classification intents. Also, they reported the prediction of calcified plaques considering only the entire artery. A pixelwise classification approach is often more useful for identifying local aspects of the artery to aggregate pixels as a single region representing the lesion's calcium burden. Atherosclerotic lesions are assumed to be abnormal structures inside the affected arteries, especially considering the appraisal of the plaque's specific components. Considering the feature extraction directly from the image, the number of pixels related to the calcification component may be too low in comparison to the total number of pixels inside the assessed artery, leading to an imbalanced dataset. In this context, algorithms designed to detect anomalous behavior in data may present some advantages regarding standard identification methods. Such a statement holds regarding the OPF variant for anomaly detection, i.e., OPF-AD, as observed in Section 6.4.

6.2.2 Optimum-path forest

This section provides a brief description of the optimum-path forest classifier, as well as four variants, i.e., Probabilistic-OPF, OPF-AD, Fuzzy OPF, and OPF_{knn}.

6.2.2.1 Optimum-path forest classifier

Suppose $\mathscr{T} = \{(x_1, y_1), (x_2, y_2), \ldots, (x_m, y_m)\}$ denotes a data set composed of training instances such that $x_i \in \mathbb{R}^n$ and $y_i \in \{-1, +1\}$. The optimum-path forest classifier [29,30] is a graph-based algorithm that models each sample from $\mathscr{T}$ as a node in a fully-connected graph whose edges are weighted by the distance between each pair of samples. Further, the most representative nodes, i.e., adjacent instances with distinct labels, are selected as prototypes and perform a competition among themselves to conquer the remaining nodes, providing them an optimum-path cost, described as follows:

$$C(r) = \min_{\forall q \in \mathscr{T}} \{\max\{C(q), d(q, r)\}\}, \tag{6.1}$$

where q stands for the training instance that conquered the node r, and $d(q, r)$ represents the distance between samples q and r.

6.2.2.2 Probabilistic optimum-path forest

The first change provided for probabilistic classification through OPF [16] comprises approximating the posterior class probability, which is performed as follows:

$$P(\hat{y} = y|x) \approx P_{A,B}(C(x)) = \frac{1}{1 + \exp(AyC(x) + B)}, \tag{6.2}$$

where y and $\hat{y}$ stand for the true and predicted labels, respectively, and A and B denote the parameters to be learned in order to adjust the probabilities. The training process is performed by minimizing the classification error, as follows:

$$E(A, B) = \sum_{x, y \in \mathscr{V}} (tq + \log(1 + \exp(-AyC(x) - B))), \tag{6.3}$$

where $\mathscr{V}$ denotes the validation set, t is related to the number of y labeled samples, and $q = C(x) + B$.

6.2.2.3 Optimum-path forest-based approach for anomaly detection

The variant of the optimum-path forest designed for anomaly detection, i.e., OPF-AD [18,34], learns the behavior of "normal" samples presented in training set for further identifying testing instances whose conduct differs too much from expected. Briefly speaking, the model performs the unsupervised OPF to cluster the training data, composed of "normal" samples only, according to their similarities. In the sequence, instances from the testing set, comprising both "normal" and "abnormal" examples, are connected to the nearest cluster through a k-nearest neighbor-based approach, and their densities are computed as follows:

$$\rho(q) = \frac{1}{\sqrt{2\pi\sigma^2}|\mathscr{A}_k(q)|} \sum_{\forall r \in \mathscr{A}_k(q)} \exp\left(\frac{-d^2(q, r)}{2\sigma^2}\right), \tag{6.4}$$

where $\mathscr{A}_k(q)$ denotes the set composed of the k-nearest nodes from q, and $\sigma = \frac{d_f}{3}$, where d_f is the maximum arc weight between q and all samples in $\mathscr{A}_k(q)$.

Finally, each testing sample's density is compared to a threshold. Density values above this threshold imply the instance is located in a populous area, and thus classified as a "normal" and assigned the cluster label. On the other hand, samples with density values below this threshold are suggested as outliers since they are located far from most training instances, performing an abnormal behavior.

6.2.2.4 Fuzzy optimum-path forest

The Fuzzy OPF [47] combines both the supervised and the unsupervised versions of the optimum-path forest with fuzzy logic concepts to create a model that considers each sample's pertinence on the classification process. In short, the model initially performs the unsupervised OPF to cluster similar samples together. Further, each instance is assigned with a membership value, considering its pertinence in the surrounding clusters. The following equation describes the process:

$$F_\Theta(x) = (1 - \varepsilon)\left(\frac{\rho(x) - \rho_{min}}{\rho_{max} - \rho_{min}}\right)^2 + \varepsilon, \tag{6.5}$$

where ε denotes the lower bound parameter, $\rho(x)$ represents the density of the sample x, computed using Eq. (6.4), and ρ_{min} and ρ_{max} represents the minimum and maximum densities among all training samples, respectively. Besides, $\Theta = \{\varepsilon, \rho_{min}, \rho_{max}\}$ stands for the set of function parameters.

Finally, Eq. (6.1) is rewritten to accommodate the membership, as follows:

$$C(r) = \min_{\forall q \in \mathscr{I}} \{F_\Theta(r) * \max\{C(q), d(q, r)\}\}, \tag{6.6}$$

6.2.2.5 Optimum-path forest based on k-connectivity

The main difference between the standard OPF classifier and OPF_{knn} [31] relies on three main aspects:

1. while the standard OPF classifier weights only the graph edges as the distance between connected nodes, OPF_{knn} also weights each node with its respective density, which is computed using Eq. (6.4);

2. while the standard OPF classifier estimates its prototypes as the nodes located at the frontier of the classes, OPF_{knn} estimates its prototypes as the nodes with highest values of density, whose location is generally in the central region of the cluster;

3. while the standard OPF classification process aims to minimize the cost of every sample using a path-cost function that computes the maximum arc-weight along a path, the OPF_{knn} classification process aims at maximizing the cost of every instance using a path-cost function that estimates the minimum value between the cost of a training sample and the density of a test node.

6.3 Methodology

This section describes the data set and the collection of features extracted for this work. Also, we further define the setup utilized to conduct the experiments.

6.3.1 Data set

The experiments were performed over a set of features extracted from CTA images of the carotid artery. Such images were previously used in the study conducted by van Engelen et al. [15] and cordially provided by the authors under request. All the images were acquired to meet the requirements of a study approved by the Medical Committee of the Erasmus Medical Center. Notice all the assessed patients offered a written agreement to use the medical images [15].

A registration procedure was employed to align the CTA images with histological images of the plaques excised from the affected patients via a surgical procedure. Once the alignment is completed, the CTA images are cropped to attain only the interest region that highlights the carotid artery. In total, the work employs 184 CTA images with their corresponding manual delineations of the lumen, carotid wall countors, and atherosclerotic lesions. From this set, the manual shapes of the atherosclerotic components are available in 177 images. Fig. 6.1 illustrates the whole procedure for obtaining the pixels inside the carotid wall boundary in the CTA image by using the ground truth obtained from the corresponding histological image.

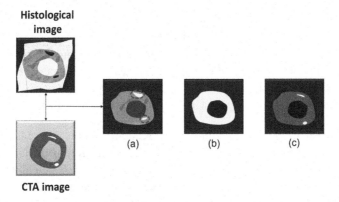

Figure 6.1 Illustration of the registration procedure between the CTA image and the corresponding histological image along with the ground truths. (a) the ground truth obtained from the histological image; (b) the binary image with pixels inside the carotid wall in white; (c) part of the carotid wall region in the CTA image obtained through the binary mask in (b). Calcified regions are the ones covered by red (dark gray in print version) circles in the ground truth image displayed in (a). One can notice the matching with the location of the brightest regions shown in the CTA images, which represent the calcification of the lesion. The images shown here were manually drawn for illustration purposes only and, therefore, not representing the original ones from the data set.

The manual contours of the calcified components were obtained by using a fixed threshold value on the micro-CT images acquired from the excised plaques. The micro-CT images were also aligned with the corresponding CTA images through the registration procedure mentioned above. The reader is invited to check the research of van Engelen et al. [15] for more details.

6.3.2 Features set

Table 6.1 shows the 27 features obtained from each pixel of the CTA images that fall inside the region between the contours of the lumen and the carotid wall boundaries.

Besides the original CTA image intensity, we also used a combination of filters for image enhancement purposes. Noise removal, for instance, is attained through the application of the Gaussian and mean filters. The sigmoid filter is often useful for highlighting a range of grayscale intensities in the image, thereby helping the calcified components' increasing brightness. Gradient magnitude helps to detect the edges of the structures of interest, which is useful to get the calcified regions' boundaries. We used the well-known Sobel filter for edge detection purposes.

Table 6.1 Features.

Description	
Intensity of the original image	Average intensity sigmoid filter
Intensity of the image (Gaussian filter)	Standard deviation sigmoid filter
Intensity of the image (mean filter)	Minimum intensity original intensity
Intensity of the image (gradient magnitude)	Minimum intensity Gaussian filter
Intensity of the image (sigmoid filter)	Minimum intensity mean filter
Average intensity original image	Minimum intensity gradient magnitude
Standard deviation original image	Minimum intensity sigmoid filter
Average intensity Gaussian filter	Maximum intensity original intensity
Standard deviation Gaussian filter	Maximum intensity Gaussian filter
Average intensity mean filter	Maximum intensity mean filter
Standard deviation mean filter	Maximum intensity gradient magnitude
Average intensity gradient magnitude	Maximum intensity sigmoid filter
Standard deviation gradient magnitude	X and Y coordinates of the pixel

* Features extracted from a 3 × 3 neighborhood centered at each pixel of the original and filtered CTA images.

Each pixel inside the carotid wall region (Fig. 6.1(c)) is centered at a 3 × 3 template for feature extraction from the original CTA image and images resulting from the application of the mentioned filters. Each pixel is assigned 1 if it represents a calcification, and 0 otherwise. Such labels are marked in the template that defines the ground truth of the histological image (Fig. 6.1(a)). Afterward, all features were normalized through a normal distribution scaler that subtracts each sample's mean to scale it in a unit variance.

The feature set is highly imbalanced, so the number of noncalcified pixels is much higher than those representing the calcification of the lesion. From the 52,070 pixels extracted from the images, 48,853 represent the noncalcium component.

6.3.3 Metrics

This chapter considers three metrics, i.e., accuracy, F1 score, and Interception over Union (IoU), to evaluate the feasibility of the OPF-based approaches to perform the task classification over features extracted from atherosclerotic lesion image pixels. In general, accuracy denotes the standard metric for classification purposes. However, such a metric is not robust enough to evaluate imbalanced data sets. In this context, the F1 score is more suitable for the task, since it considers the data distribution per class, providing a weighted score of the results. Such an evaluation is relevant for pixelwise binary classification, especially under such circumstances, once the number of pixels in the region without atherosclerotic lesion is higher than the number of pixels in the carotid wall area. As an alternative, the Interception over Union is also considered for imbalanced data sets since it acknowledges the number of correct predictions, as well as the number of false positives and false negatives. Moreover, since pixelwise classification can be viewed as a semantic segmentation task, the use of metrics such as IoU is relevant because it can measure how good the predicted segmentation is compared to the known ground truth.

6.3.4 Experimental setup

This chapter employs the optimum-path forest classifier, as well as four variations, i.e., the Probabilistic-OPF, OPF-AD, Fuzzy OPF, and OPF_{knn}, to the task of detecting the atherosclerosis calcification in carotid arteries. Besides, the radial-basis function support vector machine is also considered a baseline for comparison purposes. Experiments were conducted over a data set composed of 52,070 samples comprising 27 features extracted from CTA images. Moreover, the data set was randomly split into three subsets for training (60%), testing (20%), and validation (20%) for hyperparameter tuning purposes. In this context, a grid-search optimization was employed considering the following ranges of values[1]:

- **Probabilistic-OPF:** $A \times B$ defined within $[-5, 5] \times [-5, 5]$;
- **OPF-AD:** $k_{max} \in [1, 100]$ with step size of 5 and threshold value ranges from 100 to 2,300 with a step size of 100;
- **Fuzzy OPF:** $k_{max} \in [1, 150]$ with step size of 10 and $\varepsilon \in [0.2, 1.2]$ with a step size of 0.2.
- **SVM:** $C \in \{1, 10, 100, 1000\}$ and $\gamma \in \{0.001, 0.01, 0.1, 1\}$.

For a fair comparison, the experiments were performed during 20 runs, and the Wilcoxon Signed-rank test [52] with 5% of significance was considered for statistically comparing the most accurate technique, i.e., the one that obtained the highest F1 score, against all other algorithms individually. Besides, we also performed a post hoc analysis using the Nemenyi test [27] after computing the Friedman test with $\alpha = 0.05$, aiming to evaluate the critical difference (CD) among all techniques.

---

[1] Notice OPF classifier and OPF_{knn} have no hyperparameters to be tuned.

Finally, all the OPF-based approaches were implemented and conducted over the C-based library LibOPF.[2] Regarding SVM, we employed the Scikit-learn [35] implementation. Besides, the computational environment comprises a 2×1.6 GHz Intel Xeon processor with 32 GB of RAM, running over an Ubuntu 16.04 Linux machine.

6.4 Experimental results

This section presents the results and discussion regarding the task of classification, a statistical analysis considering such outcomes, and the computational burden.

6.4.1 Classification

Table 6.2 presents the F1 score, accuracy, and intersection over union concerning each OPF variant and the SVM. One can observe OPF-AD outperformed the other techniques considering the F1 score. Such a result reveals the anomaly detection concept's effectiveness while considering the presence of calcified areas in the carotid artery wall as anomalies. Besides, the number of calcified pixels is significantly smaller than the total area of the carotid wall region, thereby leading to small spots of abnormal structures inside the assessed artery. The fact reinforces the OPF-AD ability to deal with highly imbalanced data sets by treating minority class samples as anomalies. Notice the problem of anomaly detection in imaging data sets was recently highlighted in the work of Costa et al. [13].

Table 6.2 Results obtained from each OPF-variant.

Metric	Statistic	OPF	Probabilistic-OPF	OPF-AD	Fuzzy OPF	OPF$_{knn}$	SVM
F1 score	Avg.	0.9466	0.9466	**0.9635**	0.9489	0.9507	0.9592
	Std.	±0.0019	±0.0019	±0.0034	±0.0021	±0.0022	±0.0016
Accuracy	Avg.	94.7743	94.7643	93.8736	94.9544	95.0941	95.6131
	Std.	±0.1844	±0.1839	±0.2485	±0.2019	±0.2139	±0.1648
IoU	Avg.	0.9456	0.9455	0.9385	0.9475	0.9490	0.9547
	Std.	±0.0019	±0.0019	±0.0025	±0.0021	±0.0022	±3.05388

Despite the imbalanced distribution of the data set, the attained results are excellent, since all techniques provided results with over 93% of precision in all metrics. Disregarding the F1 score where OPF-AD outperformed all variants, OPF$_{knn}$ also deserves some attention since it obtained

---

[2] https://github.com/jppbsi/LibOPF.

the best results considering both accuracy and IoU values, disregarding the SVM approach. OPF$_{knn}$ success is probably associated with the proximity relation provided by the limited connection between the closest instances. Finally, it can also be observed that Fuzzy OPF offers attractive results, outperforming the standard and probabilistic OPF in all cases. Such capability is provided by the pertinence relation attributed to each training sample, thus designing an architecture robust against anomalous and imbalanced data sets.

6.4.2 Statistical analysis

This section considers an alternative statistical analysis considering the Nemenyi test [27]. The method performs a post hoc approach to find critical differences among all techniques considering the Friedman test as the statistical baseline for multiple comparisons. Results presented in Fig. 6.2 depict the OPF variants and the SVM's average rank in a horizontal bar where lower ranks are positioned in the rightmost side of the diagram, describing the best approaches considering the F1 score. Notice that methods connected do not differ statistically among themselves [14].

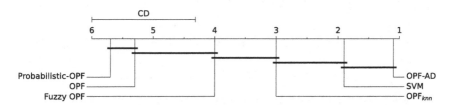

Figure 6.2 Comparison of Nemenyi test concerning all techniques' average F1 score. CD stands for the critical difference among all the techniques.

The test highlights three main conclusions: (i) the OPF-AD is the most accurate techniques for the task, followed by SVM; (ii) OPF$_{knn}$ and Fuzzy OPF also outperformed the standard OPF classifier, even though it could not provide results as precise as OPF-AD and SVM; and (iii) computing the probabilities from each sample did not offer any improvement to the classification. Contrariwise, it granted the worst results overall, suggesting most of the instances are well-defined regarding their labels. The results emphasize the advantages of improved versions of the OPF classifier to deal with imbalanced data sets comprising anomalous samples.

6.4.3 Computational burden

Table 6.3 presents the average elapsed time required for training the OPF classifier and its four variants, as well as the radial-basis function SVM. Standard OPF and OPF$_{knn}$ resulted in the lowest computational burden compared to the other techniques, which is expected since both variants do not require hyperparameter tuning. Regarding SVM, OPF-AD, and the Fuzzy OPF, the high computational cost demand lies in the optimization step, performed to tune the models' hyperparameters. Despite the optimization procedure, Fuzzy OPF is also implemented in a two-step procedure, i.e., the model performs an unsupervised strategy to compute each sample's membership value, and further executes a supervised classification step, thus implying in the most costly method.

Table 6.3 Computational burden (in minutes).

Statistic	OPF	Probabilistic-OPF	OPF-AD	Fuzzy OPF	OPF$_{knn}$	SVM
Avg.	2.4812	26.1350	446.5608	835.1608	8.1104	91.5529
Std.	±0.0082	±0.4549	±1.1068	±3.4442	±0.0341	±2.0601

6.5 Conclusions and future works

The correct assessment of atherosclerotic lesions in images has been an intense topic of research in numerous studies of the literature, especially the ones that include computer medical systems and machine learning for pattern classification in structures through several imaging modalities. In this sense, this chapter proposed identifying calcified pixels in CTA images of the carotid artery through the optimum-path forest classifier and four of its variants. Experiments conducted in a large dataset composed of more than 52,000 samples proved the effectiveness of the OPF-based models in the context of vascular diseases, namely the employment of the OPF-based algorithm for anomaly detection, outperforming the well-known support vector machines considering the F1 score, which is suitable to evaluate the classifiers' performance over imbalanced data sets. Besides, OPF$_{knn}$ and Fuzzy OPF also presented favorable results, especially compared to the standard OPF and the probabilistic OPF variants.

Futures studies include the image reconstruction of the classified calcium burden for the area and volume analysis purposes. Furthermore, we also intend to consider assessing other components of the lesion through the OPF-based models in images of alternative imaging modalities.

References

[1] Cardiovascular diseases, https://www.who.int/health-topics/cardiovascular-diseases. (Accessed 13 September 2020).

[2] L.C.S. Afonso, L.A. Passos, J.P. Papa, Enhancing brain storm optimization through optimum-path forest, in: 2018 IEEE 12th International Symposium on Applied Computational Intelligence and Informatics (SACI), IEEE, 2018, pp. 000,183–000,188.

[3] A.M. Alaa, T. Bolton, E. Di Angelantonio, J.H.F. Rudd, M. van der Schaar, Cardiovascular disease risk prediction using automated machine learning: a prospective study of 423,604 UK biobank participants, PLoS ONE 14 (5) (2019) 1–17.

[4] M.S. Amin, Y.K. Chiam, K.D. Varathan, Identification of significant features and data mining techniques in predicting heart disease, Telematics and Informatics 36 (2019) 82–93.

[5] A.M. Arias-Lorza, J. Petersen, A. van Engelen, M. Selwaness, A. van der Lugt, W.J. Niessen, M. de Bruijne, Carotid artery wall segmentation in multispectral mri by coupled optimal surface graph cuts, IEEE Transactions on Medical Imaging 35 (3) (2016) 901–911.

[6] S. Balocco, C. Gatta, F. Ciompi, A. Wahle, P. Radeva, S. Carlier, G. Unal, E. Sanidas, J. Mauri, X. Carillo, T. Kovarnik, C.W. Wang, H.C. Chen, T.P. Exarchos, D.I. Fotiadis, F. Destrempes, G. Cloutier, O. Pujol, M. Alberti, E.G. Mendizabal-Ruiz, M. Rivera, T. Aksoy, R.W. Downe, I.A. Kakadiaris, Standardized evaluation methodology and reference database for evaluating IVUS image segmentation, Computerized Medical Imaging and Graphics 38 (2) (2014) 70–90, https://doi.org/10.1016/j.compmedimag.2013.07.001.

[7] H.E. Barrett, K. Van der Heiden, E. Farrell, F.J. Gijsen, A.C. Akyildiz, Calcifications in atherosclerotic plaques and impact on plaque biomechanics, Journal of Biomechanics 87 (2019) 1–12.

[8] A. Boi, A.D. Jamthikar, L. Saba, D. Gupta, A. Sharma, B. Loi, J.R. Laird, N.N. Khanna, J.S. Suri, A survey on coronary atherosclerotic plaque tissue characterization in intravascular optical coherence tomography, Current Atherosclerosis Reports 20 (7) (2018) 33.

[9] J.M. Cai, Classification of human carotid atherosclerotic lesions with in vivo multicontrast magnetic resonance imaging, Circulation 106 (11) (2002) 1368–1373, https://doi.org/10.1161/01.CIR.0000028591.44554.F9.

[10] M. Cilla, J. Martinez, E. Pena, M.Á. Martínez, Machine learning techniques as a helpful tool toward determination of plaque vulnerability, IEEE Transactions on Biomedical Engineering 59 (4) (2012) 1155–1161.

[11] C. Cortes, V. Vapnik, Support vector machine, Machine Learning 20 (3) (1995) 273–297.

[12] R. Corti, V. Fuster, Imaging of atherosclerosis: magnetic resonance imaging, European Heart Journal 32 (14) (2011) 1709–1719, https://doi.org/10.1093/eurheartj/ehr068.

[13] K.A.P. Costa, J.P. Papa, L.A. Passos, D. Colombo, J. Del Ser, K. Muhammad, V.H.C. de Albuquerque, A critical literature survey and prospects on tampering and anomaly detection in image data, Applied Soft Computing (2020) 106727.

[14] J. Demšar, Statistical comparisons of classifiers over multiple data sets, Journal of Machine Learning Research 7 (2006) 1–30.

[15] A. van Engelen, W.J. Niessen, S. Klein, H.C. Groen, H.J.M. Verhagen, J.J. Wentzel, A. van der Lugt, M. de Bruijne, Atherosclerotic plaque component segmentation in combined carotid MRI and CTA data incorporating class label uncertainty, PLoS ONE 9 (4) (2014) 1–14, https://doi.org/10.1371/journal.pone.0094840.

[16] S.E. Fernandes, D.R. Pereira, C.C. Ramos, A.N. Souza, D.S. Gastaldello, J.P. Papa, A probabilistic optimum-path forest classifier for non-technical losses detection, IEEE Transactions on Smart Grid 10 (3) (2018) 3226–3235.

[17] K.L. Furie, S.M. Smimakis, W.J. Koroshetz, J.P. Kistler, Stroke due to large artery atherosclerosis, in: K.L. Furie, P.J. Kelly (Eds.), Handbook of Stroke Prevention in Clinical Practice, Current Clinical Neurology, Humana Press, 2004, pp. 151–165.

[18] R.R. Guimarães, L.A. Passos, R. Holanda Filho, V.H.C. de Albuquerque, J.J. Rodrigues, M.M. Komarov, J.P. Papa, Intelligent network security monitoring based on optimum-path forest clustering, IEEE Network 33 (2) (2018) 126–131.

[19] H.R. Hemmati, M. Alizadeh, A. Kamali-Asl, S. Shirani, Semi-automated carotid lumen segmentation in computed tomography angiography images, Journal of Biomedical Research 31 (6) (2017) 548.

[20] G.A. Holzapfel, J.J. Mulvihill, E.M. Cunnane, M.T. Walsh, Computational approaches for analyzing the mechanics of atherosclerotic plaques: a review, Journal of Biomechanics 47 (4) (2014) 859–869.

[21] D.S. Jodas, A.S. Pereira, J.M.R. Tavares, A review of computational methods applied for identification and quantification of atherosclerotic plaques in images, Expert Systems with Applications 46 (2016) 1–14.

[22] Y. Kan, W. He, B. Ning, H. Li, S. Wei, T. Yu, The correlation between calcification in carotid plaque and stroke: calcification may be a risk factor for stroke, International Journal of Clinical and Experimental Pathology 12 (3) (2019) 750.

[23] P.K. Kumar, T. Araki, J. Rajan, J.R. Laird, A. Nicolaides, J.S. Suri, State-of-the-art review on automated lumen and adventitial border delineation and its measurements in carotid ultrasound, Computer Methods and Programs in Biomedicine 163 (2018) 155–168, https://doi.org/10.1016/j.cmpb.2018.05.015.

[24] A. Madani, A. Bakhaty, J. Kim, Y. Mubarak, M.R.K. Mofrad, Bridging finite element and machine learning modeling: stress prediction of arterial walls in atherosclerosis, Journal of Biomechanical Engineering 141 (8) (2019), https://doi.org/10.1115/1.4043290.084502.

[25] M. Miralles, J. Merino, M. Busto, X. Perich, C. Barranco, F. Vidal-Barraquer, Quantification and characterization of carotid calcium with multi-detector ct-angiography, European Journal of Vascular and Endovascular Surgery 32 (5) (2006) 561–567.

[26] S. Mohan, C. Thirumalai, G. Srivastava, Effective heart disease prediction using hybrid machine learning techniques, IEEE Access 7 (2019) 81,542–81,554.

[27] P. Nemenyi, Distribution-Free Multiple Comparisons, Princeton University, 1963.

[28] D. Owen, A. Lindsay, R. Choudhury, Z. Fayad, Imaging of atherosclerosis, Annual Review of Medicine 62 (2011) 25–40.

[29] J.P. Papa, A.X. Falcão, V.H.C. Albuquerque, J.M.R.S. Tavares, Efficient supervised optimum-path forest classification for large datasets, Pattern Recognition 45 (1) (2012) 512–520.

[30] J.P. Papa, A.X. Falcão, C.T.N. Suzuki, Supervised pattern classification based on optimum-path forest, International Journal of Imaging Systems and Technology 19 (2) (2009) 120–131.

[31] J.P. Papa, S.E.N. Fernandes, A.X. Falcao, Optimum-path forest based on k-connectivity: theory and applications, Pattern Recognition Letters 87 (2017) 117–126.

[32] L.A. Passos, D.S. Jodas, L.C. Ribeiro, T. Moreira, J.P. Papa, O^2PF: oversampling via optimum-path forest for breast cancer detection, in: 2020 IEEE 33rd International Symposium on Computer-Based Medical Systems (CBMS), IEEE Computer Society, 2020, pp. 498–503.

[33] L.A. Passos, C.R. Pereira, E.R.S. Rezende, T.J. Carvalho, S.A.T. Weber, C. Hook, J.P. Papa, Parkinson disease identification using residual networks and optimum-path forest, in: 2018 IEEE 12th International Symposium on Applied Computational Intelligence and Informatics (SACI), 2018, pp. 000,325–000,330.

[34] L.A. Passos, C.C.O. Ramos, D. Rodrigues, D.R. Pereira, A.N. de Souza, K.A.P. da Costa, J.P. Papa, Unsupervised non-technical losses identification through optimum-path forest, Electric Power Systems Research 140 (2016) 413–423.

[35] F. Pedregosa, G. Varoquaux, A. Gramfort, V. Michel, B. Thirion, O. Grisel, M. Blondel, P. Prettenhofer, R. Weiss, V. Dubourg, J. Vanderplas, A. Passos, D. Cournapeau, M. Brucher, M. Perrot, E. Duchesnay, Scikit-learn: machine learning in Python, Journal of Machine Learning Research 12 (2011) 2825–2830.

[36] R. Pini, G. Faggioli, S. Fittipaldi, F. Vasuri, M. Longhi, E. Gallitto, G. Pasquinelli, M. Gargiulo, A. Stella, Relationship between calcification and vulnerability of the carotid plaques, Annals of Vascular Surgery 44 (2017) 336–342.

[37] U. Rajendra Acharya, K.M. Meiburger, J.E. Wei Koh, J. Vicnesh, E.J. Ciaccio, O. Shu Lih, S.K. Tan, R.R.A.R. Aman, F. Molinari, K.H. Ng, Automated plaque classification using computed tomography angiography and Gabor transformations, Artificial Intelligence in Medicine 100 (2019) 101,724, https://doi.org/10.1016/j.artmed.2019.101724.

[38] C.C.O. Ramos, A.N. Souza, J.P. Papa, A.X. Falcão, A new approach for nontechnical losses detection based on optimum-path forest, IEEE Transactions on Power Systems 26 (1) (2011) 181–189.

[39] P.B. Ribeiro, L.A. Passos, L.A. Silva, K.A. Costa, J.P. Papa, R.A. Romero, Unsupervised breast masses classification through optimum-path forest, in: 2015 IEEE 28th International Symposium on Computer-Based Medical Systems, IEEE, 2015, pp. 238–243.

[40] D. Rodrigues, L.A. Pereira, R.Y. Nakamura, K.A. Costa, X.S. Yang, A.N. Souza, J.P. Papa, A wrapper approach for feature selection based on bat algorithm and optimum-path forest, Expert Systems with Applications 41 (5) (2014) 2250–2258, https://doi.org/10.1016/j.eswa.2013.09.023.

[41] G.H. Rosa, K.A.P. Costa, L.A. Passos, J.P. Papa, A.X. Falcão, J.M.R.S. Tavares, On the training of artificial neural networks with radial basis function using optimum-path forest clustering, in: 2014 22nd International Conference on Pattern Recognition, IEEE, 2014, pp. 1472–1477.

[42] T. Saam, M.S. Ferguson, V.L. Yarnykh, N. Takaya, D. Xu, N.L. Polissar, T.S. Hatsukami, C. Yuan, Quantitative evaluation of carotid plaque composition by in vivo MRI, Arteriosclerosis, Thrombosis, and Vascular Biology 25 (2005), https://doi.org/10.1161/01.ATV.0000149867.61851.31.

[43] L. Saba, H. Gao, E. Raz, S.V. Sree, L. Mannelli, N. Tallapally, F. Molinari, P.P. Bassareo, U.R. Acharya, H. Poppert, J.S. Suri, Semiautomated analysis of carotid artery wall thickness in MRI, Journal of Magnetic Resonance Imaging 39 (6) (2014) 1457–1467, https://doi.org/10.1002/jmri.24307.

[44] V. Sandfort, J.A. Lima, D.A. Bluemke, Noninvasive imaging of atherosclerotic plaque progression: status of coronary computed tomography angiography, Circulation: Cardiovascular Imaging 8 (7) (2015) e003,316.

[45] J.P. Schadé, The Complete Encyclopedia of Medicine & Health, Foreign Media Books, Franklin Park, NJ, 2006.

[46] L.A.D. Souza, L.C.S. Afonso, C. Palm, J.P. Papa, Barrett's esophagus identification using optimum-path forest, in: 2017 30th SIBGRAPI Conference on Graphics, Patterns and Images (SIBGRAPI), 2017, pp. 308–314.

[47] R.W.R. Souza, J.V.C. Oliveira, L.A. Passos, W. Ding, J.P. Papa, V.H. Albuquerque, A novel approach for optimum-path forest classification using fuzzy logic, IEEE Transactions on Fuzzy Systems (2019).

[48] H.C. Stary, A.B. Chandler, R.E. Dinsmore, V. Fuster, S. Glagov, W. Insull Jr, M.E. Rosenfeld, C.J. Schwartz, W.D. Wagner, R.W. Wissler, A definition of advanced types of atherosclerotic lesions and a histological classification of atherosclerosis: a report from the committee on vascular lesions of the council on arteriosclerosis, American heart association, Circulation 92 (5) (1995) 1355–1374.

[49] J.M. Tarkin, M.R. Dweck, N.R. Evans, R.A. Takx, A.J. Brown, A. Tawakol, Z.A. Fayad, J.H. Rudd, Imaging atherosclerosis, Circulation Research 118 (4) (2016) 750–769.

[50] B. Wang, G. Sha, P. Yin, X. Liu, Automated segmentation of carotid artery vessel wall in mri, in: International Conference on Advanced Hybrid Information Processing, Springer, 2017, pp. 275–286.

[51] D.O. Wiebers, V.L. Feigin, R.D. Brown, Handbook of Stroke, 2nd edn., Board Review Series, Lippincott Williams & Wilkins, Philadelphia, PA, 2006.

[52] F. Wilcoxon, Individual comparisons by ranking methods, Biometrics Bulletin 1 (6) (1945) 80–83.

[53] F. Zhao, B. Wu, F. Chen, X. Cao, H. Yi, Y. Hou, X. He, J. Liang, An automatic multiclass coronary atherosclerosis plaque detection and classification framework, Medical & Biological Engineering & Computing 57 (1) (2019) 245–257.

CHAPTER 7

Learning to weight similarity measures with Siamese networks: a case study on optimum-path forest[☆]

Gustavo H. de Rosa and João Paulo Papa
Department of Computing, São Paulo State University, Bauru, Brazil

7.1 Introduction

Increasing demand in autonomous systems and decision-making assisting tools has fostered Artificial Intelligence (AI) [2] throughout the last decade. Additionally, specific computing hardware, such as Graphics Processing Units (GPU) and Tensor Processing Units (TPU), eased the development and training of Machine Learning (ML) algorithms, allowing their application in a wide range of tasks, such as image segmentation [6] and classification [8], object recognition [24], medical imaging [16], remote sensing [15], among others.

A common approach regarding classification and recognition tasks is to employ supervised learning, which consists of learning mathematical functions capable of mapping inputs to outputs, i.e., learn patterns from sets of data and classify them according to their corresponding labels. Throughout the years, well-known classifiers, such as Logistic Regression (LR) [11], Decision Trees (DT) [23], Support Vector Machines (SVM) [4], Artificial Neural Networks (ANN) [7], were developed to tackle such problems, attaining state-of-the-art results in several applications.

Although they have obtained remarkable results throughout several problems, the crescent tasks' complexity has led to poor performance and inconsistent results, mainly due to the high-dimensional feature vectors and the necessity of using vast amounts of data. A recent approach denoted as

☆ The authors appreciate São Paulo Research Foundation (FAPESP) grants #2013/07375-0, #2014/12236-1, #2017/25908-6, #2018/15597-6, #2018/21934-5 and #2019/02205-5, and CNPq grants 307066/2017-7 and 427968/2018-6.

155

Optimum-Path Forest (OPF) [21] is a graph-based classifier that aims to find prototype nodes responsible for defining the classes and conquering the remaining nodes through connectivity functions. Such an approach has obtained state-of-the-art results with high computational time, although it did not employ higher-dimensional feature spaces (SVMs) or deep architectures (ANNs) [20]. A recurring OPF's setback stands for using a distance measure, such as the Euclidean norm, to weigh the connectivity function during the prototypes' definition and the nodes' conquering. Such a necessity carries an enormous computational load and might not be ideal when working with exceedingly similar data as their output would tend to zero and not weigh arcs appropriately, making the same prototypes conquer samples from distinct classes.

Recently, a new type of neural network denoted as Siamese network [3] has been proposed to find similarities between samples' pairs. It is essentially composed of twin architectures that share their weights and are trained according to a similarity-based object, such as the contrastive loss [10]. For instance, Melekhov et al. [19] proposed to learn new feature vectors by using matching and nonmatching image pairs guided by a contrastive loss in Convolutional Neural Networks (CNN), while Jindal et al. [12] fed pairs of chromosomes' feature vectors to learn new embedded representations and better discriminate them. Zhan et al. [27] used CNNs guided by a contrastive loss to detect pixel changes in optical aerial images, while Chen et al. [5] proposed a two-step change detection framework using deep Siamese networks, where the former obtains the corresponding samples through unsupervised learning, and the latter detects whether there were changes or not. Furthermore, Wang et al. [17] introduced a few-short learning leaves classifier, where Siamese networks embeds features in new spaces that better distinguish between similar and dissimilar leaves, while a spatial structure optimizer helps in guiding the objective. Finally, Sun et al. [25] introduced a Siamese network classification framework to map risk and risk-free data and alleviate the problem of imbalanced data.

This work proposes to find similarity-based measures using Siamese networks and further applying them to the OPF's supervised classification. In short, the Siamese network will learn a similarity matrix between a set of samples and provide it to OPF, where it will be used instead of calculating the distance between the same set of samples. To the best of the authors' knowledge, no work in the literature employs Siamese networks to find similarity-based measures to weigh OPF's connectivity function. Therefore the main contributions of this work are three-fold: (i) to introduce a similarity-based measure to OPF, (ii) to remove the burden of OPF's distance calculation, and (iii) to fill the lack of research regarding Siamese networks and optimum-path forests.

The remainder of this paper is organized as follows. Section 7.2 introduces a brief discussion regarding optimum-path forests and Siamese networks, while Section 7.3 discusses the evaluated tasks, data sets, and experimental setup. Finally, Section 7.4 presents the experimental results and Section 7.5 states the conclusions and future works.

7.2 Theoretical background

This section introduces a theoretical background regarding optimum-path forest and Siamese networks.

7.2.1 Optimum-path forest

Papa et al. [21] proposed the optimum-path forest, a multiclass graph-based classifier capable of segmenting the feature space without massive data. Essentially, the OPF aims at constructing a complete graph, where an arc connects every pair of nodes. During its training phase, OPF defines a set of prototype[1] nodes and let them compete between themselves to conquer the remaining nodes, i.e., finding the best path (lowest cost). Afterward, during the testing phase, OPF inserts a new sample in the graph and finds a minimum cost prototype, defining its label. Fig. 7.1 illustrates such behavior.

Let $\mathcal{Z}$ be a data set composed of training and testing sets denoted as $\mathcal{Z}_1$ and $\mathcal{Z}_2$, respectively. One can define a graph $G = (\mathcal{V}, \mathcal{A}),$[2] which belongs to $\mathcal{Z}$ such that $v(s) \in \mathcal{V}$, where s stands for a sample in data set $\mathcal{Z}$ and $v(\cdot)$ stands for a feature extraction function. Additionally, let $\mathcal{A}$ be an adjacency relation that connects samples in $\mathcal{V}$, as well as let $d : \mathcal{V} \times \mathcal{V} \to \mathfrak{R}^+$ be a distance function that weigh edges in $\mathcal{A}$.

Training step

Let π_s be a path in G that ends in node $s \in \mathcal{V}$ and let $\langle \pi_s \cdot (s, t) \rangle$ be the nexus between path π_s and arc $(s, t) \in \mathcal{A}$. The optimum-path forest classifier aims at establishing a set of prototypes nodes $\mathcal{S} \subseteq \mathcal{V}$ using a cost function f

---

[1] Master node that represents a specific class and conquers other nodes.
[2] Note that one can also define $G_1 = (\mathcal{V}_1, \mathcal{A}_1)$ and $G_2 = (\mathcal{V}_2, \mathcal{A}_2)$ from $\mathcal{Z}_1$ and $\mathcal{Z}_2$, respectively.

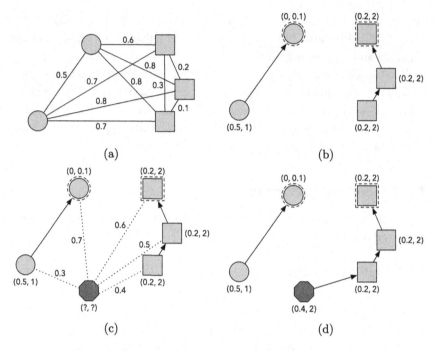

Figure 7.1 (a) Complete weighted graph given a training set. (b) Optimum-path forests for f_{max} and two prototypes (outlined nodes). Note that (x, y) denotes the cost and label of the samples. (c) Test sample (hexagon) and its connections (dashed lines). (d) Optimum-path from test sample to most strongly prototype.

defined by Eq. (7.1) as follows:

$$f_{max}(\langle s \rangle) = \begin{cases} 0 & \text{if } s \in S, \\ +\infty & \text{otherwise} \end{cases}$$

$$f_{max}(\pi_s \cdot \langle s, t \rangle) = \max\{f_{max}(\pi_s), d(s, t)\}, \tag{7.1}$$

where $f_{max}(\pi_s \cdot \langle s, t \rangle)$ is the maximum distance between adjacent samples along the path $\pi_s \cdot \langle s, t \rangle$. Thus, its training algorithm minimizes f_{max} for every sample $t \in \mathcal{Z}_1$, assigning an optimum-path $P(t)$ with a minimum cost defined by Eq. (7.2) as follows:

$$C(t) = \min_{\forall \pi_t \in (\mathcal{Z}_1, \mathcal{A})} \{f_{max}(\pi_t)\}. \tag{7.2}$$

Finally, Algorithm 7.1 describes the f_{max} minimization procedure.

Algorithm 7.1: OPF training algorithm

Input: Training set $\mathcal{Z}_1$, prototypes $\mathcal{S} \subseteq \mathcal{Z}_1$, priority queue Q,
   current cost c.
Output: Optimum-path forest P and cost map C.
for $s \in \mathcal{Z}_1$ **do**
    $C(s) \leftarrow +\infty$;
for $s \in \mathcal{S}$ **do**
    $C(s) \leftarrow 0$;
    $P(s) \leftarrow -1$;
    Insert s in Q;
while Q *is not empty* **do**
    Remove s from Q such that $C(s)$ is minimum;
    for $t \in \mathcal{Z}_1$, *such that* $t \neq s$ *and* $C(t) > C(s)$ **do**
        $c \leftarrow \max\{C(s), d(s, t)\}$;
        if $c < C(t)$ **then**
            if $C(t) \neq +\infty$ **then**
                Remove t from Q;
            $P(t) \leftarrow s$;
            $C(t) \leftarrow c$;
            Insert t in Q;

Testing step

During the testing phase, each sample t will be connected to a sample $s \in \mathcal{V}_1$, becoming part of the original graph. The algorithm's goal is to find an optimum-path $P(t)$ that connects a prototype to node t, which is achieved by evaluation the path through an optimum-cost function denoted by Eq. (7.3) as follows:

$$C(t) = \min_{\forall s \in \mathcal{Z}_1} \{\max\{C(s), d(s, t)\}\}. \tag{7.3}$$

7.2.2 Siamese networks

Siamese networks, often called twin networks, consist of a pair of neural networks that share their weights and aims at computing similarity functions. Essentially, their main objective is to identify whether a pair of data is dissimilar or not. Fig. 7.2 illustrates an example of a Siamese network architecture.

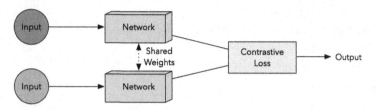

Figure 7.2 Example of a Siamese network architecture.

An interesting point lies in the fact that Siamese networks can be composed of networks like multilayer perceptrons, convolutional neural networks, and even recurrent neural networks. Such an ability enhances their applicability, being fruitful when coped with diverse applications such as handwriting recognition, automatic detection of faces, and matching queries with indexes documents.

Let $\mathcal{X}$ be the set of training data, where a single sample is represented by a pair $(\mathbf{x}, \hat{\mathbf{x}})$, such that $\mathbf{x} \in \mathcal{X}$, $\hat{\mathbf{x}} \in \mathcal{X}$ and $\mathbf{x} \neq \hat{\mathbf{x}}$. The so-called contrastive loss, denoted by L, usually conducts the Siamese network's learning process described by Eq. (7.4):

$$L = (1 - y) \cdot d^2 + y \cdot \max(0, m_g - d)^2, \tag{7.4}$$

where y is the true label (0 for dissimilar and 1 for similar) of the data pair $(\mathbf{x}, \hat{\mathbf{x}})$, d is the Euclidean distance between $\mathbf{x}$ and $\hat{\mathbf{x}}$, and m_g is the margin that defines the similarity radius. Hence, throughout the learning process, the network learns how to identify whether a pair of data is similar or not.

7.3 Methodology

This section presents the proposed approach, as well as the employed data sets and the experimental setup.

7.3.1 Proposed approach

Although optimum-path forest classifiers are implemented in supervised and unsupervised algorithms, we opted to employ its supervised version applied to classification tasks. The proposed approach aims to learn similarity functions between pairs of data and employ them as the distance measure used by the OPF classifier. Let $\mathcal{X}_1$ and $\mathcal{X}_2$ be the training and testing sets, respectively. Additionally, let S be the Siamese network and let O be the optimum-path forest classifier.

The first step is to learn a similarity function by training S over random data pairs drawn from the training set $\mathcal{X}_1$. After completing the training procedure, S can be used to compute the similarities between all pairs of data present in $\mathcal{X}_1$ and $\mathcal{X}_2$, i.e., a squared matrix with length equals to n^2, where n stands for the number of samples found in both training and testing sets. Furthermore, it is possible to use the similarity matrix throughout OPF learning step,[3] thus providing similarity values instead of calculating the distance measure between pairs of data present in $\mathcal{X}_1$ and $\mathcal{X}_2$. Finally, one can compare the output metrics obtained from the similarity-based OPF against its traditional distance-based version.

7.3.2 Data sets

We considered four data sets to evaluate the proposed approach, being three image and one text-based:

- BBC News [9]: formed by 2,225 text articles and divided into 5 categories (labels). The texts had their stop-words removed and were tokenized, stemmed, lemmatized, and preprocessed for blank spaces and lower cases. Finally, 1,024 features (most frequent words) were extracted using the term frequency-inverse document frequency;
- Caltech101 Silhouettes [18]: constituted of binary silhouettes from the Caltech 101 data set, comprising 8,671 images from 101 classes with 28×28 resolutions;
- MPEG-7 [14]: composed of 1,400 binary images with 32×32 resolutions. The images represents objects divided into 70 classes, with 20 samples per class;
- Semeion [1]: formed by 1,593 grayscale images from handwritten digits "0" – "9" written in two ways: standard (accurately) and fast (no accuracy). Afterward, pixels were binarized with a 0.5 threshold, and images were stretched into 16×16 resolutions.

7.3.3 Experimental setup

In this work, we opted to employ a Convolutional Neural Network[4] as a base architecture to construct the Siamese networks. It is a three-layered

---

[3] Note that the learning step follows the same algorithm depicted in Section 7.2.1.

[4] https://github.com/gugarosa/dualing/blob/master/dualing/models/base/cnn.py.

network using $32(5) - 64(3) - 128(1)$ convolutional units (kernel) followed by max pooling operators and 128 output units.[5] It has been trained from scratch using normalized data, the Adam [13] optimizer with a learning rate equal to 0.0001 and batch size equal to 128. Additionally, it has been trained with the contrastive loss, using an L_2 distance and the margin equal to 1. Notice that the optimum-path forest classifier does not need any parameters. To assess the influence of more robust training, we opted to consider the number of epochs and the number of training pairs as hyperparameters. Therefore, Table 7.1 describes the employed model configurations.

Table 7.1 Model   hyperparameters configuration.

Acronym	Epochs	Training Pairs
α_1	10	1,024
α_2	25	1,024
α_3	50	1,024
β_1	10	2,048
β_2	25	2,048
β_3	50	2,048
γ_1	10	4,096
γ_2	25	4,096
γ_3	50	4,096

Furthermore, to provide statistical analysis over the proposed experiments, we conducted a 2-fold cross-validation approach with 25 runnings, i.e., each data set has been equally split into training and testing sets with 25 distinct seeds, and the final metrics had their mean and standard deviation computed. Additionally, we opted to use the Wilcoxon signed-rank test [26] with a significance of 0.05 to verify statistically significant differences between the evaluated experiments. The source code used to implement this work's experiments is available at GitHub,[6] while the OP-Fython [22] package implements the optimum-path forest classifiers and the Dualing[7] package implements the Siamese Networks. Finally, the Support Vector Machines (SVM), Logistic Regressors (LR), and Decision Trees (DT) are the standard ones implemented by Scikit-Learn.[8]

---

[5] The input units vary according to the data set.
[6] https://github.com/gugarosa/opf_siamese.
[7] https://github.com/gugarosa/dualing.
[8] https://scikit-learn.org.

7.4 Experimental results

This section presents the experimental results and their analysis concerning the proposed approach.

7.4.1 BBC News

Table 7.2 describes the evaluation metrics over the BBC News testing set, where the underlined cells stand for the highest means. First, one can observe that none of the similarity-based OPF classifiers could produce comparable results to the standard ones, being roughly 55% inferior in the worst case (α_1) and 28% inferior in the best case (γ_3). Regarding the similarity-based OPF classifiers, it is possible to perceive that they struggled mainly due to the low amount of training pairs compared to the number of training examples. On the other hand, an increasing number of training epochs assisted the Siamese networks in learning more proper representations as depicted by α_3, β_3, and γ_3 models. Additionally, networks trained with more pairs, such as γ-based models, could outperform their corresponding α and β models, reinforcing that these networks may benefit more from a higher number of training pairs.

Table 7.2 Evaluation metrics over BBC News testing set.

Model	Accuracy	Precision	Recall	F1-Score
α_1	43.99 ± 1.21	43.81 ± 1.23	43.82 ± 1.23	43.72 ± 1.22
α_2	45.28 ± 1.21	45.08 ± 1.26	45.09 ± 1.23	44.97 ± 1.24
α_3	46.17 ± 1.28	45.94 ± 1.23	45.90 ± 1.19	45.80 ± 1.24
β_1	45.24 ± 1.28	45.07 ± 1.33	45.11 ± 1.30	44.98 ± 1.31
β_2	47.56 ± 1.18	47.29 ± 1.21	47.31 ± 1.23	47.19 ± 1.23
β_3	51.93 ± 2.39	51.56 ± 2.36	51.45 ± 2.39	51.39 ± 2.41
γ_1	47.83 ± 1.78	47.56 ± 1.79	47.59 ± 1.72	47.47 ± 1.78
γ_2	53.28 ± 2.13	52.85 ± 2.14	52.71 ± 2.11	52.67 ± 2.13
γ_3	69.54 ± 2.50	69.36 ± 2.55	69.04 ± 2.53	69.05 ± 2.55
DT	80.92 ± 1.71	80.87 ± 1.79	80.66 ± 1.68	80.67 ± 1.72
LR	96.63 ± 0.52	96.67 ± 0.48	96.49 ± 0.55	96.57 ± 0.52
OPF	91.03 ± 0.67	90.97 ± 0.74	90.92 ± 0.72	90.89 ± 0.72
SVM	$\underline{96.74 \pm 0.45}$	$\underline{96.75 \pm 0.44}$	$\underline{96.63 \pm 0.48}$	$\underline{96.68 \pm 0.46}$

Fig. 7.3 depicts a Wilcoxon signed-rank test heat map, where red (dark gray in print version) cells stand for dissimilar models according to the test, and yellowish cells stand for statistically equivalent architectures. In such a

figure, it is possible to observe that SVM was solely the best architecture considering the BBC News data set.

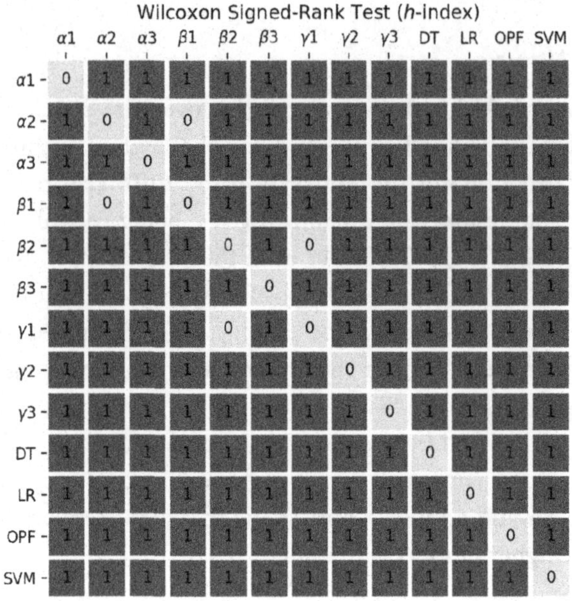

Figure 7.3 Wilcoxon signed-rank test comparison between classification models over BBC data set.

Finally, Fig. 7.4 illustrates the training loss convergence considering all similarity-based models and corroborates the hypothesis mentioned above. Every depicted curve seems to follow a convergence trend and may benefit from more training epochs, especially those represented in Fig. 7.4(c).

7.4.2 Caltech101 Silhouettes

Table 7.3 describes the evaluation metrics over the Caltech101 Silhouettes testing set. Although similarity-based OPF classifiers could not achieve the best metrics, they could produce competitive results, roughly 8% inferior to SVM.

Additionally, according to the Wilcoxon signed-rank test, α, β, and γ models have been statistically similar (Fig. 7.5). Thus it is impossible to observe a different trend regarding a specific number of training pairs and training epochs in such a data set.

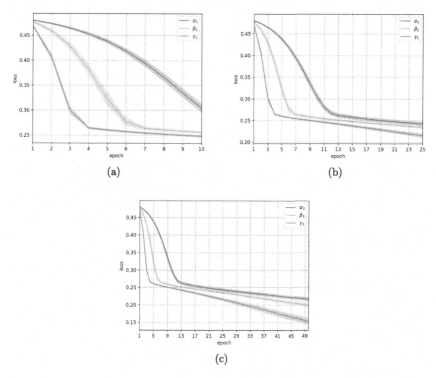

Figure 7.4 Siamese network training loss convergence over BBC data set using: (a) 10 epochs, (b) 25 epochs, and (c) 50 epochs.

Table 7.3 Evaluation metrics over Caltech101 Silhouettes testing set.

Model	Accuracy	Precision	Recall	F1-Score
α_1	55.25 ± 0.84	44.94 ± 1.16	44.41 ± 0.97	43.62 ± 0.96
α_2	55.61 ± 0.74	44.98 ± 1.11	44.55 ± 0.73	43.80 ± 0.83
α_3	55.16 ± 1.03	43.99 ± 1.28	43.60 ± 0.85	42.86 ± 1.02
β_1	55.92 ± 0.84	45.10 ± 1.05	44.96 ± 0.90	44.04 ± 0.90
β_2	55.58 ± 1.13	44.52 ± 1.49	44.33 ± 1.02	43.45 ± 1.18
β_3	55.51 ± 0.89	44.13 ± 1.15	43.95 ± 0.87	43.05 ± 0.88
γ_1	55.69 ± 0.52	44.78 ± 0.82	44.57 ± 0.41	43.74 ± 0.43
γ_2	55.86 ± 0.70	44.71 ± 1.04	44.56 ± 0.49	43.68 ± 0.62
γ_3	55.04 ± 1.15	43.78 ± 1.53	43.41 ± 1.02	42.67 ± 1.11
DT	41.30 ± 0.60	27.66 ± 0.85	27.50 ± 0.84	27.00 ± 0.76
LR	58.51 ± 0.52	49.56 ± 0.76	47.33 ± 0.65	47.23 ± 0.60
OPF	58.58 ± 0.55	50.98 ± 0.73	$\underline{48.07 \pm 0.51}$	46.91 ± 0.57
SVM	$\underline{60.67 \pm 0.63}$	$\underline{58.82 \pm 1.45}$	47.40 ± 0.79	$\underline{48.26 \pm 0.81}$

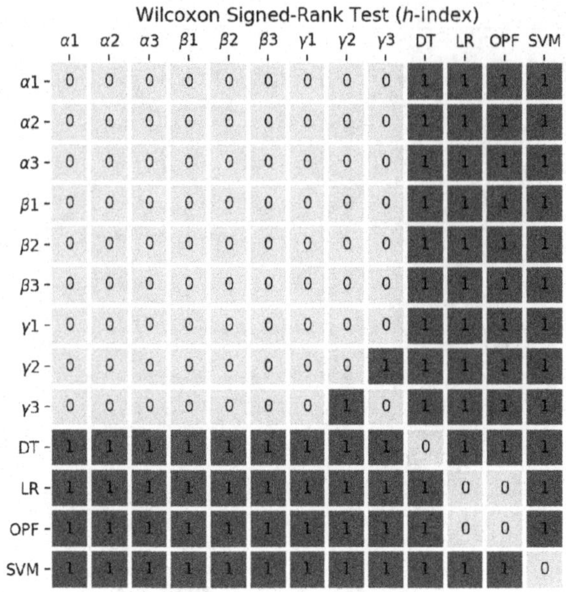

Wilcoxon Signed-Rank Test (h-index)

	α1	α2	α3	β1	β2	β3	γ1	γ2	γ3	DT	LR	OPF	SVM
α1	0	0	0	0	0	0	0	0	0	1	1	1	1
α2	0	0	0	0	0	0	0	0	0	1	1	1	1
α3	0	0	0	0	0	0	0	0	0	1	1	1	1
β1	0	0	0	0	0	0	0	0	0	1	1	1	1
β2	0	0	0	0	0	0	0	0	0	1	1	1	1
β3	0	0	0	0	0	0	0	0	0	1	1	1	1
γ1	0	0	0	0	0	0	0	0	0	1	1	1	1
γ2	0	0	0	0	0	0	0	0	1	1	1	1	1
γ3	0	0	0	0	0	0	0	1	0	1	1	1	1
DT	1	1	1	1	1	1	1	1	1	0	1	1	1
LR	1	1	1	1	1	1	1	1	1	1	0	0	1
OPF	1	1	1	1	1	1	1	1	1	1	0	0	1
SVM	1	1	1	1	1	1	1	1	1	1	1	1	0

Figure 7.5 Wilcoxon signed-rank test comparison between classification models over Caltech101 Silhouettes data set.

One interesting remark lies in Fig. 7.6, where the loss convergence curves have been smoother than BBC-based ones and strengthen Siamese networks' ability to be improved when trained with additional training pairs and epochs.

7.4.3 MPEG-7

Table 7.4 exhibits the evaluation metrics over the MPEG-7 testing set. As such data set has a low number of training examples, every similarity-based OPF could produce a competitive result and even surpass the traditional classifiers in some cases, such as β_2, γ_1, γ_2, and γ_3. The interesting point is that models with 25 training epochs could achieve better evaluation metrics than models with 50 training epochs in two out of three cases.

On the other hand, an increased number of training pairs enabled γ_2 to achieve the best results in this particular data set, outperforming every other similarity-based OPF, as well as traditional OPF, DT, LR, and SVM. Additionally, according to the Wilcoxon signed-rank test depicted by Fig. 7.7, γ_2 has not been statistically similar to any other experiment, thus allowing us to conclude that it was indeed the best model. Finally, by glancing at Fig. 7.8, it is possible to observe that the loss convergence curves followed

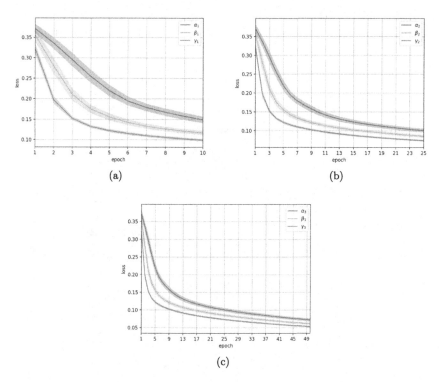

Figure 7.6 Siamese network training loss convergence over Caltech101 Silhouettes data set using: (a) 10 epochs, (b) 25 epochs, and (c) 50 epochs.

Table 7.4 Evaluation metrics over MPEG-7 testing set.

Model	Accuracy	Precision	Recall	F1-Score
α_1	75.07 ± 1.81	76.02 ± 1.88	75.86 ± 1.76	74.27 ± 1.78
α_2	77.76 ± 1.87	78.61 ± 1.79	78.60 ± 1.87	77.23 ± 1.81
α_3	78.18 ± 2.03	79.37 ± 1.90	79.01 ± 1.84	77.73 ± 1.90
β_1	77.92 ± 1.65	78.71 ± 1.35	78.73 ± 1.40	77.32 ± 1.41
β_2	79.27 ± 1.84	80.29 ± 1.69	80.18 ± 1.54	78.87 ± 1.68
β_3	78.83 ± 1.63	80.24 ± 1.38	79.71 ± 1.38	78.65 ± 1.45
γ_1	79.53 ± 1.42	80.42 ± 1.47	80.27 ± 1.32	79.08 ± 1.40
γ_2	$\underline{80.49 \pm 1.69}$	82.00 ± 1.59	$\underline{81.27 \pm 1.63}$	$\underline{80.28 \pm 1.69}$
γ_3	79.60 ± 1.83	81.45 ± 1.76	80.30 ± 1.70	79.67 ± 1.73
DT	54.74 ± 2.03	55.12 ± 2.11	55.87 ± 1.89	53.17 ± 1.97
LR	78.43 ± 1.70	79.35 ± 1.58	79.20 ± 1.27	77.34 ± 1.53
OPF	78.95 ± 1.59	81.43 ± 1.32	79.47 ± 1.20	77.46 ± 1.43
SVM	74.18 ± 1.78	79.50 ± 2.06	76.27 ± 1.56	74.15 ± 1.71

the same patterns depicted before, which allows us to draw some insights related to whether these networks could still benefit from more training pairs and training epochs.

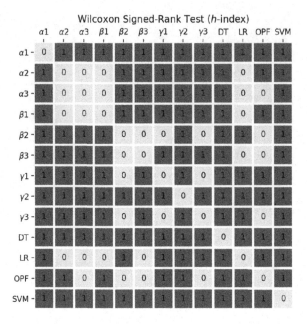

Figure 7.7 Wilcoxon signed-rank test comparison between classification models over MPEG-7 data set.

7.4.4 Semeion

Table 7.5 describes the evaluation metrics over the Semeion testing set. On such a data set, it is clear that similarity-based models with a high number of training epochs could outperform their counterparts, achieving the highest evaluation metrics. Additionally, an increased number of training pairs also benefited such models, allowing γ_3 to achieve the best evaluation metrics when compared across all experiments. Furthermore, three similarity-based models (β_3, γ_2 and γ_3) outperformed the best non-similarity classifier (SVM), while two out of those three (β_3 and γ_3) were statistically equivalent according to the Wilcoxon signed-rank test, depicted by Fig. 7.9.

Fig. 7.10 illustrates the training loss convergence between similarity-based models over the Semeion data set. Such a figure has the same behavior as the previous ones, where γ-based models achieved the lowest losses, and

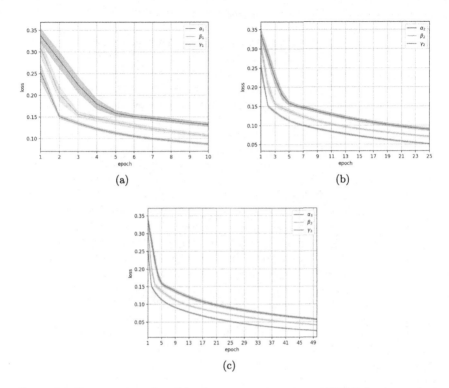

(a)

(b)

(c)

Figure 7.8 Siamese network training loss convergence over MPEG-7 data set using: (a) 10 epochs, (b) 25 epochs, and (c) 50 epochs.

Table 7.5 Evaluation metrics over Semeion testing set.

Model	Accuracy	Precision	Recall	F1-Score
α_1	84.89 ± 2.02	85.10 ± 2.04	84.99 ± 1.99	84.83 ± 2.03
α_2	89.59 ± 1.59	89.79 ± 1.58	89.66 ± 1.53	89.58 ± 1.56
α_3	93.12 ± 1.10	93.22 ± 1.04	93.17 ± 1.07	93.11 ± 1.07
β_1	89.33 ± 1.34	89.54 ± 1.30	89.41 ± 1.27	89.33 ± 1.29
β_2	93.85 ± 0.99	93.92 ± 0.94	93.89 ± 0.99	93.84 ± 0.97
β_3	95.09 ± 0.64	95.16 ± 0.61	95.13 ± 0.64	95.09 ± 0.64
γ_1	92.62 ± 0.94	92.73 ± 0.94	92.69 ± 0.93	92.62 ± 0.94
γ_2	95.19 ± 0.75	95.26 ± 0.75	95.20 ± 0.74	95.18 ± 0.76
γ_3	95.51 ± 0.85	95.59 ± 0.84	95.53 ± 0.87	95.51 ± 0.86
DT	70.55 ± 1.53	70.59 ± 1.65	70.55 ± 1.60	70.29 ± 1.61
LR	91.28 ± 1.06	91.42 ± 0.99	91.30 ± 1.04	91.26 ± 1.03
OPF	87.79 ± 1.01	88.44 ± 0.94	87.72 ± 0.92	87.60 ± 0.99
SVM	94.09 ± 0.90	94.22 ± 0.85	94.13 ± 0.90	94.10 ± 0.89

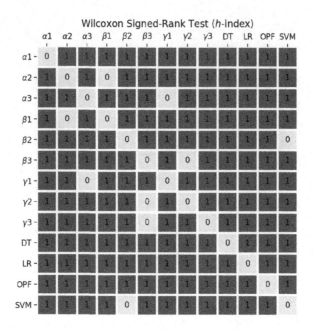

Figure 7.9 Wilcoxon signed-rank test comparison between classification models over Semeion data set.

every curve could benefit from more training epochs. Additionally, it is possible to observe that models trained with 10 epochs had a higher standard deviation (the shaded area around the curve), leading to a conclusion that such training was unstable across the evaluated runnings.

7.5 Conclusion

This work introduced a similarity-based measure to optimum-path forest classifiers' training process, replacing their standard distance-based measures. The similarity measure was estimated by pairs of Siamese networks and then used across the data set's samples before OPF's graph creation. Additionally, such a work compared the proposed approach against state-of-the-art classifiers, such as decision tree, logistic regression, support vector machine, and the standard optimum-path forest.

In two out of four data sets (MPEG-7 and Semeion), similarity-based OPF classifiers outperformed the baseline classifiers, achieving superior results over the evaluated metrics according to the Wilcoxon signed-rank test with 5% significance. Nevertheless, in the remaining data sets (BBC News

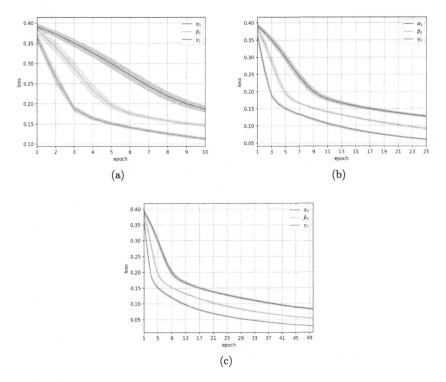

(a)   (b)

(c)

Figure 7.10 Siamese network training loss convergence over Semeion data set using: (a) 10 epochs, (b) 25 epochs, and (c) 50 epochs.

and Caltech101 Silhouettes), similarity-based models could not produce satisfactory results and underperformed compared to the state-of-the-art classifiers. One possible problem of such data sets lies in their increased number of available samples, requiring a higher number of training pairs and more training epochs to establish a proper convergence. Additionally, similarity-based models obtained higher standard deviations than the baseline classifiers, allowing us to remark that their training was unstable across the evaluated runnings.

Regarding future works, we aim to expand the evaluated experiments with more training epochs and training pairs and employ the proposed approach in additional data sets. Moreover, we believe that specific Siamese network architectures might achieve more satisfying results according to the evaluated tasks, i.e., deeper CNN-based models when working with image data sets and RNN-based models when working with text data sets.

References

[1] Semeion handwritten digit data set, Tech. Rep., Semeion Research Center of Sciences of Communication, via Sersale 117, 00128 Rome, Italy, Tattile Via Gaetano Donizetti 1-3-5, 25030 Mairano (Brescia), Italy, 2008.

[2] S.V. Albrecht, P. Stone, Autonomous agents modelling other agents: a comprehensive survey and open problems, Artificial Intelligence 258 (2018) 66–95.

[3] J. Bromley, I. Guyon, Y. LeCun, E. Säckinger, R. Shah, Signature verification using a "Siamese" time delay neural network, in: Advances in Neural Information Processing Systems, 1994, pp. 737–744.

[4] C.C. Chang, C.J. Lin, Libsvm: a library for support vector machines, ACM Transactions on Intelligent Systems and Technology 2 (3) (2011) 1–27.

[5] H. Chen, C. Wu, B. Du, L. Zhang, Deep Siamese multi-scale convolutional network for change detection in multi-temporal vhr images, in: 2019 10th International Workshop on the Analysis of Multitemporal Remote Sensing Images (MultiTemp), 2019, pp. 1–4.

[6] S.S. Chouhan, A. Kaul, U.P. Singh, Soft computing approaches for image segmentation: a survey, Multimedia Tools and Applications 77 (21) (2018) 28483–28537.

[7] D.C. Cireşan, U. Meier, L.M. Gambardella, J. Schmidhuber, Deep, big, simple neural nets for handwritten digit recognition, Neural Computation 22 (12) (2010) 3207–3220.

[8] P. Druzhkov, V. Kustikova, A survey of deep learning methods and software tools for image classification and object detection, Pattern Recognition and Image Analysis 26 (1) (2016) 9–15.

[9] D. Greene, P. Cunningham, Practical solutions to the problem of diagonal dominance in kernel document clustering, in: Proc. 23rd International Conference on Machine Learning (ICML'06), ACM Press, 2006, pp. 377–384.

[10] R. Hadsell, S. Chopra, Y. LeCun, Dimensionality reduction by learning an invariant mapping, in: 2006 IEEE Computer Society Conference on Computer Vision and Pattern Recognition (CVPR'06), Vol. 2, IEEE, 2006, pp. 1735–1742.

[11] D.W. Hosmer Jr, S. Lemeshow, R.X. Sturdivant, Applied Logistic Regression, Vol. 398, John Wiley & Sons, 2013.

[12] S. Jindal, G. Gupta, M. Yadav, M. Sharma, L. Vig, Siamese networks for chromosome classification, in: Proceedings of the IEEE International Conference on Computer Vision (ICCV) Workshops, Oct 2017.

[13] D.P. Kingma, J. Ba, Adam: a method for stochastic optimization, arXiv preprint, arXiv: 1412.6980, 2014.

[14] L.J. Latecki, R. Lakamper, Shape similarity measure based on correspondence of visual parts, IEEE Transactions on Pattern Analysis and Machine Intelligence 22 (10) (2000) 1185–1190.

[15] Y. Li, H. Zhang, X. Xue, Y. Jiang, Q. Shen, Deep learning for remote sensing image classification: a survey, Wiley Interdisciplinary Reviews: Data Mining and Knowledge Discovery 8 (6) (2018) e1264.

[16] G. Litjens, T. Kooi, B.E. Bejnordi, A.A.A. Setio, F. Ciompi, M. Ghafoorian, J.A. Van Der Laak, B. Van Ginneken, C.I. Sánchez, A survey on deep learning in medical image analysis, Medical Image Analysis 42 (2017) 60–88.

[17] X. Liu, Y. Zhou, J. Zhao, R. Yao, B. Liu, Y. Zheng, Siamese convolutional neural networks for remote sensing scene classification, IEEE Geoscience and Remote Sensing Letters 16 (8) (2019) 1200–1204.

[18] B. Marlin, K. Swersky, B. Chen, N. Freitas, Inductive principles for restricted Boltzmann machine learning, in: Proceedings of the Thirteenth International Conference on Artificial Intelligence and Statistics, 2010, pp. 509–516.

[19] I. Melekhov, J. Kannala, E. Rahtu, Siamese network features for image matching, in: 2016 23rd International Conference on Pattern Recognition (ICPR), 2016,
pp. 378–383.

[20] J.P. Papa, A.X. Falcão, V.H.C. Albuquerque, J.M.R.S. Tavares, Efficient supervised
optimum-path forest classification for large datasets, Pattern Recognition 45 (1) (2012)
512–520.

[21] J.P. Papa, A.X. Falcão, C.T.N. Suzuki, Supervised pattern classification based on
optimum-path forest, International Journal of Imaging Systems and Technology 19
(2009) 120–131.

[22] G.H. de Rosa, J.P. Papa, A.X. Falcão, Opfython: A Python-Inspired Optimum-Path
Forest Classifier, 2020.

[23] S.R. Safavian, D. Landgrebe, A survey of decision tree classifier methodology, IEEE
Transactions on Systems, Man and Cybernetics 21 (3) (1991) 660–674.

[24] C. Sukanya, R. Gokul, V. Paul, A survey on object recognition methods, International
Journal of Science, Engineering and Computer Technology 6 (1) (2016) 48.

[25] D. Sun, Z. Wu, Y. Wang, Q. Lv, B. Hu, Risk prediction for imbalanced data in cyber
security: a Siamese network-based deep learning classification framework, in: 2019
International Joint Conference on Neural Networks (IJCNN), 2019, pp. 1–8.

[26] F. Wilcoxon, Individual comparisons by ranking methods, Biometrics Bulletin 1 (6)
(1945) 80–83.

[27] Y. Zhan, K. Fu, M. Yan, X. Sun, H. Wang, X. Qiu, Change detection based on
deep Siamese convolutional network for optical aerial images, IEEE Geoscience and
Remote Sensing Letters 14 (10) (2017) 1845–1849.

CHAPTER 8

An iterative optimum-path forest framework for clustering

David Aparco-Cardenas, Pedro Jussieu de Rezende, and
Alexandre Xavier Falcão
Institute of Computing, University of Campinas (UNICAMP), Campinas, São Paulo, Brazil

8.1 Introduction

A vast amount of data is generated by a wide range of sources in the current digital age. This data needs to be processed, analyzed, and transformed into valuable insights to support decision-making tasks [31]. Due to its extensive availability, intensive computing resources and sophisticated techniques are required to efficiently and effectively extract useful information. Conventionally, these techniques are categorized into supervised, unsupervised, and semisupervised methods based on their degree of dependency on labeled data. Unsupervised methods do not require labeled samples and play a key role in mining and generating information from data sets.

Clustering is a fundamental unsupervised learning procedure that seeks to identify the intrinsic grouping in a set of unlabeled data based on some similarity measure. It has become, throughout the years, a ubiquitous pattern recognition technique due to its ability to find hidden patterns in the data without using any prior information. Clustering has a variety of applications in a wide range of domains, including plant and animal ecology, sequence analysis, human genetic clustering, medical imaging, market research, social network analysis, image segmentation, evolutionary algorithms, crime analysis, petroleum geology, physical geography, and so forth [16].

The goal of clustering is to partition a set of unlabeled objects into disjoint subsets (clusters), such that those falling within the same subset are more closely related (similar) to each other than to those falling in distinct subsets. Clusters can be found in a variety of shapes, sizes, and densities (see Fig. 8.1). Thus a relevant research topic is the design of practical clustering algorithms aiming to maximize intra-subset similarity and inter-subset dissimilarity according to a similarity metric. A great diversity of cluster-

Optimum-Path Forest
https://doi.org/10.1016/B978-0-12-822688-9.00016-5
175

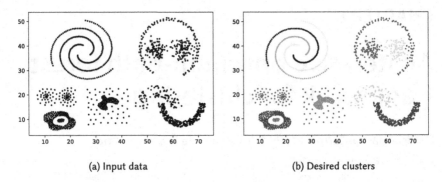

(a) Input data   (b) Desired clusters

Figure 8.1 Diversity of clusters. The clusters in (a) (indicated by distinct colors in (b)) differ in shape, size, and density. Adapted from [27].

ing algorithms addressing this problem through different approaches can be found in the literature [39,47]. Nevertheless, no single algorithm can handle all kinds of cluster shapes and structures [23].

Furthermore, only a few clustering algorithms explore optimum connectivity between samples, which is relevant for a variety of problems [38, 42,43]. These algorithms can be comprehensively categorized into *hierarchical* and *partitional* based on their solving strategies. Hierarchical clustering algorithms attempt to recursively find nested clusters representing the clustering result as *dendrograms* or binary trees. In contrast, partitional algorithms aim to simultaneously discover groups by decomposing the data set into disjoint subsets [27].

The k-means algorithm, a partitional clustering solution, stands out as one of the most commonly used algorithms for clustering in the literature, mainly because of its simplicity of implementation and intuitiveness. It is a numerical, nondeterministic, and iterative method that approximates each cluster's center by representing the objects as data points in the Euclidean space and measuring the dissimilarity between two points by their Euclidean distance [27]. It (*i*) starts with an initial set of seed samples from a given data set, (*ii*) partitions the data set by assigning each remaining sample to the group of its most similar (closest) seed and (*iii*) recomputes the seed set so that each new seed is the centroid of its group, repeating steps (*ii*) and (*iii*) until some convergence criterion is met. The objective of k-means is to minimize the sum of squared distances between every point and its nearest centroid, also known as *sum-of-squared-errors* (SSE). However, some variants of k-means aim to minimize different objective functions. Despite being widely used, k-means presents some shortcomings [33], such as: (*i*) the clustering result depends heavily on the initial centers being prone to local optimum convergence, (*ii*) it can only identify spherical-shaped clusters, and (*iii*) it scales poorly for large data sets. Several extensions have been proposed to overcome these limitations [19,36,42], addressing, however, only a subset of these issues.

Recently, a graph-based iterative framework called *Iterative Spanning Forest* (ISF) [44] was proposed for superpixel segmentation. An ISF-based solution entails the selection of four fundamental components: (*i*) a seed set sampling strategy, (*ii*) a connectivity function, (*iii*) an adjacency relation, and (*iv*) a seed set recomputation scheme. It consists of a sequence of *Image Foresting Transforms* (IFTs) [21] from seed sets spawned by (*iv*). By selecting those components, the user can design different ISF-based methods suitable for particular applications. The ISF framework exploits optimum connectivity and has proven to be effective at creating superpixel segmentation methods that are either competitive or superior to several other state-of-the-art solutions [8,32]. Another recent work is the *Dynamic IFT* (DynIFT) [10], an IFT-based method for object segmentation, which dynamically estimates the arc weights of the image graph while extracting object information as the trees evolve from the seed set. This approach has been shown to significantly improve interactive object segmentation in comparison to several other graph-based counterparts.

On the other hand, a graph-based clustering algorithm called *Iterated Watersheds* (IW) [43], hereafter referred to as IW, was introduced as an extension of *k*-means, introducing the notion of optimum connectivity between a set of prototypes and the remaining samples of a data set. As with ISF, it also works through multiple executions of *Optimum-Path Forests* (OPFs) [34] (*i.e.*, IFT generalized to the feature space) with graph topology restrictions following an iterative procedure until convergence is reached. The initial set of prototypes is chosen randomly from the data set, and a prototype recomputation procedure is carried out at the end of each OPF execution. The IW algorithm, from its design, can be regarded as an ISF-based method generalized to the feature space.

Accordingly, the motivation for creating a graph-based clustering framework based on an iterative approach stems from the following considerations. In [43], the study of IW is restricted to the additive connectivity function (f_{sum}) and the employment of the general OPF algorithm as the main component of the iterative solution. Thus the use of both a different connectivity function (f_{max}) and the OPF algorithm with dynamic arc-weight estimation under an iterative clustering scheme remains unexplored. Therefore, we believe that its generalization to encompass a broader set of configurations is a plausible research direction. Moreover, its applicability was narrowed to graphs whose adjacency relations are either already defined or intuitively derived from the nature of the problem (e.g., image segmentation). Hence, defining a graph topology for data sets with no evident relationship among the samples becomes challenging. Furthermore, since the clustering result of seed-based algorithms (e.g., k-means) relies heavily on the choice of the initial seeds, the formulation of a strategy for the selection of the initial set of prototypes is necessary.

In this context, this work aims to explore graph-based clustering solutions through the proposal of a novel graph-based iterative clustering framework based on a sequence of OPFs executions on a graph derived from the data set. The data set is interpreted as a graph, whose nodes are the samples, and arcs are defined by some *adjacency relation* between samples. A *connectivity function* stipulates a value to any path in the graph, and the OPF algorithm partitions the graph into optimum-path trees (clusters) rooted at a given set of prototypes. Thus, different graph-based clustering algorithms that exploit optimum connectivity can be devised by the combination of different choices of adjacency relations and connectivity functions. Henceforth, we call this framework *Iterative Optimum-Path Forest* (IOPF).

Usually, OPF-based clustering algorithms may find groups of densely connected samples and partition a graph into optimum-path trees (clusters) rooted at the maxima of a probability density function [38]. In IOPF, however, the number of desired clusters is an input parameter, and multiple executions of the OPF algorithm are often required to improve the initial set of prototypes. Applications of the OPF algorithm to supervised [34], unsupervised [38], and semisupervised learning [6] are well known as extensions of the IFT algorithm from the image domain to the feature space. Therefore we expect the IOPF framework can be explored beyond clustering applications in the future.

The first objective of this work is to formally present the IOPF framework, which can be regarded as a generalization of the ISF framework from the image domain to the feature space. IOPF, through the different selection of its components, can create a variety of clustering solutions by exploiting optimum connectivity between a set of prototypes and the remaining samples of the data set.

Once the IOPF framework has been established and explained, our second objective is to study and analyze the applications of IOPF-based solutions under different graph topologies while showcasing its flexibility, extensibility, and applicability to a wide variety of problems. Furthermore, we plan to explore different approaches toward defining the graph topology based on the context of the problem. For instance, road networks or image processing problems offer enough information about the relationship between the samples in the data set to build a graph. In contrast, generic data sets do not present an intuitive way to identify the relationships between samples, requiring the introduction of strategies to create a suitable graph representation.

Furthermore, we also aim to analyze the effect of using OPF with dynamic arc-weight estimation under an unsupervised iterative scheme. Previous works [9,10] have shown the effectiveness of using IFT with dynamic arc-weight estimation in superpixel and interactive object segmentation. However, the generalization of this strategy to the feature space is still unaddressed.

The remainder of this work is organized as follows. Section 8.2 reviews different graph-based clustering algorithms proposed in the literature, including those that take advantage of OPF to perform clustering while exploiting optimum connectivity. Section 8.3 introduces the IOPF framework describing its constituent components and its application in the image domain. Section 8.4 validates our framework through a series of experiments involving different graph-based clustering applications.

8.2 Related work

Graph-based clustering algorithms use the concepts and properties of graph theory, such that the clustering problem can be described as a graph partition problem. The nodes of a weighted graph represent the data set samples in the feature space, while arcs are built through spatial proximity reflecting a potential relationship between each pair of samples.

Graph-based methods can be applied in both hierarchical and partitional clustering, for instance, both single linkage and complete linkage clustering can be described as a graph problem equivalent to seeking maximally connected subgraphs (components) and maximally complete subgraphs (cliques), respectively [28]. *Chameleon* [30] is an agglomerative hierarchical clustering algorithm based on the k-nearest neighbor (k-NN) graph. It starts by partitioning the k-NN graph into a set of subclusters with the minimal edge cut. Next, the characteristics of potential clusters are explored through the computation of relative interconnectivity and relative closeness. Then such small subsets are merged, ending up with the final graph partition.

In the context of partitional clustering, Zhan [48] proposed a graph-based clustering algorithm consisting of identifying and discarding inconsistent edges in the *minimum spanning tree* (MST) from an input weighted graph to partition it into compact subgraphs. Hartuv and Shamir [25] presented *Highly Connected Subgraphs* (HCS) where "highly connected" is equivalent to say that the connectivity (i.e., the minimum number of edges to remove to disconnect the graph) of a subgraph is at least half as great as the number of vertices. HCS determines these subgraphs recursively using the minimum cut approach. CLICK [41] is another algorithm that can be regarded as an adaptation of the HCS algorithm on weighted similarity graphs. The graph edges are weighted using a probability approach, and clusters are formed based on the computation of the minimum-weight cut.

Spectral clustering methods constitute another strategy, which may be divided into three steps: (*i*) create a weighted graph, with samples as nodes and arcs between adjacent samples, (*ii*) compute the first k eigenvectors of its Laplacian matrix to define a feature vector for each sample in the $\mathbb{R}^k$ space, and (*iii*) execute the k-means algorithm in the $\mathbb{R}^k$ space to identify and label the groups [13]. A more detailed list of graph-based clustering algorithms may be found in the works by Aggarwal [4] and Schaeffer [40].

All graph-based clustering algorithms above do not exploit optimum connectivity between samples and a set of prototypes for cluster definition. In this context, several OPF-based clustering algorithms have been introduced to bridge this gap under different approaches. The OPF-based clustering solutions can be broadly categorized into density-based and centroid-based algorithms. Density-based algorithms depend on the computation of a *probability density function* (pdf), while centroid-based algorithms aim to improve an initial set of prototypes through an iterative scheme.

Rocha et al. [38] introduced a first clustering method based on optimum connectivity—the maxima of a pdf compete among themselves to conquer the remaining samples of the data set, and each maximum (dome of the pdf) defines a cluster as an optimum-path tree rooted on it. The pdf is estimated from a k-nearest neighbor (k-NN) graph, and the choice of k is attained by finding the solution that minimizes a normalized graph-cut measure. This algorithm relies on the pdf estimation for a suitable choice of an interval $[k_{min}, k_{max}]$ in which the best value of k must be found; however, the pdf estimation may become computationally prohibitive for large data sets. Moreover, it does not provide user control determining the number of desired clusters. The selection of the best value of k within an interval $[k_{min}, k_{max}]$ is usually carried out through exhaustive search, which may become computationally intractable for data sets with millions of samples. Costa et al. [15] propose nature-inspired optimization techniques to speed up the selection of k for the pdf estimation with applications to intrusion detection for computer networks.

Cappabianco et al. [11] extended the OPF-based clustering approach for large data sets by subsampling training samples, generating candidate solutions, and selecting the most plausible one. The authors demonstrated the advantages of the method for MR-brain tissue segmentation.

Montero and Falcão [17] proposed a two-level divide-and-conquer clustering approach based on density-based OPF clustering. This algorithm is well suited to handle large data sets. First, the data set is divided into a reasonable number of disjoint blocks. Next, OPF-based clustering is used to cluster the samples in each block, such that each block ends with a set of prototypes that summarize the block's information. These prototypes are then joined together to create a new data set in which OPF-based clustering is executed once again, obtaining a good approximation of the original data set's underlying partition. Lastly, label propagation occurs in a cascade manner, from prototypes to the remaining elements in each block.

Chen et al. [12] presented an improved version of density-based OPF-based clustering for segmentation of remote sensing images. It works on the principle that cluster centers display high local densities, while samples surrounding centers usually exhibit relatively low local densities. In addition, cluster centers are often located far away from samples with higher local densities. Following this line of thought, the probability density function of OPF-based clustering is modified for each sample in the data set to include the distance to samples with higher densities.

Afonso et al. [2] introduced a multilayered OPF-based clustering algorithm inspired by hierarchical clustering. This algorithm, called *Deep Optimum-Path Forest* (Deep OPF), builds a model comprised of a fixed number of stacked layers, such that the last layer contains the desired number of clusters. Each layer of the model partitions the input data set, consisting of the prototypes obtained from the previous layer's clustering, into an optimum-path forest using density-based OPF-based clustering. This procedure is repeated until the last layer is reached. Recently, this algorithm was used in [3] to design visual dictionaries for the automatic identification of Parkinson's disease.

Soor et al. [43] proposed *Iterated Watersheds* (IW), a graph-based clustering algorithm based on iterative applications of watershed transforms in a feature space. This algorithm is a modified version of k-means with connectivity constraints, which turns out to be a particular configuration of the IOPF framework proposed herein.

8.3 The iterative optimum-path forest framework

An IOPF-based method consists of four steps: (*i*) sampling of an initial seed set S, (*ii*) graph partition by OPF from S in a graph derived from the data set, (*iii*) recomputation of S based on the previous graph partition, and after multiple executions of steps (*ii*) and (*iii*), (*iv*) selection of the forest with the lowest total path-cost across all iterations.

Let Z be a data set such that for every sample $s \in Z$ there is a feature vector $v(s) \in \mathbb{R}^n$. For a given adjacency relation $A \subseteq Z \times Z$, the pair $G = (Z, A)$ defines a graph. The adjacency relation A can be defined in different ways, based on the definition of the problem. In some cases, the adjacency relation of the graph is given beforehand, whereas in some other cases it must be built from scratch. For instance, if Z is the set of pixels $s = (x_s, y_s)$ in the bidimensional domain of an image, A may be defined as $A = \{(s, t) \in Z \times Z \mid 1 \leq \|(x_t, y_t) - (x_s, y_s)\| \leq r\|\}$. In this regard, the most notable adjacency relations on this domain are A_1 and $A_{\sqrt{2}}$, referred to 4- and 8-neighborhood, respectively. As r increases, the local image feature space is explored with less spatial constraint. On the other hand, for arbitrary data sets, we may define A as follows:

(1) $A = \{(s, t) \in Z \times Z \mid s, t \in Z$ and $s \neq t\}$, so that G represents a complete graph; or

(2) $A = \{(s, t) \in Z \times Z \mid v(t)$ is a k-nearest neighbor of $v(s)\}$, for a fixed k.

However, in (2), it is essential to make sure that all nodes in Z are reachable from any seed in the seed set S. Therefore, two conditions should be met: (*i*) if $(s, t) \in A$, then $(t, s) \in A$, and (*ii*) G must be a single component.

A *simple path* with terminus t is a sequence of samples $\pi_t = \langle s_1, s_2, \ldots, s_n = t \rangle$, $(s_i, s_{i+1}) \in A$, $i \in \{1, 2, \ldots, n - 1\}$, whereas $\pi_t = \langle t \rangle$ is called a *trivial path*. We consider two types of connectivity functions, f_{max} and f_{sum}, with the same rule f_*, $* \in \{max, sum\}$, for trivial paths:

$$f_*(\langle t \rangle)) = \begin{cases} 0 & \text{if } t \in S \subset Z \\ +\infty & \text{otherwise} \end{cases}$$

$$f_{max}(\pi_s \cdot \langle s, t \rangle) = \max\{f_{max}(\pi_s), w(s, t)\} \tag{8.1}$$

$$f_{\text{sum}}(\pi_s \cdot \langle s, t \rangle) = f_{\text{sum}}(\pi_s) + w(s, t), \tag{8.2}$$

where $w(s, t)$ is an arc-weight of $\langle s, t \rangle$ and $\pi_s \cdot \langle s, t \rangle$ is the concatenation of π_s and $\langle s, t \rangle$, with the two instances of s merged into one. The OPF algorithm minimizes a path-cost map $C(t) = \min_{\forall \pi_t \in \Pi_t} \{ f_*(\pi_t) \}$, where Π_t is the set of all possible paths rooted at $\mathcal{S}$ with terminus t, while it outputs an *optimum-path forest* P; *i.e.*, an acyclic map that assigns to each $t \in \mathcal{Z}$ either its predecessor $P(t) \in \mathcal{Z}$ in the optimum path π_t^* rooted at $\mathcal{S}$ or a distinct marker *nil* if t is a *root* of the map (*i.e.*, $t \in \mathcal{S}$). Thus, each seed $t \in \mathcal{S}$ defines an optimum-path tree $\mathcal{T}_t$ (*i.e.*, cluster) in P, and may also propagate its corresponding label $L(t) \in \{1, 2, \ldots, k\}$ to its most strongly connected samples in $\mathcal{T}_t$.

An IOPF-based solution aims to estimate the graph partition that minimizes the total path-cost given by the sum of path costs between samples and their most strongly connected seeds in G. The minimization of this objective function is addressed following an iterative approach consisting in, given a fixed number of clusters k, partitioning the graph G into k optimum-path trees by multiple OPF executions from enhanced sets of seeds. Each OPF execution will output a triplet (L, C, P) consisting of a label map L, a cost map C, and a predecessor map P, leading to the computation of the total path-cost given by $\sum_{\forall s \in \mathcal{Z}} C(s)$. The set of enhanced seeds is computed, selecting the samples closest to each optimum-path tree's mean feature vector. The iterative procedure is repeated until either seed set convergence is achieved or a fixed maximum number of iterations is exhausted. Fig. 8.2 depicts the pipeline of the IOPF framework where initial seeds are selected randomly, and seed convergence is achieved at the fourth iteration. In this example, the third iteration minimizes $\sum_{\forall s \in \mathcal{Z}} C(s)$, and hence it is returned as the final clustering.

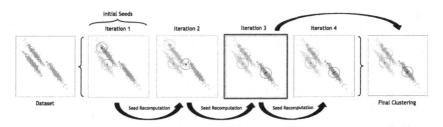

Figure 8.2 IOPF pipeline. Initial seeds are selected randomly and seeds recomputed at the end of each single OPF execution. In the example, seed convergence is attained at the fourth iteration. Lastly, the partition that minimizes $\sum_{\forall s \in \mathcal{Z}} C(s)$ across all iterations is returned as the final clustering.

8.3.1 Seed set selection

The performance of seed-based algorithms, like k-means, is susceptible to the choice of the initial seed set, given that these techniques rely on a local optimization approach. Thus, the initial seed set selection represents a critical element in the framework design. In this work, we present two strategies to address this problem.

Algorithm 8.1: Seed set selection algorithm for f_{sum}

Input : Graph $G = (\mathcal{Z}, \mathcal{A})$, number of seeds $k \geq 1$, and estimated percentage of outliers $0 < h < 1$

Output : Seed set $\mathcal{S}$

Auxiliar: Priority queue $\mathcal{Q} = \emptyset$, maps C and P, and variables *tmp* and *first-time*

1 $\mathcal{S} \leftarrow$ random element from $\mathcal{Z}$, *first-time* $\leftarrow$ **true**
2 **while** $|\mathcal{S}| < k$ **do**
3   **foreach** $s \in \mathcal{Z}$ **do**
4          $C(s) \leftarrow +\infty, P(s) \leftarrow nil$
5   **if** $s \in \mathcal{S}$ **then**
6 | $C(s) \leftarrow 0$
7   Insert s in $\mathcal{Q}$
8   **while** $\mathcal{Q} \neq \emptyset$ **do**
9   Remove s from $\mathcal{Q}$, such that $s = \text{argmin}_{t \in \mathcal{Q}}\{C(t)\}$
10   **if** $h \times |\mathcal{Z}| \geq |\mathcal{Q}|$ **then**
11   **if** *first-time* **then**
12 | $\mathcal{S} \leftarrow \{s\}$, first-time $\leftarrow$ **false**
13   **else**
14 | $\mathcal{S} \leftarrow \mathcal{S} \cup \{s\}$
15           $\mathcal{Q} \leftarrow \emptyset$ and **break**
16   **foreach** $(s, t) \in \mathcal{A} \mid q \in \mathcal{Q}$ **do**
17           $w(s, t) = \|v(t) - v(s)\|$
18           $tmp \leftarrow C(s) + w(s, t)$
19   **if** $tmp < C(t)$ **then**
20 | $C(t) \leftarrow tmp, P(t) \leftarrow s$
21 **return** $\mathcal{S}$

For a fixed number of groups, k, the IOPF framework starts off by selecting a set of samples $\mathcal{S} \subset \mathcal{Z}$, such that $|\mathcal{S}| = k$. The first strategy selects the elements of $\mathcal{S}$ randomly. This initialization technique provides a different result for each run, therefore improving results through repetition (restarting) of the algorithm.

As a second strategy, we propose an initial seed set sampling that builds $\mathcal{S}$, with one seed per object, by searching the least strongly connected samples (after discarding outliers) by a sequence of OPF executions. Algorithm 8.1 outlines such an iterative procedure.

Given a graph $G = (\mathcal{Z}, \mathcal{A})$, number of seeds $k \geq 1$, an estimated percentage of outliers $0 < h < 1$, and the sum path-cost function (f_{sum}). The algorithm starts in Line 1 with an initial seed set $\mathcal{S}$ consisting of an arbitrary node $s \in \mathcal{Z}$, which is discarded after the first OPF execution to obtain more statistically consistent seeds. Thus, only the seeds acquired at the end of each OPF execution are considered towards establishing the initial seed set $\mathcal{S}$. During each iteration in lines 2–20, the OPF execution is interrupted after $(1 - h) \times |\mathcal{Z}|$ nodes have been processed (*i.e.*, nodes removed from priority queue $\mathcal{Q}$) in lines 10–15. Next, in line 14, the last node s removed from $\mathcal{Q}$ is selected as the next seed and inserted into $\mathcal{S}$. This procedure is repeated with the updated seed set $\mathcal{S}$ until the desired number of seeds is attained and lastly, the seed set $\mathcal{S}$ is returned in Line 21. The nodes are removed from $\mathcal{Q}$ in nondecreasing order of their path-cost values. Hence, all nodes left in $\mathcal{Q}$ have a path-cost value greater than or equal to the path-cost value of the last removed node s. These nodes are "farther" away from the seeds contained in $\mathcal{S}$ than is s and therefore can be regarded as outliers. Fig. 8.3 depicts the functioning of the seed selection algorithm where the initial seed is selected randomly and discarded after the first seed was identified by means of an OPF execution. Later, the seed set is progressively built based on a sequence of OPF executions.

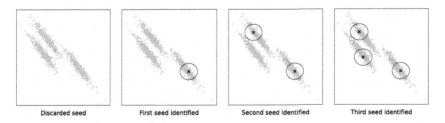

| Discarded seed | First seed identified | Second seed identified | Third seed identified |

Figure 8.3 Seed selection procedure. It starts by randomly choosing a seed, which is then discarded after the first seed has been identified. Next, the second and third seeds are progressively identified and the resultant seed set is returned.

8.3.2 Clustering by optimum-path forest

Once the initial seed set S has been finally established, an iterative procedure based on a sequence of OPF executions is carried out until either convergence or a preset maximum number of iterations $T > 0$ is achieved. In this context, convergence is attained when the seed sets obtained in consecutive iterations are equal (*i.e.*, have the same elements) since this will lead to the same graph partition.

Given a fixed number of groups k, the objective of each single OPF execution is to exploit optimum connectivity by partitioning the graph $G = (Z, A)$ into k optimum-path trees (clusters) $T_i, i \in \{1, 2, \ldots, k\}$, which altogether form an optimum-path forest. Each optimum-path tree T_i is rooted at seed $s_i \in S$, $i \in \{1, 2, \ldots, k\}$, such that the nodes constituting T_i are more strongly connected to s_i, than to any other seed in S.

Let $C_i \subset Z$ be the cluster defined by optimum-path tree $T_i, i \in \{1, 2, \ldots, k\}$, such that $\cup_{i=1}^{k} C_i = Z$ and $\cap_{i=1}^{k} C_i = \emptyset$. By assigning a distinct group label $i \in \{1, 2, \ldots, k\}$ to each seed $s \in S$, the OPF algorithm propagates the corresponding label $L(s)$ to its most closely connected samples in Z, creating a label map L.

In this work, we address two ways of determining the arc-weights, namely *fixed* and *dynamic* arc-weights. The arc-weight for an edge $(s, t) \in A$ is represented by $w(s, t)$. For fixed arc-weights, it is determined through the Euclidean distance of the feature vectors of s and t, i.e., $w(s, t) = \|v(t) - v(s)\|$, whereas for dynamic arc-weights we use instead

$$w(s, t) = \|v(t) - \mu_{L(s)}\|,$$
$$\mu_{L(s)} = \frac{1}{|C_{L(s)}|} \sum_{\forall x \in C_{L(s)}} v(x) \tag{8.3}$$

where $C_L(s)$ is the growing cluster (optimum-path tree) that contains s by the time a path $\pi_s \cdot \langle s, t \rangle$ reaches a node $t \in Z \setminus \cup_{i=1}^{k} C_i$ under evaluation. The dynamic approach leverages cluster information as the trees grow from the seed set, aiming to obtain more compact clusters since centroids are recomputed as the trees grow, and optimum connectivity is evaluated between such centroids and the remaining samples.

8.3.3 Seed recomputation

The seed recomputation stage occurs after each single OPF execution. This procedure aims to obtain enhanced seed sets using clustering information. The seeds are recomputed by selecting the sample whose feature vector is the closest to the mean feature vector of their corresponding cluster. This seed recomputation strategy stems from the idea that seeds that minimize the total path-cost may be located in dense regions of nodes. Therefore\an approximation of such regions can be obtained through the centroid estimation for each cluster.

For a fixed number of groups k, let $T_{ij}, i \in \{1, 2, \ldots, k\}$ be the k optimum-path trees generated by the seed set S_j after a single OPF execution during iteration j. The nodes comprising the optimum-path tree T_{ij} define the cluster C_{ij} for all $i \in \{1, 2, \ldots, k\}$. Therefore, each element $s_{i,j+1}, i \in \{1, 2, \ldots, k\}$ of the seed set for the next iteration S_{j+1} is calculated as

$$s_{i,j+1} = \underset{s \in C_{ij}}{\mathrm{argmin}} \{ \| v(s) - \mu_{ij} \| \},$$

$$\mu_{ij} = \frac{1}{|C_{ij}|} \sum_{\forall x \in C_{ij}} v(x) \tag{8.4}$$

8.3.4 Returning the forest with lowest total path-cost

Since the objective of the proposed framework is to minimize the objective function given by the total path-cost $\sum_{\forall s \in Z} C(s)$, the triplet (L, C, P) consisting of label map L, cost map C, and predecessor map P, that leads to the lowest total path-cost must be returned.

This stage is carried out once either seed set convergence has been achieved or the maximum number of iterations has been exhausted. Conversely to IW, the triplet corresponding to the last iteration is not returned since the total path-cost between consecutive iterations is not monotonically decreasing. Therefore, a search must be carried out across the triplets of all iterations to identify the one that leads to the lowest total path cost.

8.3.5 Algorithm outline

Algorithm 8.2 depicts the pseudocode of IOPF with dynamic arc-weight estimation for $f_{\max}$. The algorithm starts off by initializing the cost map C^*, label map L^*, and predecessor map P^* in lines 1–2. These maps are updated throughout the execution of the algorithm aiming to minimize the total path-cost value derived from C^*. Later, in Line 3, k seeds $r_i \in Z$, $i \in \{1, 2, \ldots, k\}$ are picked, such that each is uniquely identified as belonging to one among k clusters.

In lines 4–24, Algorithm 8.2 computes k optimum-path trees (clusters) from a seed set S, recomputes the seed set S in lines 18–20, and repeats

---

Algorithm 8.2: IOPF for f_{max} and dynamic arc-weight estimation

---

Input   : Graph $G = (\mathcal{Z}, \mathcal{A})$, seed set $\mathcal{S}$ with labeling function λ, number of seeds $k \geq 1$, and maximum number of iterations $T \geq 1$

Output : Label L^*, cost C^*, and predecessor P^* maps

Auxiliar: Priority queue $\mathcal{Q}$, dynamic sets $\mathcal{C}_i$, $\forall r_i \in \mathcal{S}$, $i = 1, 2, \ldots, k$, maps C, L and P, and variables *iter*, *converged* and *tmp*

---

1 **foreach** $s \in \mathcal{Z}$ **do**
2 | $C^*(s) \leftarrow +\infty, L^*(s) \leftarrow 0, P^*(s) \leftarrow nil$
3 Pick k seeds from $\mathcal{Z}$: $\mathcal{S} = \{r_1, r_2, \ldots, r_k\}$, iter $\leftarrow 1$, converged $\leftarrow$ **false**
4 **while** *iter* $\leq T$ **and** *converged* = **false do**
5 | $\mathcal{C}_i \leftarrow \emptyset, \forall i \in \{1, 2, \ldots, k\}$
6 | $\mathcal{Q} = \emptyset$
7 | **foreach** $s \in \mathcal{Z}$ **do**
8 | $C(s) \leftarrow +\infty, L(s) \leftarrow 0, P(s) \leftarrow nil$
9 | **if** $s = r_i \in \mathcal{S}$, $i \in \{1, 2, \ldots, k\}$ **then**
10 | $C(s) \leftarrow 0, L(s) \leftarrow i$
11 | Insert s in $\mathcal{Q}$
12 | **while** $\mathcal{Q} \neq \emptyset$ **do**
13 | Remove s from $\mathcal{Q}$, so that $s = \text{argmin}_{t \in \mathcal{Q}}\{C(t)\}$ and $\mathcal{C}_{L(s)} \leftarrow \mathcal{C}_{L(s)} \cup \{s\}$
14 | **foreach** $(s, t) \in \mathcal{A} \mid t \in \mathcal{Q}$ **do**
15 | $tmp \leftarrow \max\{C(s), \|v(t) - \mu_{L(s)}\|\}$
16 | **if** $tmp < C(t)$ **then**
17 | $C(t) \leftarrow tmp, L(t) \leftarrow L(s), P(t) \leftarrow p$
18 | $\mathcal{S}_{prev} \leftarrow \mathcal{S}, \mathcal{S} \leftarrow \emptyset$
19 | **foreach** $i \in \{1, 2, \ldots, k\}$ **do**
20 | $r_i \leftarrow \text{argmin}_{s \in \mathcal{C}_i}\{\|v(s) - \mu_i\|\}$ and $\mathcal{S} \leftarrow \mathcal{S} \cup \{r_i\}$
21 | converged $\leftarrow (\mathcal{S} = \mathcal{S}_{prev})$
22 | **if** $\sum_{\forall s \in \mathcal{Z}} C(s) < \sum_{\forall s \in \mathcal{Z}} C^*(s)$ **then**
23 | $(L^*, C^*, P^*) \leftarrow (L, C, P)$
24 | iter $\leftarrow$ iter $+ 1$
25 **return** (L^*, C^*, P^*)

---

both operations until either the convergence criterion is met or a preset maximum number of iterations T is reached. In line 5, it sets the dynamic sets $C_i, i \in \{1, 2, \ldots, k\}$ to empty. In lines 8–11, it initializes label map L, cost map C, and predecessor map P, and inserts all nodes into a priority queue $\mathcal{Q}$. In lines 12–17, the algorithm maintains the dynamic sets $C_i, i \in \{1, 2, \ldots, k\}$, label map L, cost map C, and predecessor map P. At each iteration of this loop, a node s of minimum cost $C(s)$ is removed from $\mathcal{Q}$ and inserted into the corresponding dynamic set $C_{L(s)}$ in line 13. At this moment, the current path π_s is optimum (*i.e.*, its cost is minimum among all possible paths with terminus s and rooted at $\mathcal{S}$). In lines 14–17, node s offers an extended path $\pi_s \cdot \langle s, t \rangle$ to a node $t \in \mathcal{Q}$ (*i.e.*, $t \in \mathcal{Z} \setminus \cup_{i=1}^{k} C_i$). The path value $f_{max}(\pi_s \cdot \langle s, t \rangle)$ is computed and stored in *tmp* in line 15. If *tmp* is less than the cost $C(t)$ of the current path π_t in P, then π_t is replaced by $\pi_s \cdot \langle s, t \rangle$ in line 17 by updating the values of the predecessor $P(t)$, cost $C(t)$, and label $L(t)$ corresponding to t to s, *tmp*, and $L(s)$, respectively.

In lines 18–20, the algorithm saves the current seed set $\mathcal{S}$ into $\mathcal{S}'$, resets the seed set $\mathcal{S}$ to empty and then recomputes it by selecting the nodes $r_i \in C_i$ that are closest to the mean feature vector of their resulting optimum-path tree $\mathcal{T}_i, i \in \{1, 2, \ldots, c\}$. The mean feature vector is defined as the arithmetic mean of the feature vectors of the elements contained in C_i. Next, in line 21, $\mathcal{S}'$ is compared to $\mathcal{S}$ to test for convergence and the result of this comparison is saved in *converged*. In lines 22–23, we test whether the map C provides a lesser total path-cost value than the map C^*, if that is so, then L^*, C^*, and P^* are updated with the maps L, C, and P, respectively. Lastly, the tuple (L^*, C^*, P^*) with minimum total path-cost value among all iterations is returned in line 25.

The algorithm for IOPF with fixed arc-weights differs only in line 15, where the arc-weight between nodes s and t is estimated as $\|v(t) - v(s)\|$. Thus line 15 should be modified to $tmp \leftarrow \max\{C(s), \|v(t) - v(s)\|\}$.

In order to reduce the complexity of the algorithm, we can store the mean feature vector of each dynamic set and its size so that these measures can efficiently be updated during label propagation. Therefore each time a new element s is added to the dynamic set, the mean feature vector and the dynamic set size are updated as in Eq. (8.5), where $v(s)$ represents the feature vector of s, μ_{prev} and μ_{next} are the previous and next mean feature vectors, while n_{prev} and n_{next} represent the size of the dynamic set before and after the update.

$$\mu_{next} = \mu_{prev} + \frac{v(s) - \mu_{prev}}{n_{prev} + 1}$$

$$n_{next} = n_{prev} + 1$$

(8.5)

8.3.6 Application to object delineation

Since IOPF is a generalization of the ISF framework from the image domain to the feature space, its application to image segmentation is straightforward. We call the methods for object delineation *Iterative Dynamic Trees* (IDT). A two-dimensional image is a pair $(\mathcal{D}_{\mathcal{I}}, \mathbf{I})$, such that $\mathbf{I}(p)$ assigns local image features (*e.g.*, color space components) for each pixel $p \in \mathcal{D}_{\mathcal{I}} \subset \mathbb{Z}^2$. An image can be rendered as a graph $(\mathcal{N}, \mathcal{A})$ under various configurations, depending upon how nodes $\mathcal{N} \subseteq \mathcal{D}_{\mathcal{I}}$ and adjacency relation $\mathcal{A} \subset \mathcal{N} \times \mathcal{N}$ are defined. We define pixels as nodes ($\mathcal{N} = \mathcal{D}_{\mathcal{I}}$), such that $\mathbf{I}(p)$ represents the CIELab color components of pixel p, and the 8-neighborhood relation defines the arcs.

Given a seed set $\mathcal{S}$, we wish to partition the image into objects such that the pixels enclosed by an object are more closely connected to the seed within the object than to any other seed. A unique object identifier is given to each seed $p \in \mathcal{S}$ by a labeling function $\lambda(p) \in \{1, 2, \ldots, c\}$, where c is the number of objects.

Therefore this application focuses on object delineation as a superpixel segmentation task that defines each object by a single superpixel. The IDT algorithm consists of four steps: (*i*) initial seed estimation with one seed per object, (*ii*) object delineation as an optimum-path tree, (*iii*) seed set improvement, and the loop of steps (*ii*)–(*iii*) for a preset number of iterations or up to seed set convergence. After that, step (*iv*) completes the process by selecting the optimum-path forest from loop (*ii*)–(*iii*) whose total path cost is minimum. The IDT algorithm may be regarded as a new method based on the *Iterative Spanning Forest* (ISF) framework [44], which adds step (*iv*) and drastically reduces the number of superpixels to the number of objects. In ISF, more accurate delineation can be achieved by dynamic arc-weight estimation as the optimum-path trees grow—a strategy that has been demonstrated for superpixel segmentation [9] and interactive object segmentation [10]. In IDT, we exploit this property in ISF for unsupervised object segmentation for the first time.

All of the framework components presented in previous sections are valid for this application. However, given the nature of the problem, some other strategies can be introduced as components for the framework. Following this line of thought, we present a new seed recomputation strategy in the image domain. In Section 8.3.3, during iteration j, new seeds are selected as the nodes closest to the mean feature vector for each optimum-path tree $\mathcal{T}_{ij}, i \in \{1, 2, \ldots, k\}$. Nevertheless, in the image domain, we may also select the new seeds as the nodes closest to the mean pixel of each optimum-path tree. The mean pixel is defined as the arithmetic mean of pixel coordinates of the elements of clusters $\mathcal{C}_{ij}, i \in \{1, 2, \ldots, k\}$. Thus, each seed $r_{i,j+1}, i = 1, 2, \ldots, n$ for iteration $j + 1$ is determined as

$$r_{i,j+1} = \underset{p \in \mathcal{C}_i}{\operatorname{argmin}} \{ \| p - \frac{1}{|\mathcal{C}_i|} \times \sum_{\forall q \in \mathcal{C}_i} q \| \} \qquad (8.6)$$

Fig. 8.4 depicts the application of the IDT algorithm from a randomly selected initial seed set and a maximum number of iterations set to 20. The seed set is recomputed at the end of each iteration, and the optimum-path forest with the lowest total cost is returned as the final output.

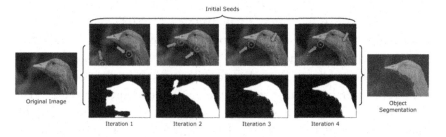

Figure 8.4 Object segmentation using the IDT algorithm.

8.4 Experimental results

In this section, we present three applications to show the robustness and flexibility of the IOPF framework by designing suitable and effective IOPF-based methods for each problem context. The first application in Section 8.4.1 addresses the problem of object delineation following an unsupervised approach. The second application in Section 8.4.2 addresses the analysis of road networks by establishing emergency stations in strategic locations, such that the distance between reference points and emergency stations is minimized. Lastly, the third application in Section 8.4.3 addresses the problem of clustering synthetic two-dimensional data sets presenting a wide variety of shapes and distributions.

8.4.1 Object delineation by iterative dynamic trees

To demonstrate the advantages of step (*iv*) and random seed sampling in step (*i*) in the context of object delineation, we compare four versions of IDT. IDT_1 is the proposed version, as described in Section 8.3.6 using the connectivity function f_{max}. IDT_2 is IDT_1 without step (iv); it selects the last optimum-path forest after T iterations, as proposed in the original ISF framework and adopted by all previous ISF-based methods, such as DISF [9]. IDT_3 is IDT_1 with grid sampling (seed sampling with uniform distance among seeds) in step (*iii*), as used in some ISF-based approaches, such as DISF [9] and most superpixel segmentation methods. IDT_4 is IDT_1 with seed recomputation based on the mean feature vector instead of the mean pixel, as is detailed in Section 8.3.3.

To demonstrate the improvement of IDT for object delineation, we compare it against DISF and IW [43] with two path-cost functions in the IFT algorithm: IW-max computes the cost of a path as the maximum arc weight along it, for fixed arc weights $\|\mathbf{I}(q) - \mathbf{I}(p)\|$, and IW-sum computes the cost of a path as the sum of its arc weights. Like IDT_1 and IDT_2, both IW-based methods start from a random seed set of size equal to the number of desired objects (and background) [43]. DISF begins from a set with 150 seeds selected by grid sampling for all images and reduces the seed set size at every iteration until it reaches the number of desired objects [9]. IW has already been demonstrated to be superior to spectral clustering [46], isoperimetric partitioning [24], and k-means in the task of object delineation.

For evaluation of object segmentation, we use the Weizmann 1-Object and 2-Object data sets [5], containing 100 images each, along with ground-truth segmentations. Images in these data sets (available at http://www.wisdom.weizmann.ac.il/~vision/Seg_Evaluation_DB/) depict one or two objects in the foreground. For assessment of the methods, we use four popular effectiveness measures: (*i*) *Adjusted Mutual Information* (AMI) [45], which is an adjustment of the Mutual Information (MI) score to account for chance, (*ii*) *Adjusted Rand Index* (ARI) [26], which determines the Rand index (RI) score adjusted for chance, (*iii*) *Boundary Recall* (BR), which measures boundary adherence [1], and (*iv*) *Cluster Accuracy* [20], which measures the degree of intersection between predicted and ground-truth segmentation.

The experiments were conducted using the same sets of initial seeds for IDT_1, IDT_2, IDT_4, IW-max, and IW-sum. To guarantee the best result from each algorithm, they are executed 20 times for each image, from which the best object segmentation is selected according to the evaluation metrics. Next, mean and standard deviation are computed from these values across all images for each data set.

Table 8.1 shows the effectiveness of object segmentation for all methods according to four different metrics (AMI, ARI, BR, and CA). Fig. 8.5 depicts a bar chart where the bar height represents the average value for each of the metrics, which are evaluated for each algorithm. IDT_1 is the best approach, being worse than IDT_2 in only a single case, according to ARI for the 2-object segmentation task. IDT_1 exhibits superior results than IDT_4, suggesting that the seed recomputation based on the mean pixel is the best option in the context of image segmentation.

Table 8.1 AMI, ARI, Boundary Recall, and Cluster Accuracy (Mean +/- Std. Deviation) for Weizmann 1-Object and 2-Object data sets for IDT variants, DISF, IW-max, and IW-sum.

	Method	AMI	ARI	BR	CA
1-Object	IDT_1	**0.564673 ± 0.283**	**0.613058 ± 0.317**	**0.657833 ± 0.241**	**0.908387 ± 0.091**
	IDT_2	0.344623 ± 0.270	0.363208 ± 0.323	0.433819 ± 0.276	0.841895 ± 0.114
	IDT_3	0.366932 ± 0.307	0.372370 ± 0.363	0.458131 ± 0.285	0.860064 ± 0.107
	IDT_4	0.471829 ± 0.281	0.512906 ± 0.319	0.586976 ± 0.243	0.885122 ± 0.097
	DISF	0.304520 ± 0.282	0.282088 ± 0.347	0.398606 ± 0.296	0.836631 ± 0.112
	IW–max	0.397320 ± 0.278	0.419055 ± 0.318	0.473212 ± 0.276	0.856288 ± 0.112
	IW–sum	0.352781 ± 0.257	0.373990 ± 0.300	0.330048 ± 0.243	0.847699 ± 0.108
2-Object	IDT_1	**0.589247 ± 0.278**	0.600024 ± 0.345	**0.748527 ± 0.194**	**0.953605 ± 0.054**
	IDT_2	0.587252 ± 0.278	**0.614408 ± 0.333**	0.730065 ± 0.207	0.946522 ± 0.064
	IDT_3	0.386087 ± 0.279	0.334149 ± 0.328	0.518125 ± 0.263	0.902305 ± 0.100
	IDT_4	0.553327 ± 0.274	0.566872 ± 0.324	0.711618 ± 0.204	0.943516 ± 0.064
	DISF	0.420036 ± 0.295	0.376453 ± 0.352	0.582483 ± 0.263	0.919615 ± 0.078
	IW–max	0.435559 ± 0.330	0.544933 ± 0.311	0.615948 ± 0.231	0.921671 ± 0.086
	IW–sum	0.395757 ± 0.242	0.347743 ± 0.299	0.496769 ± 0.224	0.895421 ± 0.097

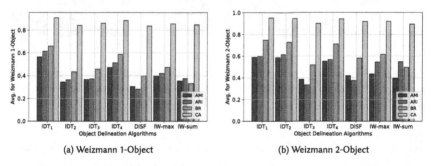

(a) Weizmann 1-Object   (b) Weizmann 2-Object

Figure 8.5 Results obtained in each data set for AMI, ARI, BR, and CA. (a) Weizmann 1-Object data set, (b) Weizmann 2-Object data set.

An important finding from the experiments showed that DISF relies heavily on the size of the initial seed set, imparting outstanding results for some images while failing for others. The results also show that random

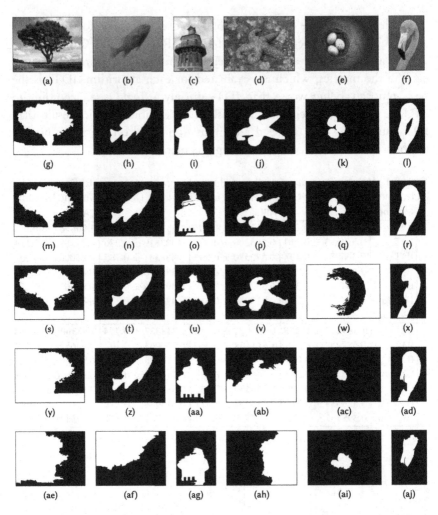

Figure 8.6 Segmentation results for Weizmann 1-Object data set. (a)–(f) Original images, (g)–(l) Ground-truth, (m)–(r) IDT_1, (s)–(x) DISF ($N_o = 150$), (y)–(ad) IW-max, and (ae)–(aj) IW-sum.

sampling suffices for step (i), and step (iv), added by the proposed approach to the ISF framework, is vital for improved object segmentation. The results raise the question of how good it would be IDT for superpixel segmentation (when the number of seeds is higher than the number of desired objects), which we will leave for future work. Figs. 8.6 and 8.7 shows the segmentation results for IDT_1, DISF, IW-max, and IW-sum on some images of Weizmann 1-Object and 2-Object data sets, respectively.

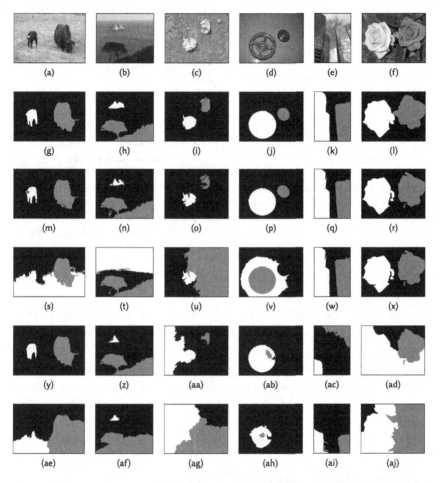

Figure 8.7 Segmentation results for Weizmann 2-Object data set. (a)–(f) Original images, (g)–(l) Ground-truth, (m)–(r) IDT_1, (s)–(x) DISF ($N_o = 150$), (y)–(ad) IW-max, and (ae)–(aj) IW-sum.

In this context, the seed set selection algorithm was also tested to determine whether it may positively affect the performance of IDT_1. IDT_1 originally starts with a random seed set. However, in this experiment, the algorithm will start with initial seed sets output by Algorithm 8.1. The seed set selection algorithm was executed with different values of h (estimated percentage of outliers) in the range of 0.05% to 30% with a step size of 2.5%. Fig. 8.8 exhibit the performance of this methodology expressed in four different metrics for both Weizmann 1-Object and 2-Object data sets. From the figure, we see that as we increase the estimated percentage

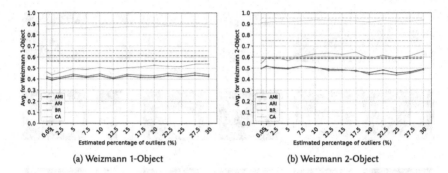

(a) Weizmann 1-Object   (b) Weizmann 2-Object

Figure 8.8 Results obtained for IDT_1 with Algorithm 8.1 under different values of estimated seed of outliers (h) in the range [0.05%, 30%] in each data set for AMI, ARI, BR, and CA. The score of IDT_1 with random initial seed set (see Table 8.1) is shown in dashed lines for all metrics. (a) Weizmann 1-Object data set, (b) Weizmann 2-Object data set.

of outliers, the algorithm's performance, assessed by BR and CA, slightly increases in both data sets.

Conversely, the algorithm's performance is barely increasing and sometimes decreasing for some values of h when assessed by AMI and ARI. Nevertheless, these scores are lower than its counterpart IDT_1 with a random initial seed set (shown in dashed lines). Therefore, this result suggests that combining the seed selection strategy with IDT_1 does not improve the original formulation where the seed set is selected randomly. Thus we can conclude that in order to attain the best performance in object delineation, IDT_1 with random seed selection is the most suitable configuration.

8.4.2 Analysis on road networks

Road networks impose a new constraint on the graph's adjacency relation since it is already predefined by the road network map where edges are defined by the roads connecting two reference points. This experiment addresses the following problem: given a road network instance, identifying appropriate points for placing emergency stations, such that emergency station reaches the point of an incident in the minimum time possible. The following points should be taken into consideration to devise a solution to this problem: (*i*) The emergency station must be reachable from the point of an incident in a short time interval (*i.e.*, the distance between these two points must be minimized), and (*ii*) the number of emergency stations spread across the map must be as low as possible to reduce the establishment costs.

A road network will induce a weighted graph $G = (\mathcal{Z}, \mathcal{A})$, where the nodes are defined by a set of reference points spread across the road map. Such points constitute the data set $\mathcal{Z}$ and are uniquely identified by a pair of coordinates $x = (x_1, x_2)$. An emergency station must be established at one of such points. The adjacency relation $\mathcal{A}$ that defines the arcs of the graph is given by the set of pairs $(x, y) \in \mathcal{Z} \times \mathcal{Z}$, such that x and y are connected by a road. The arcs are weighted by their corresponding road lengths, which are provided beforehand for this experiment.

Based on the above definition, we may formulate this problem as the discovering of a set of k emergency points $c_i \in \mathcal{Z}$, $i \in \{1, 2, \ldots, k\}$, such that sum of path-costs between each reference point $s \in \mathcal{Z}$ and its closest emergency station, i.e., $\sum_{s \in \mathcal{Z}} f(\pi_s)$, is minimized across all reference points for a given connectivity function f; therefore the application of the IOPF framework to this problem is straightforward. In this context, the problem described above may be divided into two subsequent stages or subproblems. The first stage entails discovering the set of k emergency points through the IOPF framework, which can be carried out under different combinations of connectivity functions and arc-weight estimation strategies. Next, the second stage determines the sum of path-costs between each of the emergency stations discovered during the first stage and its closest points, which is obtained through a single execution of the OPF algorithm with f_{sum} using the emergency station points as seeds. The ideal number of emergency stations is identified after repeating the experiment with a sequence of increasing values. The ideal number of stations is selected at the point where the reduction of $\sum_{s \in \mathcal{Z}} f(\pi_s)$ does not compensate the placing costs of establishing an additional emergency station.

In this experiment, our objective is to determine the IOPF configuration that suits the problem described above. Therefore we compare four versions of IOPF, where each of them presents a variation in their configurations on either the connectivity function or the arc-weight estimation strategy. IW-sum and IW-max determine the cost of a path using the f_{sum} and f_{max} connectivity functions, respectively, for fixed arc weights $\|x - y\|$. On the other hand, IOPF-dynsum and IOPF-dynmax determine the cost of a path using the f_{sum} and f_{max} connectivity functions for dynamic arc-weight estimation.

The road networks for this experiment are taken from [29] (available at https://figshare.com/articles/dataset/Urban_Road_Network_Data/2061897). In [43], a similar experiment was conducted with the road networks corresponding to the Indian cities of Mumbai, Hyderabad, Chen-

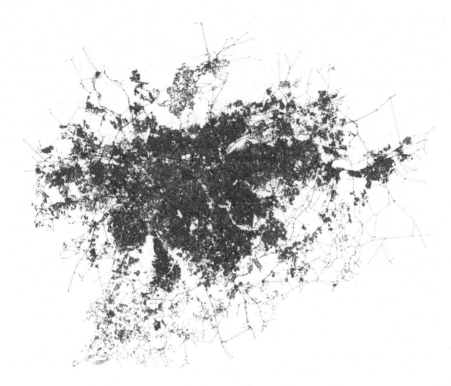

Figure 8.9 Road network of the city of São Paulo, Brazil.

nai, Bengaluru, Calcutta, and Delhi. The IW algorithm was compared to
k-means and greedy k-center, exhibiting better performance than its counterparts. This experiment uses the road networks corresponding to the
Brazilian cities of São Paulo, Rio de Janeiro, Belo Horizonte, Recife, Porto
Alegre, and Salvador. IOPF-based algorithms assume that the graph on
which are executed is connected. Therefore we need to make sure that
the graph induced by a road network is connected. To simplify this task,
we select the largest connected component in each road network as the
graph induced by the road network. Figs. 8.9, 8.10, 8.11, and 8.12 show
the graph induced by the road networks of the Brazilian cities where blue
(dark gray in print version) dots represent the nodes or reference points. In
contrast, black lines linking pairs of reference points represent the edges or
roads.

The experiments were carried out using the same sets of initial seeds
for IW-sum, IW-max, IOPF-dynsum, and IOPF-dynmax. For each city's
road network, each method is executed thirty times for a varying number of

Figure 8.10 Road network of the city of Rio de Janeiro, Brazil.

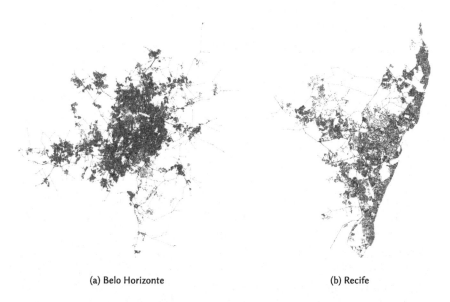

(a) Belo Horizonte   (b) Recife

Figure 8.11 Road networks of the cities of (a) Belo Horizonte and (b) Recife in Brazil.

centers. Next, the sum of path–costs across all nodes $\sum_{s\in \mathcal{Z}} f(\pi_s)$ is averaged across all executions to assess its effectiveness. Table 8.2 shows the comparison of the average values of the total path costs $\sum_{s\in \mathcal{Z}} f(\pi_s)$ with 3, 6, 9, 12, and 15 centers for each city's road network. IW-sum appears to be the most suitable IOPF-based method in most cases, achieving a lower value than its

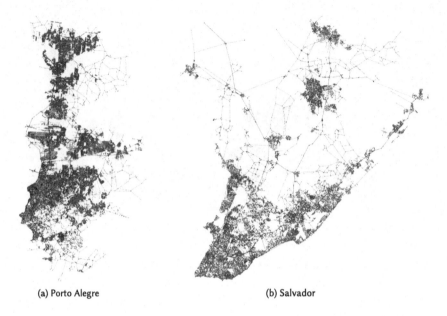

(a) Porto Alegre   (b) Salvador

Figure 8.12 Road network of the cities of (a) Porto Alegre and (b) Salvador in Brazil.

counterparts and being worse than IOPF-dynsum and IOPF-dynmax in only a few cases where the difference in values is not significant.

Furthermore, it can also be observed that both IOPF-dynsum and IOPF-dynmax obtain average values, which are very similar to those obtained by IW–sum in contrast to IW–max, which gets the largest average values. Fig. 8.13 illustrate this comparison through a line chart for each city's road network. Each line chart shows the average total path cost across an increasing number of centers for each method, where IW–sum stands out as the method that minimizes the total path cost in most settings. On the other hand, to identify whether the seed selection algorithm may improve the effectiveness of the IW–sum method, we executed the seed selection algorithm for different values of h, namely 5%, 10%, and 15%. From Fig. 8.14, we can see that some improvement is achieved when coupling the seed selection algorithm with the IW–sum method. Such behavior becomes more noticeable as the number of centers increases. We believe that this result can be further improved by incorporating local density information into the seed selection algorithm. This idea stems from the fact that seeds should be chosen from dense regions of points, however, the seed selection algorithm only considers distances along a path measured by a given connectivity function. Nevertheless, density computation for large data sets

Table 8.2 Average total path costs for the Brazilian cities of Belo Horizonte, Porto Alegre, Recife, Rio de Janeiro, Salvador, and São Paulo for the algorithms IW-sum, IW-max, IOPF-dynsum, and IOPF-dynmax with a varying number of centers.

	# Centers	IW-sum	IW-max	IOPF-dynsum	IOPF-dynmax
Belo Horizonte	3	50392.84 ± 1873.05	59173.66 ± 4721.73	49879.25 ± 441.97	**49052.51 ± 1071.37**
	6	**39271.38 ± 1024.23**	46087.54 ± 2813.85	39890.12 ± 1393.49	39326.05 ± 1186.43
	9	**32266.13 ± 1047.32**	40395.69 ± 4305.03	33035.27 ± 1223.22	32909.83 ± 1297.82
	12	**27348.55 ± 1148.55**	34701.26 ± 2364.85	28533.93 ± 1179.58	28714.03 ± 1045.76
	15	**23766.05 ± 703.01**	31133.95 ± 2348.54	25295.12 ± 1083.38	25642.89 ± 957.62
Porto Alegre	3	97407.88 ± 3809.96	121376.97 ± 24728.46	**96640.18 ± 603.42**	97018.90 ± 4720.06
	6	**70961.53 ± 3290.43**	85313.21 ± 7292.24	71178.73 ± 3009.31	73312.43 ± 5177.42
	9	54750.34 ± 4342.36	71823.30 ± 7011.44	**54571.08 ± 2361.63**	56983.83 ± 4804.08
	12	**46793.18 ± 932.39**	61733.62 ± 4060.54	47611.60 ± 1677.85	48224.04 ± 1923.37
	15	42094.06 ± 1369.52	54474.27 ± 6210.77	**41996.50 ± 1673.19**	42888.86 ± 1887.78
Recife	3	**47465.21 ± 1071.42**	56321.18 ± 5700.37	48564.26 ± 2418.34	47793.52 ± 560.23
	6	**31560.96 ± 780.89**	39324.44 ± 4542.26	31759.04 ± 497.83	32420.76 ± 1992.57
	9	**26036.27 ± 971.14**	32790.09 ± 2602.29	26178.34 ± 1167.90	26766.27 ± 1484.19
	12	**22326.89 ± 754.97**	28792.67 ± 2907.76	22475.01 ± 713.84	23276.13 ± 1102.17
	15	**19550.77 ± 430.20**	24273.99 ± 1740.91	19781.37 ± 567.09	20289.22 ± 1009.53
Rio de Janeiro	3	208968.97 ± 7704.59	308388.16 ± 83156.19	210828.25 ± 12300.04	231768.06 ± 53873.91
	6	152151.05 ± 8669.53	201568.28 ± 61683.35	151757.59 ± 7249.10	**147985.06 ± 4118.53**
	9	126027.29 ± 6118.03	149069.25 ± 14838.43	125305.51 ± 5534.58	**122329.64 ± 5945.00**
	12	105914.04 ± 3594.79	132210.23 ± 9104.88	106830.88 ± 3795.28	**105052.38 ± 4250.77**
	15	**92811.58 ± 4231.72**	112041.85 ± 8576.53	94756.97 ± 4602.93	94047.29 ± 4831.71
Salvador	3	26953.18 ± 2587.67	34741.45 ± 4769.68	**25786.45 ± 1544.62**	27255.29 ± 3135.52
	6	**17782.28 ± 648.34**	23527.57 ± 4215.90	17970.04 ± 828.34	18591.79 ± 612.93
	9	**14645.86 ± 436.67**	19189.59 ± 3306.66	14777.55 ± 646.55	15838.72 ± 1589.64
	12	**12812.38 ± 811.51**	16319.22 ± 1732.45	12857.59 ± 847.78	13392.92 ± 869.91
	15	**11037.27 ± 764.02**	14287.47 ± 1239.53	11280.82 ± 853.77	11615.92 ± 1083.61
São Paulo	3	**225694.20 ± 2862.17**	268244.34 ± 16638.99	226909.29 ± 6658.03	226372.56 ± 684.42
	6	**165991.84 ± 3441.19**	211433.73 ± 16557.69	168775.45 ± 4092.53	169531.03 ± 5047.84
	9	**142613.33 ± 2214.72**	183700.73 ± 15373.26	143098.41 ± 1907.44	143415.22 ± 3057.78
	12	**124687.04 ± 2041.82**	154775.17 ± 8153.19	126028.38 ± 2688.92	126033.73 ± 3403.75
	15	**112642.07 ± 1868.52**	142541.69 ± 11614.11	113465.35 ± 2149.23	114127.19 ± 2769.51

may become computationally expensive, impairing performance. Accordingly, research should be conducted to introduce density information into the seed selection procedure without compromising performance.

Figs. 8.15, 8.16, 8.17, and 8.18 show the clustering results of IW–sum with fifteen centers for each city's network, where each cluster is colored with a different color and the centers (*i.e.*, emergency points) are marked with a cross surrounded by a circle.

8.4.3 Experiments on synthetic data sets

In order to ascertain the performance and robustness of the IOPF framework in a broader variety of data sets, we evaluate several IOPF-based methods on synthetic data sets that exhibit a broad spectrum of shapes

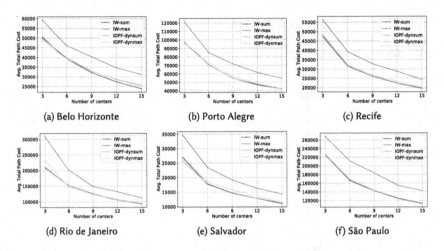

Figure 8.13 Average total path costs for the Brazilian cities of Belo Horizonte, Porto Alegre, Recife, Rio de Janeiro, Salvador, and São Paulo for the algorithms IW-sum, IW-max, IOPF-dynsum, and IOPF-dynmax with a varying number of centers.

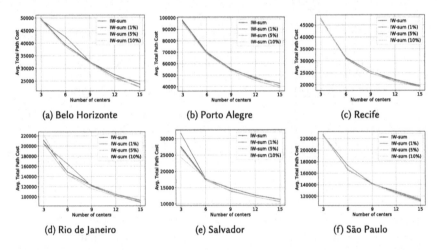

Figure 8.14 Average total path costs for the Brazilian cities of Belo Horizonte, Porto Alegre, Recife, Rio de Janeiro, Salvador, and São Paulo for IW-sum with random seed selection and IW-sum using the seed selection algorithm with estimated percentage of outliers (h) of 1%, 5%, and 10% with a varying number of centers.

and distributions. In the first part of this experiment, we use five synthetic data sets generated with *sklearn*, a Python library that implements most of the state-of-the-art machine learning algorithms and techniques. These five data sets are shown in Fig. 8.19, where it can be seen that the *noisy circles*

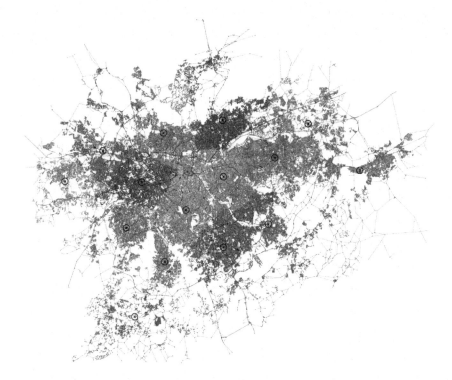

Figure 8.15 Road network of the city of São Paulo, Brazil.

Figure 8.16 Road network of the city of Rio de Janeiro, Brazil.

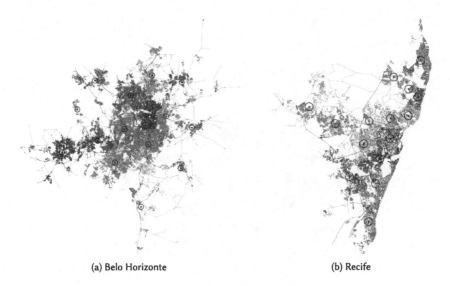

(a) Belo Horizonte   (b) Recife

Figure 8.17 Road networks of the cities of (a) Belo Horizonte and (b) Recife in Brazil.

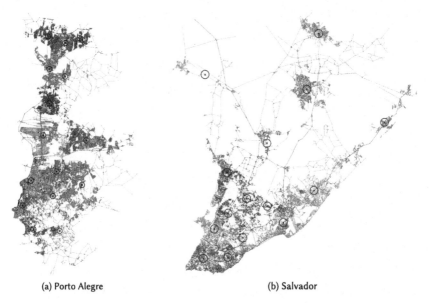

(a) Porto Alegre   (b) Salvador

Figure 8.18 Road network of the cities of (a) Porto Alegre and (b) Salvador in Brazil.

and *noisy moons* data sets comprise two groups, while the *varied*, *aniso* and *blobs* data sets comprise three groups. All these data sets consist of 1500 samples each and exhibit a diversity of shapes and distributions, which will allow us to assess the framework's robustness in these case scenarios.

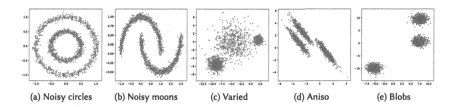

(a) Noisy circles   (b) Noisy moons   (c) Varied   (d) Aniso   (e) Blobs

Figure 8.19 Synthetic data sets created with sklearn.

In such data sets, we do not possess enough information about the underlying relationship among the samples to establish a suitable graph topology, conversely to what happens in Sections 8.4.1 and 8.4.2. Therefore, a strategy to build suitable graph topologies in the general case is still a topic under investigation. In Section 8.3, we introduced two examples of graph topologies. Let $\mathcal{Z}$ be a data set such that each sample $s \in \mathcal{Z}$ is represented in the feature space by a feature vector $v(s) \in \mathbb{R}^n$. The adjacency relation $\mathcal{A} \subseteq \mathcal{Z} \times \mathcal{Z}$ may be defined in such a way that the induced graph $G = (\mathcal{Z}, \mathcal{A})$ can be established either as a complete or a k-nearest neighbor graph. If G is defined as a complete graph, IOPF with fixed arc weights and f_{sum} connectivity function (*i.e.*, IW-sum) is expected to behave similar to k-means. In this setting, the edge connecting any seed to any of the remaining samples is selected as the path with the minimum cost over any other path connecting such a pair of samples in the graph. This fact can be explained by means of the triangle inequality extended to polygons and, therefore, its behavior matches that of k-means, which considers direct distances between centroids and samples to form the clusters.

We conducted experiments with four configurations of IOPF to ascertain its effectiveness under a complete graph topology. IW-sum and IW-max use fixed arc weights with f_{sum} and f_{max} connectivity functions, respectively. On the other hand, IOPF-dynsum and IOPF-dynmax use dynamic arc weight estimation with f_{sum} and f_{max} connectivity functions, respectively. We compare the aforementioned IOPF-based methods with k-means on the task of clustering the synthetic data sets. Fig. 8.20 shows the clustering results for k-means, IW-sum, IW-max, IOPF-dynsum, and IOPF-dynmax. For each data set, the same initial seeds are selected for all methods, which are marked with crosses (**x**), while the final medoids are marked with triangles (**▲**). From the results in Fig. 8.20, we can see that the final clusterings achieved by k-means, IW-sum, IOPF-dynsum, and IOPF-dynmax are similar for all data sets. Nevertheless, the position of the final medoids differ, and this fact is more evident for the noisy moons data set in the second row. The k-means, IW–sum, IOPF-dynsum, and IOPF-dynmax algorithms fail to separate the clusters for the noisy circles, noisy moons, varied and aniso data sets, which are represented in the first four rows of Fig. 8.20. These algorithms only succeed when separating the groups in the blobs data set, where the clusters are well-defined, well-separated, and exhibit spherical shapes.

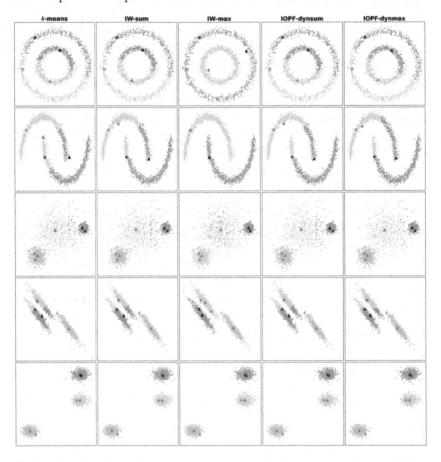

Figure 8.20 Clustering results on synthetic data sets for k-means, IW-sum, IW-max, IOPF-dynsum, and IOPF-dynmax using a complete-graph topology. The initial seeds are marked with crosses (**x**), while the final medoids are marked with triangles (**▲**). In cases where the initial seeds are equivalent to the final medoids, only the final medoids are shown.

On the other hand, the IW–max method successfully separates the groups for all synthetic data sets, albeit the final result of the clustering relies heavily on the initial seed selection. IW-max is very sensitive to isolated points or outliers, penalizes spatial gaps in the data set, and works independently of the clusters' shape. Fig. 8.21 shows the clustering results using IW-max, where it fails to separate the groups due to bad initial seeds and spatial gaps in the data set. Therefore in an effort to circumvent these cases, we employ the seed selection algorithm (see Algorithm 8.1) with estimated percentage of outliers $h = 5\%$, as shown in Fig. 8.22. It can be seen from the figure that seeds are chosen from dense regions of samples with similar interseed distances. In some cases, the algorithm starts with one seed from each cluster (which is the ideal scenario), succeeding in separating the groups. Accordingly, combining IW-max on a complete graph topology with the seed selection algorithm seems a good approach to address the clustering problem in the general case.

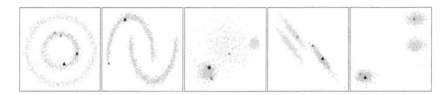

Figure 8.21 Clustering results on the synthetic data sets for IW-max where it fails at separating the groups due to bad initial seeds and spatial gaps in the data set.

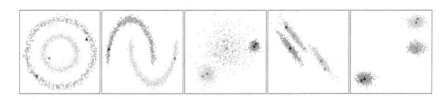

Figure 8.22 Clustering results on the synthetic data sets for IW-max where initial seeds are selected through the seed selection algorithm with estimated percentage of outliers (h) of 5%.

Alternatively, we may as well define G as a k-nearest neighbor graph, where each sample $s \in \mathcal{Z}$ is linked through an edge to its k closest neighbors for a fixed k. This construction is straightforward, however, we need to make sure that two conditions are met. If $(u, v) \in \mathcal{A}$, then $(v, u) \in \mathcal{A}$, and G must be connected. If G is not connected, the edges of the minimum spanning tree containing all samples in $\mathcal{Z}$ are added to G in increasing order of weight, joining the connected components, until there is a single connected

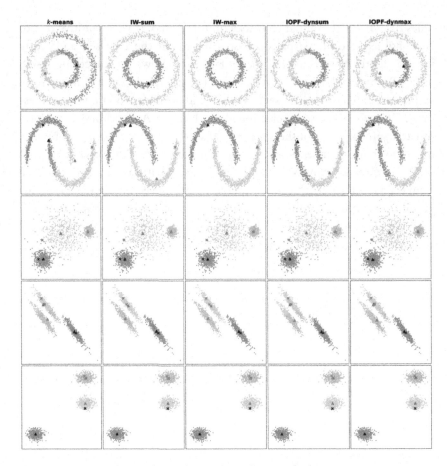

Figure 8.23 Clustering results on the synthetic data sets for k-means, IW-sum, IW-max, IOPF-dynsum, and IOPF-dynmax on a k-nearest neighbor graph topology with $k = 15$.

component in G. We conducted experiments using a k-nearest neighbor graph topology with $k = 15$ where the steps described above were applied. Fig. 8.23 shows the results of running k-means, IW–sum, IW–max, IOPF–dynsum, and IOPF–dynmax on the synthetic data sets. From the figure, it can be seen that IW–sum now is able to successfully separate the groups for the noisy circles, noisy moons, aniso, and varied data sets. Therefore, imposing restrictions in the graph topology leads to improvements in the clustering capabilities of IW–sum. On the other hand, IOPF–dynsum and IOPF–dynmax still fail at separating the groups for the noisy circles, noisy moons, varied, and aniso data sets. IW–max still performs well under this restriction on the graph topology, obtaining a similar result to the case of a complete graph.

To ascertain the framework's effectiveness and robustness against other state-of-the-art clustering algorithms, we compared IW-max using a complete graph topology, and the seed selection algorithm, with $h = 5\%$, against five popular clustering algorithms: (*i*) mean shift, (*ii*) spectral clustering, (*iii*) DBSCAN, (*iv*) Gaussian mixture, and (*v*) agglomerative clustering. Mean shift [14] is a nonparametric iterative mode-seeking clustering algorithm that works by means of maximizing the kernel density estimate to locate the modes in the data. It is widely used in pattern recognition and computer vision. Spectral clustering [46] is a graph-theoretic technique that computes the Laplacian of the graph and exploits its properties to partition the data regardless of the clusters' shapes. DBSCAN [18] is a density-based clustering technique that is capable of discovering arbitrary shape clusters and effectively handling noise and outliers during the clustering process. Gaussian mixture [37] is a parametric probability density function expressed as a weighted sum of a finite number of Gaussian distributions and determines its parameters through expectation maximization (EM). Agglomerative clustering [35] is a hierarchical clustering technique that follows a bottom-up approach to partition the data outputting a hierarchical structure progressively.

Fig. 8.24 shows the result of this comparison on the synthetic data sets. It can be seen that, in contrast to its counterparts, IW-max successfully separates the groups for all synthetic data sets. The spectral clustering algorithm is also able to separate the groups for most of the data sets, however, it fails for the aniso data set, not being able to separate the blue and green (dark gray and gray in print version) clusters. Similarly, the agglomerative clustering algorithm only fails to identify the correct groups for the aniso data set while correctly separating the groups in the rest of the cases. As expected, the Gaussian mixture algorithm correctly identifies elliptical shape clusters while failing for the noisy circles and noisy moons data sets. DBSCAN effectively works when clusters are dense and well separated by low-density regions, however, it is unsuccessful when clusters' boundaries are too close as in the cases of the varied and aniso data sets. Mean shift, on the other hand, is not able to identify the clusters in the noisy circles, noisy moons, and aniso data sets. Finally, all algorithms effectively identify the groups in the blob data set, where the clusters exhibit spherical shapes and are well separated in the feature space.

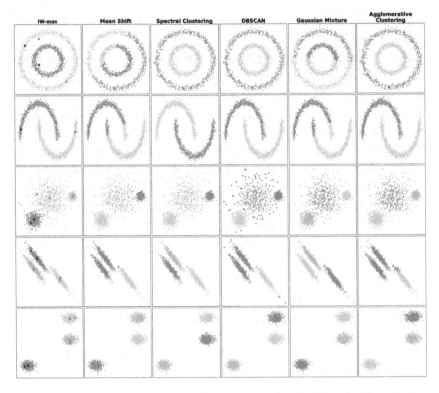

Figure 8.24 Clustering results on the synthetic data sets using IW-sum with a complete graph and the seed selection algorithm, where $h = 5\%$, against mean shift, spectral clustering, DBSCAN, Gaussian mixture, and agglomerative clustering.

To further assess the framework's performance, we employed seven additional data sets collected from [22]. Each data set presents some challenges due to their inherent structure and distribution. Fig. 8.25 shows the data sets employed in this experiment. The *Jain* and *flame* data sets comprise two clusters each, where the clusters' density in the Jain data set is not uniform. The *spiral* data sets comprise three clusters shaped as curves. The *r15, s1* and *s2* data sets consist of fifteen clusters each, with different degrees of separation. The *unbalance* data set consists of eight clusters where the three groups on the left are considerably denser than the five clusters on the right. Table 8.3 summarizes the data sets' information. We compare IW-max on a complete graph with the seed selection algorithm against k-means, mean shift, spectral clustering, DBSCAN, Gaussian mixture, and agglomerative clustering. Fig. 8.26 shows the results of the clustering experiments. Different values of the estimated percentage of outliers (h) were used for the seed selection algorithm based on the data distribution and density. For the Jain, spiral, flame, and r15 data sets, we used $h = 10\%$. For the $s1$ and $s2$ data sets, we used $h = 2\%$ and lastly, for the unbalance data set, we used $h = 1\%$. From the figure, it can be observed that IW-sum successfully separates the clusters in all data sets. Moreover, through the seed selection algorithm, we are able to locate a seed within each cluster for each data set; therefore it serves as a key tool to achieve robust clustering results.

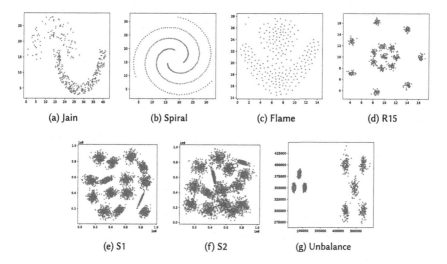

(a) Jain   (b) Spiral   (c) Flame   (d) R15

(e) S1   (f) S2   (g) Unbalance

Figure 8.25 Synthetic data sets collected from [22].

Table 8.3 Number of samples and clusters for each synthetic data set.

Data set	# of Samples	# of Clusters
Jain	373	2
Spiral	312	3
Flame	240	2
R15	600	15
S1	5000	15
S2	5000	15
Unbalance	6500	8

The clusters in the Jain data set are only correctly identified by IW-max, while its counterparts are not able to discover the groups effectively. The clusters in the spiral data set are only correctly detected by IW-max, DBSCAN, and agglomerative clustering, while for the flame data set, the IW-max and DBSCAN are the ones that stand out from the rest. For the

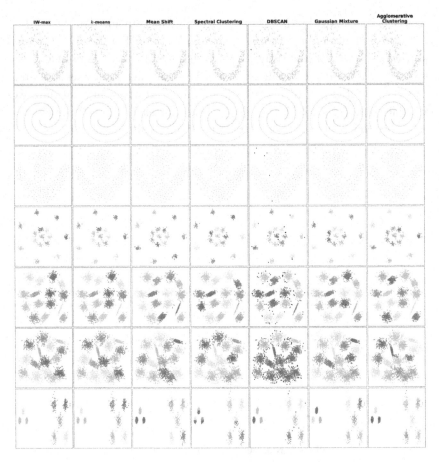

Figure 8.26 Clustering results on the synthetic data sets using IW-max with a complete graph and the seed selection algorithm against k-means, mean shift, spectral clustering, DBSCAN, Gaussian mixture, and agglomerative clustering.

r15 data set, IW-max, k-means, mean shift, and Gaussian mixture are the methods that accurately identify the groups. In the case of the s1 and s2 data sets, the only methods that correctly discover the clusters are the IW-max and Gaussian mixture techniques. Lastly, for the unbalance data set, the methods that effectively separate the groups are IW-max, k-means, DBSCAN, and Gaussian mixture. DBSCAN works effectively when the clusters are well separated and intercluster proximity is significantly larger than the distances between samples within a cluster. However, this is clearly not the case for the Jain, s1, and s2 data sets. Gaussian mixture works better for clusters of elliptical shape and when there is no intercluster overlapping.

8.5 Conclusions and future work

We introduced a flexible and robust graph-based clustering framework, called Iterative Optimum-Path Forest (IOPF), that employs subsequent executions of the optimum-path forest algorithm from reestimated seed sets to partition an input data set. Thus it allows the design of connectivity-based clustering methods by suitable choice of its components. In addition, we introduced an algorithm to select initial seeds for data clustering, improving a previous work [43]. In this context, we presented four IOPF-based clustering methods, IW-sum, IW-max, IOPF-dynsum, and IOPF-dynmax. We evaluated them for object delineation, identification of emergency stations in road networks, and group identification from synthetic data sets with different shapes and sizes in a 2D feature space.

We observed that IW-sum improves effectiveness when the graph topology is constrained to the k-nearest neighbors. On the other hand, IOPF-dynmax, previously called IDT [7], is the best approach for object delineation; IW-sum is the best approach for identification of emergency stations in road networks, and IW-max is the winner in the clustering of two-dimensional data sets. Finally, it is worth noting that the proposed versions of IW-sum and IW-max adopt the initial seed selection method introduced in Section 8.3.1 and the choice of the forest that minimizes the total path-costs, as proposed in Section 8.3.4. Therefore we can conclude that IW-sum and IW-max are relevant improvements concerning their original versions [43].

The results show that IOPF-dynmax (IDT) can be more effective than DISF [9] for object delineation, leaving as future work a comparison between them for superpixel delineation. In the identification of emergency stations in road networks, IW-sum was already shown superior to k-means [43], and now we demonstrate the advantages of IW-max over k-means, spectral clustering, DBSCAN, mean shift, Gaussian mixture models, and agglomerative clustering using synthetic data sets. Hence, we may conclude that IOPF is a flexible and robust framework being IW-sum, IW-max, and IOPF-dynmax (IDT) its best clustering methods.

We intend to investigate new techniques for seed recomputation to improve the effectiveness of the IOPF-based methods further, include local density information to identify initial seeds, and explore new applications for the IOPF-based methods.

Acknowledgments

This work was supported in part by grants from the *Brazilian National Council for Scientific and Technological Development* (CNPq), #313329/2020-6, #309627/2017-6, #303808/2018-7, *São Paulo Research Foundation* (FAPESP), #2018/26434-0, #2014/12236-1.

References

[1] R. Achanta, A. Shaji, K. Smith, A. Lucchi, P. Fua, S. Süsstrunk, Slic superpixels compared to state-of-the-art superpixel methods, IEEE Transactions on Pattern Analysis and Machine Intelligence 34 (11) (2012) 2274–2282.

[2] L. Afonso, A. Vidal, M. Kuroda, A.X. Falcão, J.P. Papa, Learning to classify seismic images with deep optimum-path forest, in: 2016 29th SIBGRAPI Conference on Graphics, Patterns and Images (SIBGRAPI), 2016, pp. 401–407.

[3] L.C. Afonso, C.R. Pereira, S.A. Weber, C. Hook, A.X. Falcão, J.P. Papa, Hierarchical learning using deep optimum-path forest, Journal of Visual Communication and Image Representation 71 (2020) 102823.

[4] C.C. Aggarwal, Graph Clustering, Springer US, Boston, MA, 2010, pp. 459–467.

[5] S. Alpert, M. Galun, R. Basri, A. Brandt, Image segmentation by probabilistic bottom-up aggregation and cue integration, in: Proceedings of the IEEE Conference on Computer Vision and Pattern Recognition, June 2007.

[6] W.P. Amorim, A.X. Falcão, J.P. Papa, M.H. Carvalho, Improving semi-supervised learning through optimum connectivity, Pattern Recognition 60 (2016) 72–85.

[7] D. Aparco-Cardenas, P.J. de Rezende, A.X. Falcão, Object delineation by iterative dynamic trees, in: Iberoamerican Congress on Pattern Recognition, 2021.

[8] F. Belém, S.J.F. Guimarães, A.X. Falcão, Superpixel segmentation by object-based iterative spanning forest, in: Iberoamerican Congress on Pattern Recognition, Springer, 2018, pp. 334–341.

[9] F.C. Belém, S.J.F. Guimarães, A.X. Falcão, Superpixel segmentation using dynamic and iterative spanning forest, IEEE Signal Processing Letters 27 (2020) 1440–1444.

[10] J. Bragantini, S.B. Martins, C. Castelo-Fernandez, A.X. Falcão, Graph-based image segmentation using dynamic trees, in: Iberoamerican Congress on Pattern Recognition, Springer, 2018, pp. 470–478.

[11] F.A. Cappabianco, A.X. Falcão, C.L. Yasuda, J.K. Udupa, Brain tissue mr-image segmentation via optimum-path forest clustering, Computer Vision and Image Understanding 116 (10) (2012) 1047–1059.

[12] S. Chen, T. Sun, F. Yang, H. Sun, Y. Guan, An improved optimum-path forest clustering algorithm for remote sensing image segmentation, Computers & Geosciences 112 (2018) 38–46.

[13] F.R. Chung, F.C. Graham, Spectral Graph Theory. Number 92, American Mathematical Soc., 1997.

[14] D. Comaniciu, P. Meer, Mean shift: a robust approach toward feature space analysis, IEEE Transactions on Pattern Analysis and Machine Intelligence 24 (5) (2002) 603–619.

[15] K.A. Costa, L.A. Pereira, R.Y. Nakamura, C.R. Pereira, J.P. Papa, A.X. Falcão, A nature-inspired approach to speed up optimum-path forest clustering and its application to intrusion detection in computer networks, Information Sciences 294 (2015) 95–108.

[16] K.S. Dar, I. Javed, W. Amjad, S. Aslam, A. Shamim, Survey of clustering applications, Journal of Network Communications and Emerging Technologies 4 (3) (2015).

[17] A. Echemendía Montero, A.X. Falcão, A divide-and-conquer clustering approach based on optimum-path forest, in: 2018 31st SIBGRAPI Conference on Graphics, Patterns and Images (SIBGRAPI), 2018, pp. 416–423.

[18] M. Ester, H.-P. Kriegel, J. Sander, X. Xu, et al., A density-based algorithm for discovering clusters in large spatial databases with noise, in: Kdd, Vol. 96, 1996, pp. 226–231.

[19] R.M. Esteves, T. Hacker, C. Rong, Competitive k-means, a new accurate and distributed k-means algorithm for large datasets, in: 2013 IEEE 5th International Conference on Cloud Computing Technology and Science, Vol. 1, 2013, pp. 17–24.

[20] A. Fahad, N. Alshatri, Z. Tari, A. Alamri, I. Khalil, A.Y. Zomaya, S. Foufou, A. Bouras, A survey of clustering algorithms for big data: taxonomy and empirical analysis, IEEE Transactions on Emerging Topics in Computing 2 (3) (2014) 267–279.

[21] A.X. Falcão, J. Stolfi, R. de Alencar Lotufo, The image foresting transform: theory, algorithms, and applications, IEEE Transactions on Pattern Analysis and Machine Intelligence 26 (1) (2004) 19–29.

[22] P. Fränti, S. Sieranoja, K-Means Properties on Six Clustering Benchmark Datasets, 2018, (Accessed 30 September 2021).

[23] A.L. Fred, A.K. Jain, Data clustering using evidence accumulation, in: Object Recognition Supported by User Interaction for Service Robots, Vol. 4, IEEE, 2002, pp. 276–280.

[24] L. Grady, E.L. Schwartz, Isoperimetric graph partitioning for image segmentation, IEEE Transactions on Pattern Analysis and Machine Intelligence 28 (3) (2006) 469–475.

[25] E. Hartuv, R. Shamir, A clustering algorithm based on graph connectivity, Information Processing Letters 76 (4) (2000) 175–181.

[26] L. Hubert, P. Arabie, Comparing partitions, Journal of Classification 2 (1) (1985) 193–218.

[27] A.K. Jain, Data clustering: 50 years beyond k-means, Pattern Recognition Letters 31 (8) (2010) 651–666.

[28] A.K. Jain, R.C. Dubes, Algorithms for Clustering Data, Prentice-Hall, Inc., 1988.

[29] A. Karduni, A. Kermanshah, S. Derrible, A protocol to convert spatial polyline data to network formats and applications to world urban road networks, Scientific Data 3 (1) (2016) 1–7.

[30] G. Karypis, E.-H. Han, V. Kumar, Chameleon: hierarchical clustering using dynamic modeling, Computer 32 (8) (1999) 68–75.

[31] N. Khan, I. Yaqoob, I.A.T. Hashem, Z. Inayat, W.K. Mahmoud Ali, M. Alam, M. Shiraz, A. Gani, Big data: survey, technologies, opportunities, and challenges, The Scientific World Journal 2014 (2014).

[32] F. Lemes Galvão, A.X. Falcão, A. Shankar Chowdhury, Risf: recursive iterative spanning forest for superpixel segmentation, in: 2018 31st SIBGRAPI Conference on Graphics, Patterns and Images (SIBGRAPI), 2018, pp. 408–415.

[33] J.P. Ortega, M. Del, R.B. Rojas, M.J. Somodevilla, Research issues on k-means algorithm: an experimental trial using Matlab, in: CEUR Workshop Proceedings: Semantic Web and New Technologies, 2009, pp. 83–96.

[34] J.P. Papa, A.X. Falcão, C.T. Suzuki, Supervised pattern classification based on optimum-path forest, International Journal of Imaging Systems and Technology 19 (2) (2009) 120–131.

[35] S. Patel, S. Sihmar, A. Jatain, A study of hierarchical clustering algorithms, in: 2015 2nd International Conference on Computing for Sustainable Global Development (INDIACom), IEEE, 2015, pp. 537–541.

[36] D. Pelleg, A.W. Moore, et al., X-means: extending k-means with efficient estimation of the number of clusters, in: Icml, Vol. 1, 2000, pp. 727–734.

[37] D.A. Reynolds, Gaussian mixture models, Encyclopedia of Biometrics 741 (2009) 659–663.

[38] L.M. Rocha, F.A. Cappabianco, A.X. Falcão, Data clustering as an optimum-path forest problem with applications in image analysis, International Journal of Imaging Systems and Technology 19 (2) (2009) 50–68.

[39] M.Z. Rodriguez, C.H. Comin, D. Casanova, O.M. Bruno, D.R. Amancio, L.d.F. Costa, F.A. Rodrigues, Clustering algorithms: a comparative approach, PLoS ONE 14 (1) (2019) e0210236.

[40] S.E. Schaeffer, Graph clustering, Computer Science Review 1 (1) (2007) 27–64.

[41] R. Sharan, R. Shamir, Click: a clustering algorithm with applications to gene expression analysis, in: Proceedings of the 8th International Conference on Intelligent Systems for Molecular Biology, Vol. 8, 2000, p. 16.

[42] S. Soor, A. Challa, S. Danda, B.S. Daya Sagar, L. Najman, Extending k-means to preserve spatial connectivity, in: IGARSS 2018 - 2018 IEEE International Geoscience and Remote Sensing Symposium, 2018, pp. 6959–6962.

[43] S. Soor, A. Challa, S. Danda, B.D. Sagar, L. Najman, Iterated watersheds, a connected variation of k-means for clustering gis data, IEEE Transactions on Emerging Topics in Computing 9 (2) (2021) 626–636.

[44] J.E. Vargas-Muñoz, A.S. Chowdhury, E.B. Alexandre, F.L. Galvão, P.A. Vechiatto Miranda, A.X. Falcão, An iterative spanning forest framework for superpixel segmentation, IEEE Transactions on Image Processing 28 (7) (2019) 3477–3489.

[45] N.X. Vinh, J. Epps, J. Bailey, Information theoretic measures for clusterings comparison: variants, properties, normalization and correction for chance, Journal of Machine Learning Research 11 (Dec. 2010) 2837–2854.

[46] U. Von Luxburg, A tutorial on spectral clustering, Statistics and Computing 17 (4) (2007) 395–416.

[47] D. Xu, Y. Tian, A comprehensive survey of clustering algorithms, Annals of Data Science 2 (2) (2015) 165–193.

[48] C.T. Zahn, Graph-theoretical methods for detecting and describing gestalt clusters, IEEE Transactions on Computers 100 (1) (1971) 68–86.

CHAPTER 9

Future trends in optimum-path forest classification

João Paulo Papa[a] **and Alexandre Xavier Falcão**[b]
[a]UNESP – São Paulo State University, School of Sciences, Bauru, Brazil
[b]Institute of Computing, University of Campinas (UNICAMP), Campinas, São Paulo, Brazil

In the past years, we have observed an increasing number of applications that require machine learning techniques to sort out problems that are not straightforward to humans. The reasons vary from information that is not clearly visible to the human eye (e.g., microscopic patterns in medical images) or the massive amount of data to analyze.

Deep learning techniques stand for the foremost approach when talking about object recognition, image classification, and speech recognition to cite a few. However, deep networks usually require a considerable amount of labeled data to achieve good results, which may be prohibitive depending on the application. Synthetic data generation has been a subject of intense study to cope with such an issue, i.e., the lack of proper data. Generative adversarial networks figure as the most prominent approach, besides not being easy to train. They tend to generate images similar to those used to feed the model, and generating high-resolution data is costly.

In this book, we gathered works that focused on the optimum-path forest classifier to address different applications. Chapter 2 surveyed many papers related to the OPF classifier, including some works that explored the synergy between CNNs and graph-based classifiers. The authors showed we could replace the softmax layer with an OPF classifier to achieve more accurate results. Chapter 3 addressed OPF in the context of intrusion detection in computer networks, more specifically, real-time intrusion detection systems.

Content-based image retrieval has been the subject of research in Chapter 4, in which unsupervised and supervised OPF approaches have been used to aid relevance feedback in medical image retrieval. Besides, active learning-driven strategies help the user select the most informative examples, thus turning the retrieval process more accurate. Chapter 5 also concerns intrusion detection, but on a larger scale. The authors proposed five variants of the OPF classifier to increase its efficiency.

Optimum-Path Forest
https://doi.org/10.1016/B978-0-12-822688-9.00017-7

217

In Chapter 6, another medical application has been addressed. The idea is to detect plaque calcifications of the carotid artery using Fuzzy OPF, a modification of the original unsupervised approach that can assign fuzzy values to the nodes' density. Chapter 7 focuses on studying the influence of different distance/similarity functions to weight OPF arcs. Also, similarity values learned through deep Siamese networks are also introduced. Finally, Chapter 8 presents a strategy to obtain a desired number of clusters using Iterative Optimum-Path Forest (IOPF)—a framework for the design of classifiers through a sequence of executions of the OPF algorithm. As shown in Chapter 8, an improved seed set is reestimated at each execution, allowing IOPF to be a robust and flexible approach to cope with clustering-driven problems.

As the take-home message, we shall say that OPF-based classifiers have gained popularity due to their simplicity and potential to create novel approaches in pattern recognition. We also state that high-dimensional and sparse feature vectors challenge such classifiers since they are based on distance calculations. Although they are not purely based on similarities like k-NN, such information is used to explore the connectivity among samples in the feature space. In view of exploring such feature spaces, usually generated by an encoder of a deep neural network, one can leverage dimensionality reduction methods to explore OPF classifiers. For instance, the t-distributed Stochastic Neighbor Embedding (t-SNE) algorithm has allowed user supervision and pseudolabel propagation by an OPF-based semisupervised classifier towards improving active learning methods [1] and training of deep neural networks with minimal user supervision [2]. Investigating other ways to reduce dimensionality and explore OPF classifiers to improve deep learning seems promising, as demonstrated by Passos et al. [3], which employed the well-known Principal Component Analysis (PCA) technique to reduce the output of a ResNet-50 deep network for Parkinson's disease identification using handwritten dynamics. Khojasteh et al. [4] used a similar approach, but in the context of exudate detection in retinal images. Last but not least, Passos et al. [5] also considered using PCA for dimensionality reduction purposes for further feeding a supervised OPF classifier, but in the context of breast mass categorization in mammographies.

Unsupervised OPF has not yet been fully explored. At the moment, we count on methodologies that can provide a given number of clusters or estimate the natural number of clusters for a given graph topology. However, we expect to see possible extensions and their use in more applications.

We also strongly encourage our readers to make use of the OPF-related libraries available out there, such as LibOPF[1] and OPFython.[2]

References

[1] B.C. Benato, J.F. Gomes, A.C. Telea, A.X. Falcão, Semi-automatic data annotation guided by feature space projection, Pattern Recognition 109 (2021) 107612, https://doi.org/10.1016/j.patcog.2020.107612.

[2] B.C. Benato, J.F. Gomes, A.C. Telea, A.X. Falcão, Semi-supervised deep learning based on label propagation in a 2d embedded space, in: Proc. of CIARP 2021, 2021, in press, arXiv:2008.00558.

[3] L.A. Passos, C.R. Pereira, E.R.S. Rezende, T.J. Carvalho, S.A. Weber, C. Hook, J.P. Papa, Parkinson disease identification using residual networks and optimum-path forest, in: 2018 IEEE 12th International Symposium on Applied Computational Intelligence and Informatics (SACI), 2018, pp. 325–330.

[4] P. Khojasteh, L.A. Passos Júnior, T. Carvalho, E. Rezende, B. Aliahmad, J.P. Papa, D.K. Kumar, Exudate detection in fundus images using deeply-learnable features, Computers in Biology and Medicine 104 (2019) 62–69.

[5] L.A. Passos, C. Santos, C.R. Pereira, L.C.S. Afonso, J.P. Papa, A hybrid approach for breast mass categorization, in: J.M.R.S. Tavares, R.M. Natal Jorge (Eds.), VipIMAGE 2019, Springer International Publishing, Cham, 2019, pp. 159–168.

[1] https://github.com/jppbsi/LibOPF/wiki.
[2] https://github.com/gugarosa/opfython/wiki.

Index

A

Accuracy
  classification, 26
  clusters, 192
  improvement, 111
Active learning (AL)
  approach, 95
  strategy, 98
AdaBoost (AB), 63, 79, 80
AdaBoostClassifier, 79
Adjacency relation, 1–3, 6, 7, 12, 14, 32,
      36, 157, 177, 178, 182, 196
Adjusted Mutual Information (AMI), 192
Adjusted Rand Index (ARI), 192
Agglomerative
  clustering, 209–211, 213
  clustering algorithm, 209
  hierarchical clustering algorithm, 179
Alcoholism detection contexts, 30
Aniso data sets, 206, 208, 209
Anomaly detection, 34, 36, 56, 59, 109,
      116, 118, 139, 141, 142, 148, 150
Artificial Intelligence (AI), 155
Artificial Neural Network (ANN), 60, 155,
      156
Atherosclerotic lesion, 137–141, 144, 146,
      150
Atherosclerotic lesion identification, 139
Attack
  class, 75
  flows, 76, 81
  scenarios, 74
  streams, 75
  surfaces, 89
Auto Color Correlogram (ACC), 101
Automated attacks, 87
Automatic
  classification, 27
  identification, 27, 181

B

Baseline classifiers, 170, 171
Bayesian classifier (BC), 5, 22, 32, 57

BBC News, 161, 163, 170
BBC News data set, 164
Benchmark data set, 130
Bernoulli NB, 75, 81, 82, 89
Betweenness centrality (BC), 112
Binary classification, 63
Boundary Recall (BR), 192
Breast mass identification context, 30

C

Calcified atherosclerotic lesion detection,
      140
Cardiovascular diseases, 137, 140
Cardiovascular diseases context, 139, 140
Carotid artery, 138, 144, 148, 150, 218
Class labels, 121
Classic attacks, 87
Classification
  accuracy, 26
  algorithms, 24, 111
  data, 1
  error, 5, 13, 79, 111, 142
  intents, 141
  models, 17, 56, 88, 90
  OPF_{cg}, 23
  OPF_{knn}, 144
  problem, 109, 121
  process, 3, 7, 24–26, 71, 143
  purposes, 146
  remote sensing, 110
  rules, 59
  step, 31
  supervised, 14, 101, 140, 150, 156
  task, 6, 24, 36, 101, 160
  task context, 33
  techniques, 67, 69, 71–74, 80, 82
Classification and regression tree (CART),
      119
Classifier
  committees, 81
  OPF, 3, 22, 24, 57, 63, 139, 140, 143,
      144, 149, 150, 161, 217, 218

OPF$_{cg}$, 24, 26
OPF$_{uns}$, 35
prototypes, 63
Clustering
  algorithms, 6, 35, 111, 123, 124, 132,
    175, 176
  applications, 178
  approach, 181
  capabilities, 208
  centroid, 96
  data, 6, 33, 213
  information, 186
  methods, 180, 213
  model, 114, 116, 118
  OPF, 104
  problem, 110, 123, 124, 132, 179, 207
  process, 209
  purposes, 34
  quality, 33
  results, 22, 176–178, 201, 205, 207
  solutions, 178
  step, 36
  task, 35
  technique, 101
Clusters
  accuracy, 192
  centers, 34, 125, 181
  information, 186
  label, 143
  shapes, 176
  structure, 120
Community detection, 120
Competition process, 1–3, 13
Complete graph, 1, 2, 12, 14, 26, 32, 36,
    157, 182, 205, 207, 209, 210
Complete graph adjacency relation, 20
Computational
  cost, 5, 150
  intelligence techniques, 66, 69–71
  intelligence techniques learning, 68
Computed tomography angiography
    (CTA), 138
  image, 141, 144–147, 150
  image intensity, 145
Computer networks, 55, 56, 67, 82, 88–90,
    109, 114
Connectivity function, 16, 156, 177, 178,
    182, 197, 200, 205

Conquering process, 19
Content-based image retrieval techniques
    (CBIR), 95, 100, 104
  approach, 97
  process, 95, 96, 101
Context
  intrusion detection, 33
  OPF, 9
Contextual information, 25
Contrastive loss, 156, 162
Convolution Neural Network (CNN), 3,
    28, 32, 156, 160
Coreset
  approach, 132
  approximation, 124
  concept, 110, 111, 123
  construction, 124, 127, 129
  size, 131
  technique, 123
Costly
  process, 121
  task, 29, 35
Critical difference (CD), 147
Cyber attacks, 110, 117–119

D
Data
  classification, 1
  clustering, 6, 33, 213
  learning, 5
  unlabeled, 175
  unlabeled training, 6
DBSCAN, 209–211, 213
Decision Tree (DT), 63, 74–76, 81, 82,
    155, 162, 166
DecisionTreeClassifier, 75
Deep learning, 28
  features, 29
  techniques, 36
Deep Siamese networks, 156
Detection
  approaches in IDS, 58
  mechanism, 62
  methodology, 55
Detection rate (DR), 109, 114, 119, 132

Disease
  detection, 138
  identification, 7
Distributed Denial of Service (DDoS)
    attacks, 56
DoS
  attacks, 82–85, 114
  Hulk, 85, 86, 88, 90
  Hulk detection, 85
  SlowHTTPTest, 84, 86, 88, 90
  SlowHTTPTest detection, 85
  Slowloris, 83–86, 88, 90
  Slowloris detection, 84
Dynamic IFT (DynIFT), 177

E

ECG arrhythmia classification, 110
Effectiveness measures, 192
Emergency station, 191, 196, 197, 213
Ensemble pruning strategies, 26
Esophagus classification, 139
Establishment costs, 196
Evaluation metrics, 163, 164, 166, 168, 192
Event classification, 31
Expectation maximization (EM), 209
Extracting features, 30, 34
Exudate detection, 30

F

False alarm rate (FAR), 109, 114, 119, 132
False negatives (FN), 65
False positives (FP), 65
Feature
  set, 145
  space, 2, 3, 5, 24, 32, 36, 115, 157,
    177–179, 182, 190, 205, 209, 213,
    218
  vector, 1, 6, 13, 37, 118, 156, 180, 183,
    186, 189, 190, 192, 218
Feature selection (FS) algorithm, 117
Finite State Machine (FSM), 59
Firefly Algorithm (FA), 56
FlowID, 70
Fraud detection, 28
Fuzzy OPF, 139, 141, 147, 149, 150, 218

G

Gaussian NB, 81, 82, 89
Genetic Algorithm (GA), 60
Graphics Processing Unit (GPU), 155
GridSearchCV technique, 75, 76, 78, 79

H

Heart arrhythmia classification, 30
Heartbleed attack, 68
Hierarchical
  clustering, 181, 209
  clustering algorithms, 176
  learning, 33
Highly Connected Subgraph (HCS), 180
Host-Based Intrusion Detection System
    (HIDS), 56, 60
Human genetic clustering, 175
Hybrid IDS, 88, 90, 111, 114, 115, 117,
    118

I

Identification prototypes, 121–123
Image Foresting Transform (IFT), 177–179,
    192
Imbalanced data sets, 146, 147, 149, 150
Incremental coreset construction, 125, 127
Inferior accuracy, 68
Infiltration attack, 68
Informative images, 96, 98
Insider attacks, 118
Interactive object segmentation, 177, 179,
    190
Intercluster proximity, 212
Intruder detection, 56
Intrusion detection, 30, 33, 35, 56, 58, 65,
    69, 89, 217
  area, 81
  context, 33, 217
  environment, 82
  model, 133
  problem, 66
  scenario, 61
Intrusion Detection and Prevention System
    (IDPS), 61
Intrusion Detection System (IDS), 55–58,
    60, 65, 67, 109–111, 114, 217

Isoperimetric partitioning, 192
Iterated Watershed (IW), 177, 182, 187, 192
Iterative Dynamic Tree (IDT), 190–192, 194
  algorithm, 190, 191
  variants, 193
Iterative Optimum-Path Forest (IOPF), 178, 187, 189, 190, 197, 205, 213, 218
  configuration, 197
  framework, 178, 179, 183, 184, 191, 197, 201
Iterative Spanning Forest (ISF), 177, 190
  framework, 177, 178, 190, 192, 194

J

Jeffrey Divergence (JD), 100

L

Label
  clusters, 143
  propagation, 21, 181, 189
Learning
  approaches, 63
  data, 5
  features, 36
  iterations, 102, 104
  mathematical, 155
  methods, 22, 24, 36, 62
  model, 97, 98
  problems, 6, 62
  process, 5, 20, 24, 30, 32, 62, 95–97, 104, 160
  rate, 79, 162
  strategies, 100
  supervised, 12, 35, 63, 109, 110, 155
  task, 6
  unsupervised, 6, 7, 20, 33, 35, 36, 63, 109, 111, 139, 156, 175
Linkage clustering, 179
Logistic Regression (LR), 155
Logistic Regressor (LR), 162

M

Machine Learning (ML), 28, 57, 59, 60, 62, 84
  algorithms, 27, 31, 56, 65, 109, 140, 141, 155, 202
  for pattern classification, 150
  models, 67, 82, 109, 139–141
  task, 6
  techniques, 6, 32, 56, 57, 65, 74, 83, 86–90, 217
Magnetic resonance imaging (MRI), 138
  examination, 138
  image modalities, 138
Majority class, 68
MapReduce approach, 111, 114, 116, 118
Markov cluster (MCL)
  algorithm, 119–121
  process algorithm, 111, 119
Massive data sets, 123, 124
Mean average precision (MAP), 101, 104
Metrics for effectiveness analysis, 65
Minimum cost, 24, 189, 205
Minimum spanning forest (MSF), 110
Minimum spanning tree (MST), 13, 63, 110, 119, 121, 127, 180
Minority class, 68, 69
Misclassification, 14, 66
Misclassification rate, 17
Misuse detection module, 118
Mixed Intrusion Detection System (MIDS), 61
Modified OPF (MOPF), 57, 110, 111, 114, 117–119, 132
Multifaceted detection, 57, 118
Multilabel semisupervised classification, 110
Multilabeled video classification data set, 26
Multiscale sequential learning, 25
Mutual information and the binary gravitational search algorithm (MI-BGSA), 117, 118
Mutual Information (MI), 192

N

Naive Bayes (NB), 57, 119
Natural Language Processing (NLP), 36
Nearest-neighbor (NN) classifier, 14
Network Behavior Analysis (NBA), 61

Network Intrusion Detection System
    (NIDS), 56, 60, 61, 89
Network traffic flow, 57, 66, 68, 70–73, 77,
    78, 82–84, 89
    classification, 67, 71, 75, 76, 78–81, 89
    features, 90
    management, 70
Noisy
    circles, 202, 206, 208, 209
    moons, 204, 206, 208, 209
    moons data sets, 204, 206, 209
Nonprototype samples, 9, 124
Nonseparable classes, 63
Nonsimilarity classifier, 168

O

Object delineation, 190–192, 196, 213
Object segmentation, 177, 192, 194
    effectiveness, 193
    task, 193
    unsupervised, 190
OPF with complete graph (OPF$_{cg}$), 13
    classification, 23
    classifier, 24, 26
    features, 32
    performance, 24, 32
    standard, 26
    working mechanism, 26
OPF-based clustering (OPFC), 114
OPF$_{knn}$
    accuracy, 17
    classification, 144
    success, 149
Optimum connectivity, 176–180, 186
Optimum-Path Forest (OPF), 1, 3, 6–8,
    11, 12, 56, 63, 78, 80
    accuracy, 3
    algorithm, 7, 12, 25, 177, 178, 183, 186,
        197, 218
    classifier, 1, 3, 22, 24, 57, 63, 139, 140,
        143, 144, 149, 150, 161, 217, 218
    clustering, 104
    context, 9
    execution, 177, 183, 185–187
    framework, 7
    model, 112, 125, 129
    supervised, 2, 30, 78, 110, 139, 217

training algorithm, 2
    training time, 3
    unsupervised, 2, 20, 33, 35, 36, 111,
        114, 139, 142, 143, 218
    working mechanism, 10
Optimum-Path Tree (OPT), 1, 9, 16, 110,
    124, 125
Overclustering issue, 21
Overlapped classes, 96

P

Parametric learning, 62
Partitional clustering, 179
    context, 180
    solution, 176
Partitioning
    methods, 124, 132
    module, 132, 133
    process, 124
    step, 128
Path cost, 9, 19, 183, 190, 200
Pattern classification, 62
Pattern recognition (PR), 1, 5–7, 11, 22,
    27, 62, 111, 175, 209, 218
Pixelwise
    binary classification, 147
    classification, 141, 147
Plugin
    configuration, 73
    startup parameters, 73
Port Scan, 82, 83, 86, 88, 90
Port Scanning, 86, 87
Predecessor
    map, 10, 18, 19
    node, 18
    set, 13
Principal Component Analysis (PCA), 218
Priority queue, 9, 10, 13, 18, 24, 189
Probabilistic classification, 139, 142
Prototypes
    classifier, 63
    identification, 121–123
    identification process, 122, 123
Proximity prestige (PR), 112
Pruning, 111–113
    algorithm, 110
    ensembles, 26

irrelevant, 23
irrelevant samples, 22
modules, 111, 112
stopping criterion, 23

Q

Query Expansion (QEX), 101, 102
Query image, 25, 95–98, 101
Query Point Movement strategy (QPM),
    100, 102

R

Rand index (RI), 192
Random Forest (RF), 63, 74, 76, 77, 81,
    140
RandomForestClassifier, 76
Reinforcement learning, 63
Relevance feedback (RF)
    loop, 96
    methods, 95
    process, 95
Remote sensing, 1, 28, 29, 155
    classification, 110
    image, 35
    image segmentation, 110
    imagery, 28
    interactive classification, 29
    segmentation, 181
Road network, 179, 191, 196–198, 200

S

Seed
    recomputation, 186, 190, 192, 193, 213
    recomputation strategy, 187
    selection algorithm, 185, 200, 207, 209,
        210
    set, 176, 177, 183, 185–187, 189–192,
        195, 218
        improvement, 190
        recomputation scheme, 177
        selection, 184
Segmentation, 16, 29, 35, 110, 138, 147
Segmentation remote sensing, 181
Semantic
    features, 34
    segmentation task, 147

Semeion
    data set, 168, 170, 171
    testing set, 168, 169
Semisupervised learning, 2, 3, 5, 6, 19, 63
Semisupervised OPF classifier (OPF_{ssp}), 20,
    32
    training phase, 32
Sequential learning, 25, 26
Siamese network, 156, 157, 159–163, 166,
    170
    architecture, 160
    classification framework, 156
Signature detection
    approaches, 61, 88
    methodologies, 56
    scheme, 66
SlowHTTPTest, 82, 84–86
SlowHTTPTest DoS, 84, 86, 88, 90
Snort, 56, 57, 61, 62, 66, 67, 69, 70, 73
    IDS accuracy, 56
    sensors, 62
Spam detection, 30
Spectral clustering, 192, 209, 210, 213
    algorithm, 209
    methods, 180
SSH Brute Force, 82, 87
SSH Brute Force attack, 87, 88, 90
Stacked sequential learning, 25
Standard
    identification methods, 141
    OPF classification, 144
    OPF_{cg}, 26
Superpixel segmentation, 177, 190, 194
    methods, 177, 192
    task, 190
Supervised
    classification, 14, 101, 140, 150, 156
    classifiers, 31, 101
    learning, 12, 35, 63, 109, 110, 155
    machine learning algorithms, 63
    machine learning techniques, 67
    OPF, 2, 30, 78, 110, 139, 217
    OPF classifier, 111, 218
    OPF versions, 22
Support Vector Machine (SVM), 5, 29, 56,
    101, 110, 155, 162
Synthetic data sets, 201, 205, 206, 208, 209

T

Temporal segmentation, 34
Tensor Processing Unit (TPU), 155
True negatives (TN), 65
True positives (TP), 65

U

Unbalanced data sets, 17
Unlabeled
  data, 6, 175
  objects, 175
  samples, 6, 20, 32, 96, 111, 112, 122
  set, 98
  training data, 6
  training samples, 20
  training set, 32

Unsupervised
  learning, 6, 7, 20, 33, 35, 36, 63, 109,
    111, 139, 156, 175
  manifold learning, 24
  object segmentation, 190
Unsupervised OPF (OPF$_{uns}$), 2, 20, 33, 35,
    36, 111, 114, 139, 142, 143, 218
  classifier, 35, 36
  parameters, 35
  version, 21

W

Wireless sensor network (WSN), 114
Wireless-based Intrusion Detection System
  (WIDS), 61

Printed in the United States
by Baker & Taylor Publisher Services